I0818491

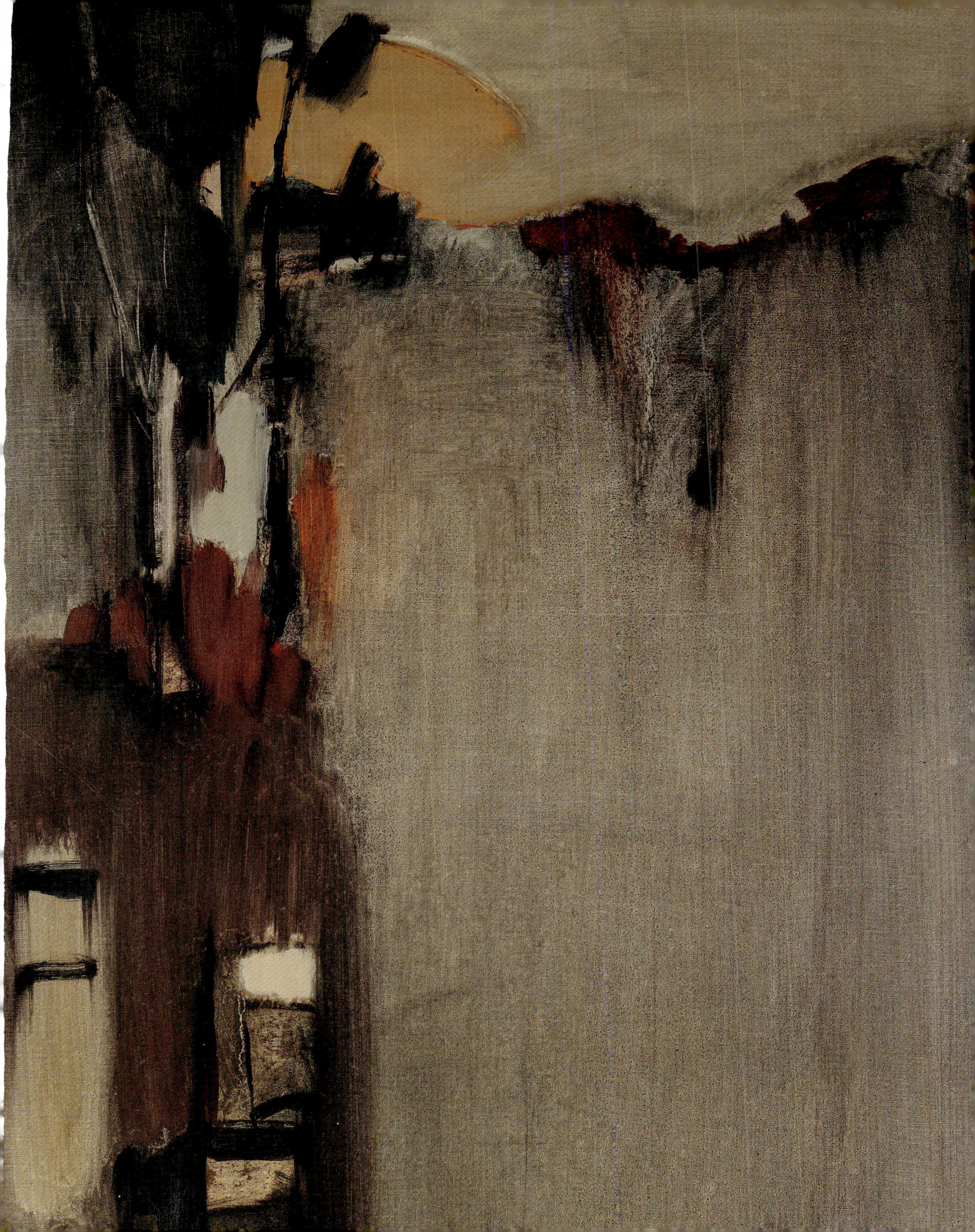

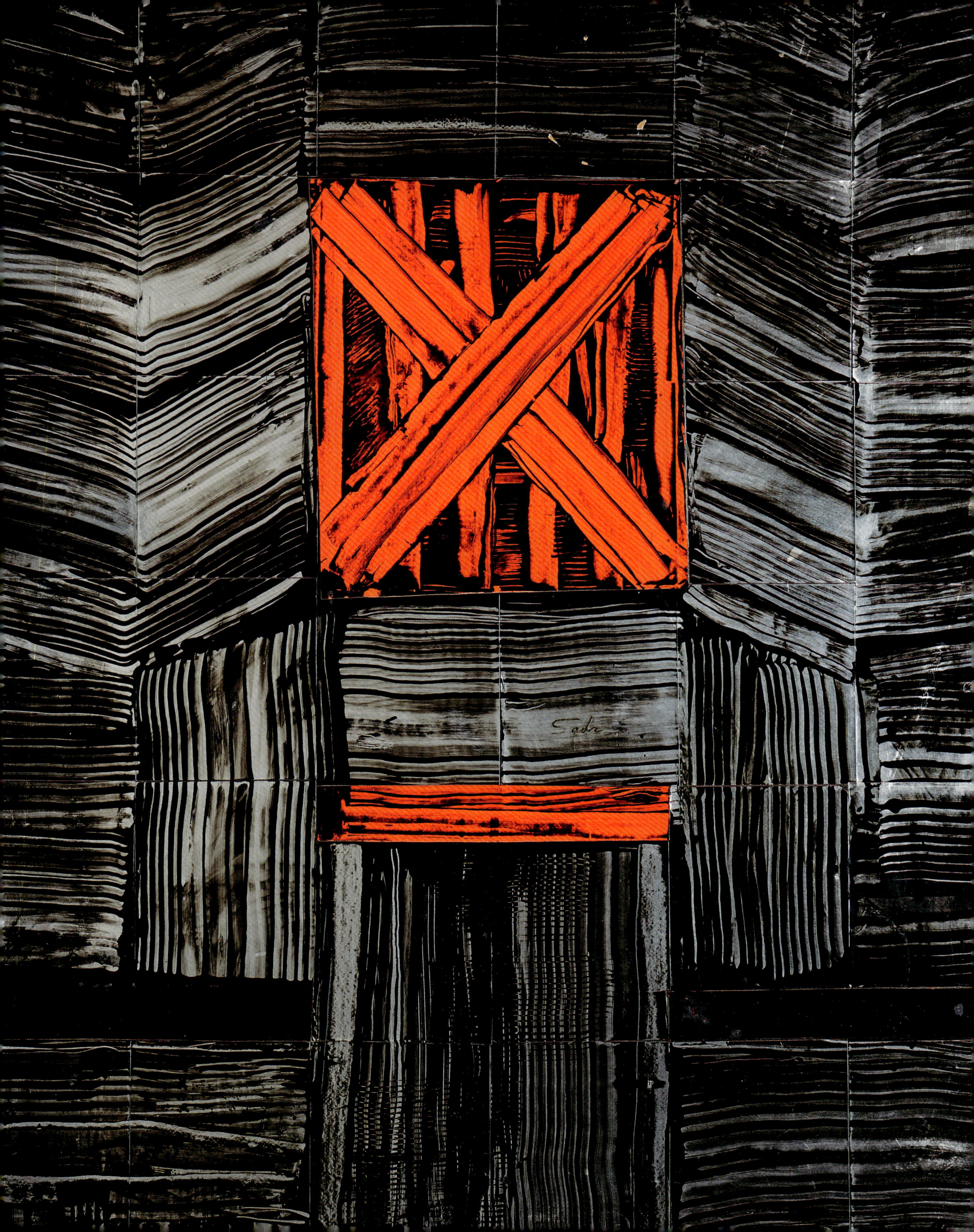

MODERN IRAN AND THE AVANT-GARDES 1948–78

Edited by Pantea Haghighi

Vancouver Artgallery HIRMER

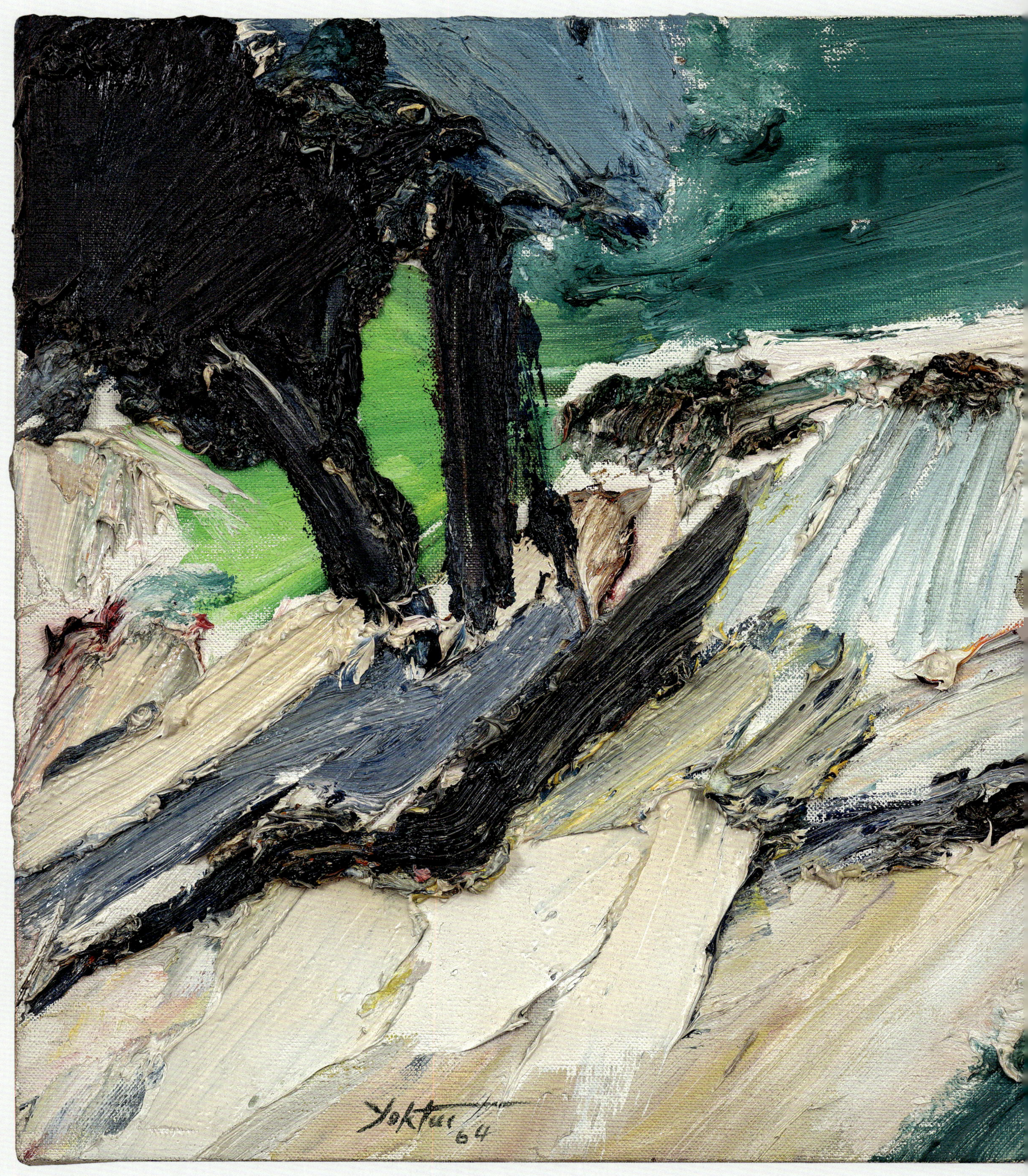

MODERN IRAN AND THE AVANT-GARDES, 1948–78

Pantea Haghighi

The modern movement in Iran was formed within an unsettled political environment that influenced the distinctly Iranian vision of modernism that emerged between 1948 and 1978. *Modern Iran and the Avant-Gardes, 1948–78* surveys the various practices and perspectives of artists who contributed to the formation of the modern movement. The diverse approaches that informed this new art were at times infused with a sense of nationalism, while at other moments they broke away from nationalism and, almost simultaneously, engaged with tradition and history. The works highlighted in the exhibition respond to a moment when struggles with notions of identity and authenticity were central to the ideas and practices of modernity. The political and economic relationship between Iran and the West remained uncertain during this period. However, the cultural dialogue between the two was less ambiguous. Many artists were in conversation with Western modes of art practices; they collaborated with artists, academics and gallerists in Europe and the United States at some point in their early years and lived in Europe or the United States. Social, cultural and economic determinants within Iran—combined with exposure to the West—factored significantly in the aesthetic decisions that these artists made in representing the modern in Iran.

In 1940, the Honarkadeh, the first Faculty of Fine Arts, was established at the University of Tehran. Here, young students were exposed to European modernism, and, until the 1960s, French culture was the dominant influence. The first graduates of this school were called, by the painter Ahmad Esfandiari, the "Pioneers of Iranian New Art." These first students included Hossein Kazemi; Manoucher Yektai, who studied in France; and Jalil Ziapour, who went to Paris in 1946 to study with the theoretician and artist André Lhote. Ziapour became familiar with European modernist art during his studies at the École des Beaux-Arts, and with Cubism, specifically, at Lhote's private art school in the city. At that time, Lhote's teachings on Cubism were intertwined with the work of the anti-rationalist philosopher Henri Bergson. Bergson's philosophy is believed to have been the underpinning for Cubist artistic language, and his theories provided the basis for the articulation of leftist nationalism. The connection between political commitment and artistic expression as presented by Bergson played a crucial role in the activities of the Fighting Rooster Association, which Ziapour and other artists

Faramarz Pilaram
Untitled, 1972 (detail)
oil on canvas

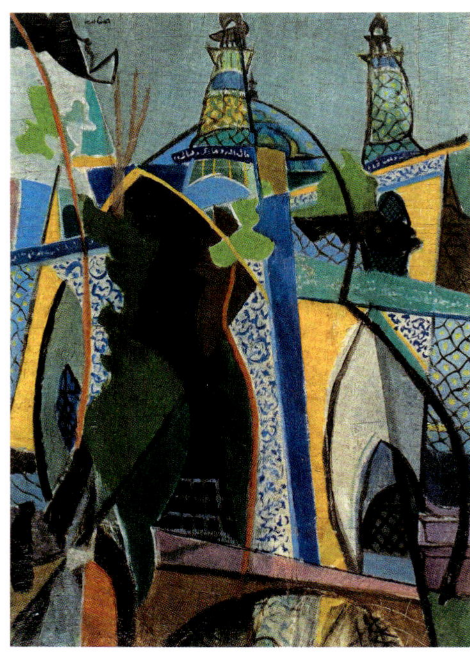

started in the late 1940s in Iran. For the artists associated with the Fighting Rooster, Bergson's theories helped establish a relationship between philosophical theories and visual practices.

The Fighting Rooster Association (Persian: انجمن هنری خروس جنگی; romanized: Anjoman-e Honari-ye Khorus Jangi) as well as the related magazine that Ziapour, writer Gholam Hossein Gharib, composer Morteza Hannaneh and playwright Hassan Shirvani founded was about their fight for recognition of modern arts with leftist tendencies. Their first publication was a poem by Nima Yushij, who was known for taking poetry out of the rituals of the royal court and bringing it to the masses. Ziapour's interest in the politically oppressed was in tune with his intention to shatter the status quo. In search of a way to represent the modern in Iran, Ziapour and the other association members became the leading promoters of Cubism and initiators of the notion of a modernism divorced from the orientalist and exotic depictions of the movement's past. When Ziapour promoted Cubism in Iran in the late 1940s, it offered him "a suitable vocabulary to elaborate an artistic subjectivity based on Iranian heritage."[1]

As a result, Cubism—which had been invented nearly forty years earlier—was not outdated as used by Ziapour. It had likewise seen a revival in France in the mid-1940s, a revival meant as a form of liberation to counter the humiliation of the Nazi occupation. Ziapour did not merely imitate this form of expression; rather, his appropriation of Cubism was translated in the Iranian context through vernacular modes such as Sufism. This became a way to make art for the time: an alternative cultural identity, rooted in Iran's spiritual heritage. As curator and scholar Fereshteh Daftari has discussed, fragmentation of the old form and imposition of the new form became Ziapour's goal.[2] Cubism's geometric vocabulary resonates with the geometric style of carpets and tile works in Iran. At the same time, Cubism was a useful way to update the local vocabulary, as seen in Ziapour's *Public Bath* (1949).

Above
Jalil Ziapour
Kaboud Mosque,
late 1940s
oil on canvas

Opposite
Jalil Ziapour with
Gholam Hossein Gharib
and Hassan Shirvani
The Fighting Rooster Association, 1949
magazine

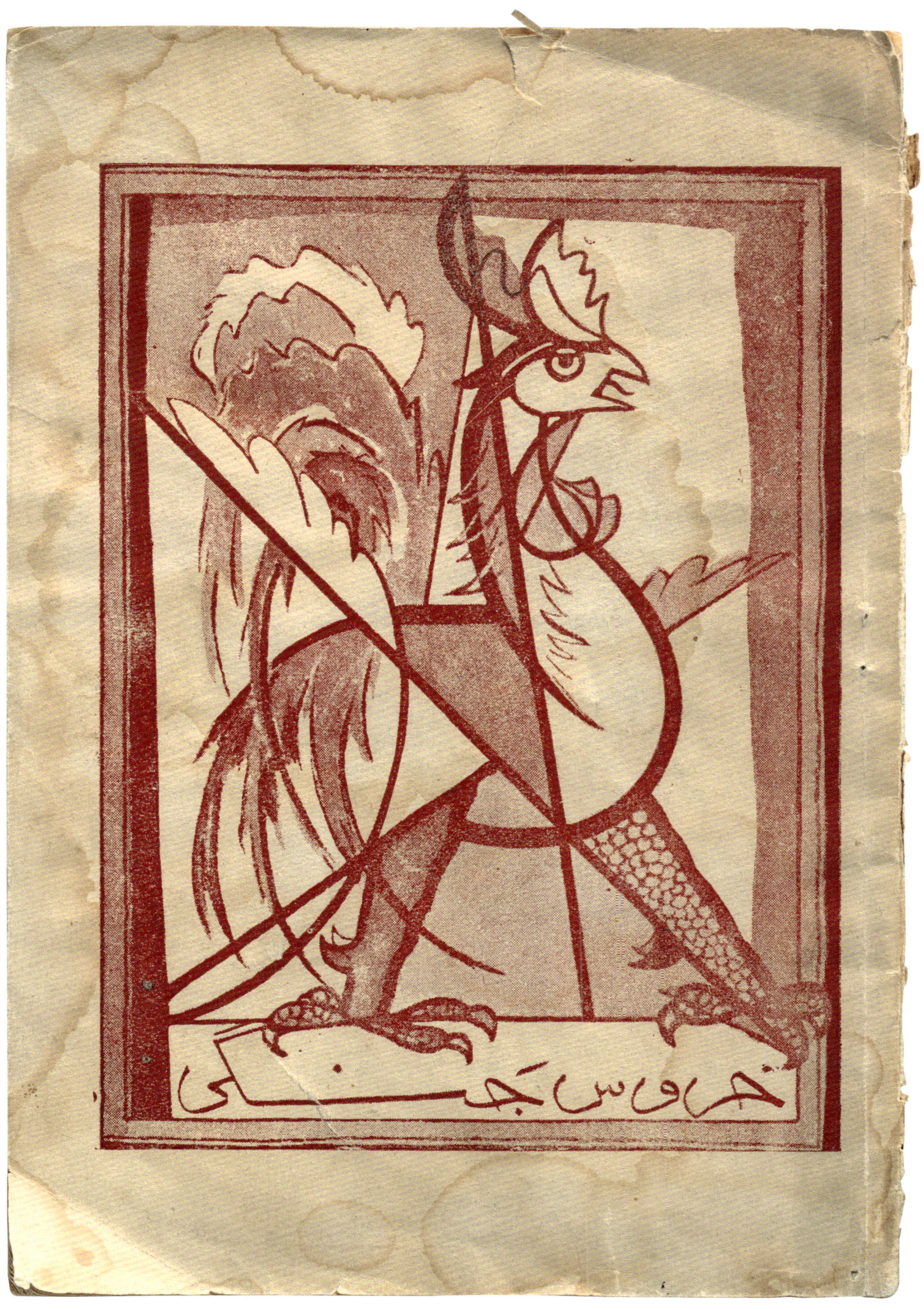
خروس جنگی

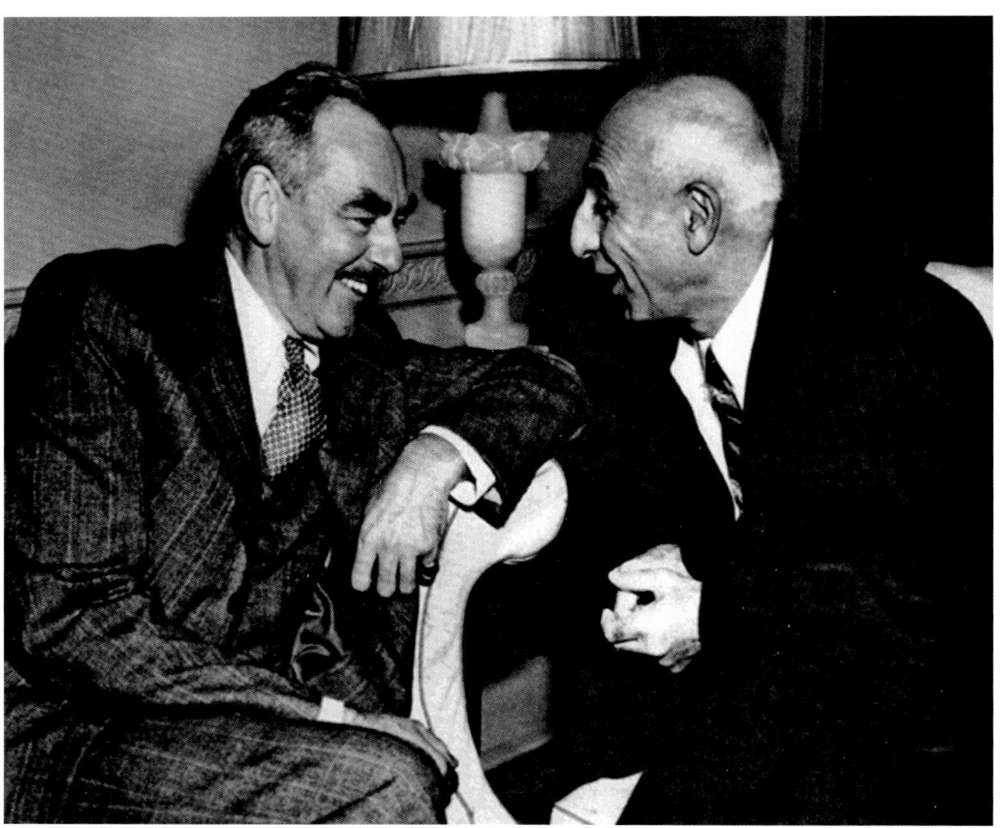

This painting, in oil on canvas, was exhibited in Tehran's Apadana Gallery in 1950 and drew criticism from art critics as a work of "Westoxication"—a term coined by writer and critic Jalal Al-e Ahmad that became popular shorthand to describe the West's influence on the artistic production of the time. Here, it implied that Ziapour and his associates were infected by the toxic ideas of the West but too intoxicated by this influence to realize it. By the end of 1951, without much support, *Fighting Rooster* no longer existed as a publication.

The year 1951 marked the beginning of major changes in Iranian politics and the country's relationship with the UK and US. In April 1951, the Iranian Parliament elected Mohammad Mosaddegh as prime minister, with a clear mandate to nationalize the British-owned Anglo-Persian Oil Company. This move sparked tension, heated debates, an economic embargo against Iranian oil and—twenty-eight months later, in 1953—a US- and British-sponsored coup d'état that overthrew the only democratic government that Iran had ever known. Historians have argued that the coup had little to do with oil and much to do with geopolitics, the fear of communism and the Soviet threat. However, I think a more telling explanation is the one put forward by historian Ervand Abrahamian, who locates it as a conflict between imperialism and nationalism: "The main concern was not so much about communism as about the dangerous repercussions that oil nationalization could have throughout the world."[3]

The 1953 coup reshaped the politics of the Middle East. The events that followed it "obliterated any possibility of a modern-secular government in Iran."[4] The new

Above
Mohammad Mosaddegh with US Secretary of State Dean Acheson, Washington, DC, October 24, 1951

Opposite
1953 Iranian coup d'état

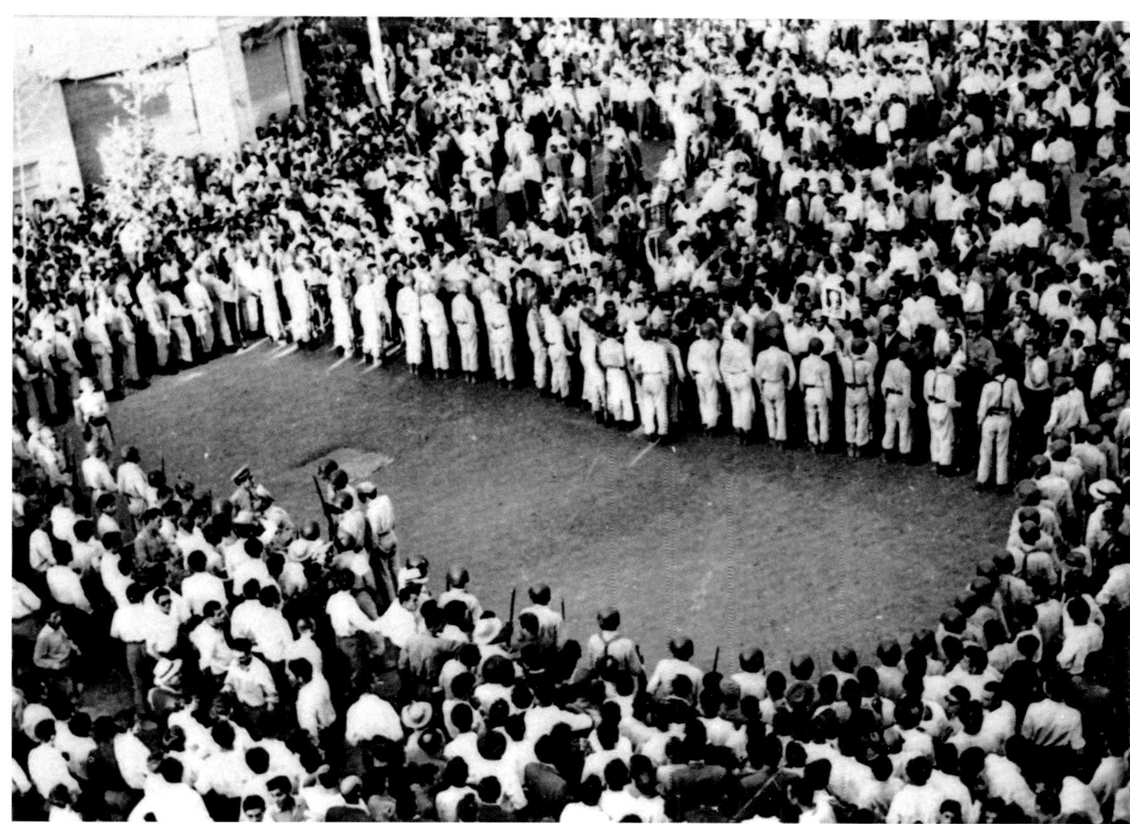

government rolled back Iran's press freedoms, civil liberties and civil society to the "draconian state since before 1941."[5] It banned all political groups—including the Tudeh (Communist) Party, which went underground—and introduced severe censorship. The political events of 1953 ensured an end to Iran's first modern avant-garde movements and artistic associations that had brought visual art, fiction and poetry together. The repressive political climate that emerged after the fall of Mossadegh made it difficult to form any modernist art societies independent of government sponsorship. It took until the middle of the following decade for a new generation of artists and writers of the modernist avant-garde to emerge.

In the climate of anti-colonial nationalism in 1950s Iran, artists such as Ziapour became part of this new avant-garde. The art critic Hal Foster characterizes the avant-garde as operating in a situation where artists' "work is never historically effective or fully significant in its initial moments," because it takes place "in the symbolic order of its time that is not prepared for it, that cannot receive it, at least not immediately, as least not without structural change."[6] The Fighting Rooster's short-lived existence could be attributed to its discontinuity with its moment. It belonged to an aggressive avant-garde, as novelist and academic Raymond Williams explains, that "saw itself as the breakthrough to the future: its members were not the bearers of a progress already repetitiously defined, but the militants of a creativity which would revive and liberate humanity."[7] Although Ziapour's was not a clear break from the past, it "could move readily towards socialist and other radical and revolutionary tendencies."[8]

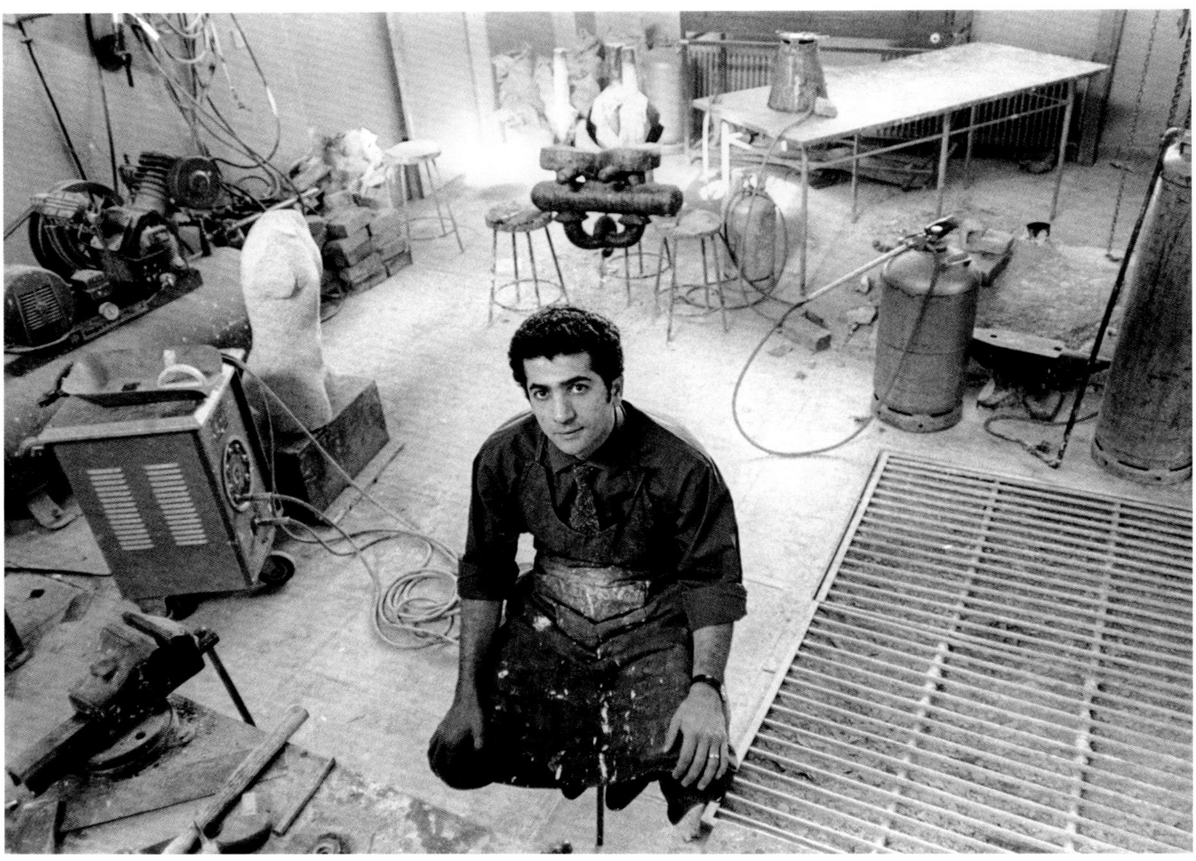

At the time of these tensions in 1953, Parviz Tanavoli was just sixteen and enrolled at the School of Fine Arts for Boys in Tehran. When he left in 1956 to further his studies in Italy, he travelled to Carrara, known for centuries as the source of marble for sculpture making. Later, he studied at the Brera Academy in Milan under the noted Italian sculptors Ugo Guidi and Marino Marini. His experiences in Italy further exposed Tanavoli to figurative work and modernist primitivism. When he returned to Iran in 1959, Tanavoli began contemplating how to create sculpture that was at once Iranian and thoroughly modern; that is, an art that dialogued with modernist art forebears and yet was radically contemporary. Although he studied outside Iran and was exposed to modernism in the West, Tanavoli was one of those artists who looked to Iranian history to create a modern sculptural language. He began to layer sacred and secular histories in his works, which became a defining aspect of his practice. This integration of the forms and philosophies of international modernism with the crafts and symbols of Iran's rich popular culture is a crucial aspect of both Tanavoli's practice and the subsequent development of modern sculpture in Iran. As Daftari explains in *Persia Reframed: Iranian Visions of Modern and Contemporary Art* (2019), Tanavoli single-handedly modernized Iranian sculpture. Through his sculptures, he developed a visual language and "symbology that would have a lasting impact on Modernism in Iran widely recognized as fully capturing the duality and interplay of Iran's pre-Islamic and Islamic cultural identities. He is the inventor of a language that is still being deciphered to this day and of a sculpture for a modern Iran."[9]

Parviz Tanavoli in his Tehran University studio, 1965

It is important to note that, in the mid-twentieth century, artists in Iran largely lacked a national tradition of art history. This was especially true in the medium of sculpture. The art critic Javad Mojabi argues that—even taking into account Achaemenian bas-reliefs and statues from the Sasanian era (224–651 CE)—Iran does not have a heritage of sculpture comparable to those of its Asian neighbours. Islamic beliefs related to image making also contributed to the lack of visual references available for inspiration, since "under Islam, three dimensional representations had virtually disappeared."[10] Instead, artists looked to poetry and mythology, which have a long and abundant history in Persian culture. As a result, poetry and folklore became the language of art that brought artists together under a unifying, national identity between 1950 and 1977.

In the early 1960s, a movement coalesced around ten artists with a shared interest in reflecting popular culture in their art. They took inspiration from artisanal bazaar objects, processional imagery, shrine motifs and other local artistic and cultural references. The artist and critic Karim Emami referred to the movement as "Saqqakhaneh"—a reference to the shrine-like niches found in some public drinking fountains, often decorated with both religious and non-religious symbols. These fountains pay tribute to Shi'a martyrs who were denied water during the Battle of Karbala in 680 CE and signify a place of refuge and healing. The term became permanently associated with the group, which included Charles Hossein Zenderoudi and Mansour Ghandriz. Despite the variety of individual approaches, the artists' practices all suggest that art can be a place that both welcomes and transcends the everyday. As with previous movements, Saqqakhaneh articulated a culturally specific modernism.

Zenderoudi studied at the School of Decorative Arts in Tehran under Shokouh Riazi and Soudabeh Ghanjei, both members of the group of artists called Pioneers of Iranian New Art. Ghanjei seems to have almost disappeared from art history, perhaps because of her death at a young age. She graduated from the École des Beaux-Arts in Paris in 1955 with a gold medal, became a teacher at the Faculty of Fine Arts in Tehran and taught many artists who later became associated with this movement. Zenderoudi studied under these women until about 1961, when he moved to Paris, where he has lived since. As judged by his canvases, he wasn't overtly influenced by the Parisian environment. Intrigued by the popular visual culture of the Shi'a religious working class, he found his inspiration instead in the streets, bazaars and back alleys of the less affluent neighbourhoods of Tehran. He looked at popular culture, talismans, zodiac signs, posters, charms, prayers and props used in mourning processions (such as the severed hand of the martyr Hazrat Abbas). Then, with a shift, he turned to the Persian alphabet in 1965, set aside Saqqakhaneh and took up calligraphic modernism. In this new phase of lyrical abstraction, Zenderoudi worked with oil on canvas, making letters the protagonists of his paintings. This move toward more abstract work brought him greater acceptance in Paris.

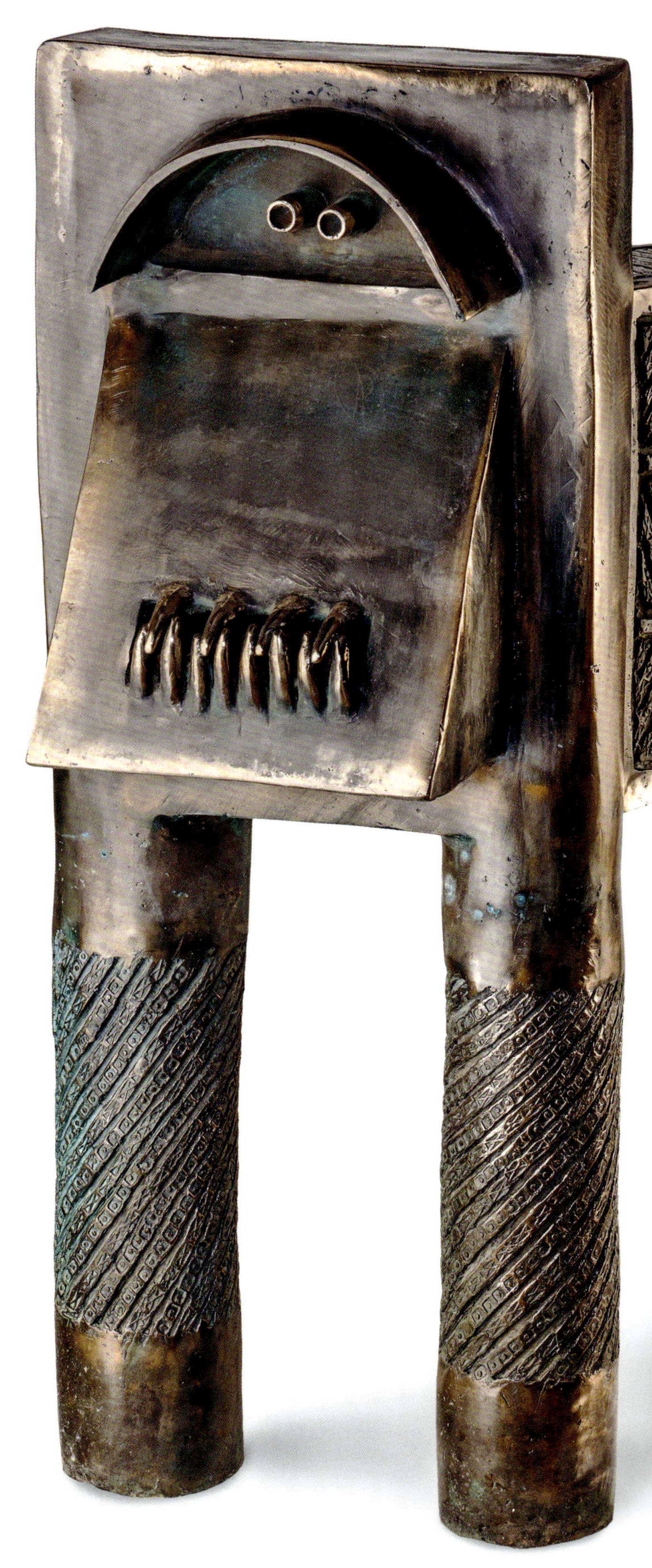

Parviz Tanavoli
Lion, 1976
bronze

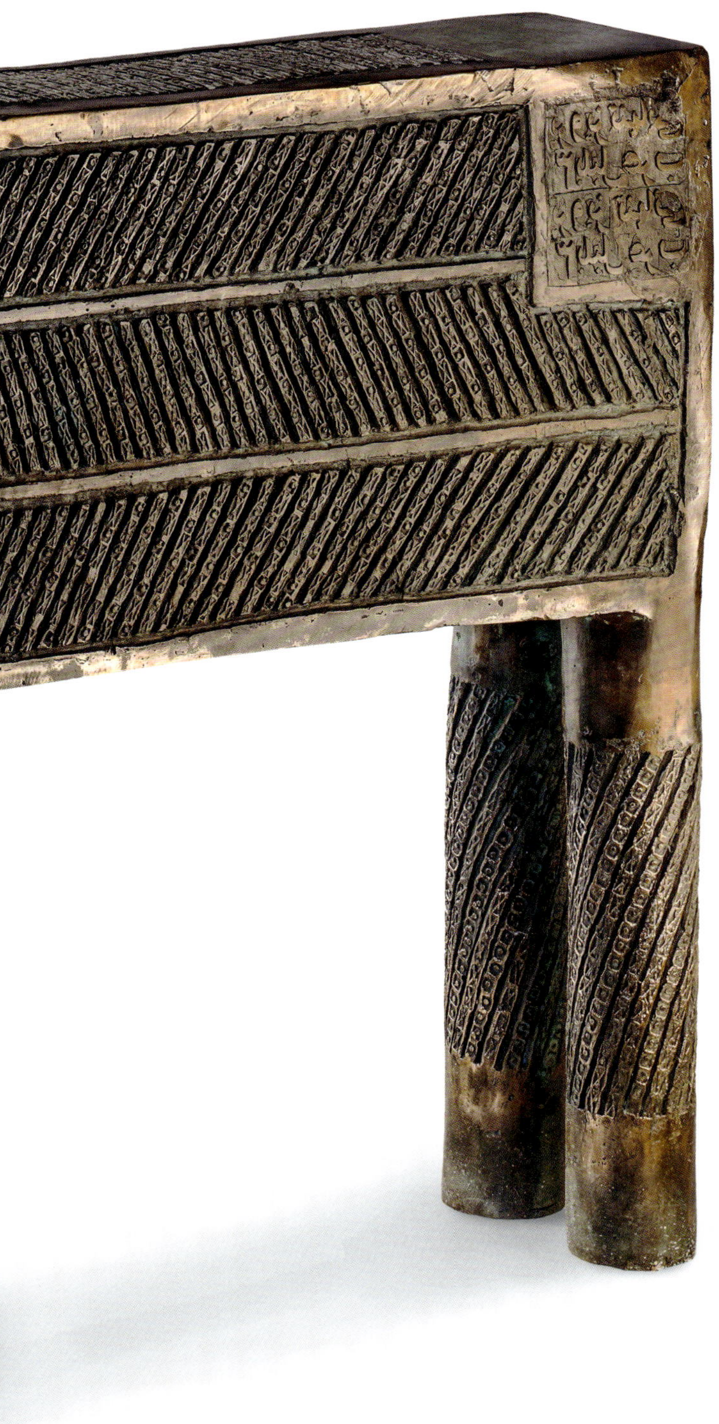

Ghandriz was a painter and printmaker known for his abstract forms of mythical creatures reminiscent of traditional Persian design. He represented ancient forms and everyday objects in a graphic, primitive style. Like the other founders of the Saqqakhaneh movement, he referenced traditional Iranian decorative art and textile patterns. Images of old Persian pottery, decorated with motifs of humans, animals or mythical creatures, often feature in his paintings.

Other Saqqakhaneh artists include Mohsen Vaziri-Moghaddam, born in Tehran in 1924, who began his art education at the Faculty of Fine Arts at the University of Tehran and continued his training at the Academy of Fine Arts in Rome between 1955 and 1963. When Iranian artists arrived in Italy in the 1950s, they encountered the Arte Informale movement, which sought a break with the past through improvisation and lyrical abstraction.[11] Italy, like France, was still emerging from the war years and rejecting the fascist aesthetics associated with the practice of representational art.[12] Vaziri-Moghaddam, who had come to Rome to study abstraction, was encouraged by Italian abstract painters to find a personal vision for his practice—a vision he found in his sand paintings, which show his relationship with the deserts of Iran and his love for Persian antiquity. For these works, he laid out sand and moved it with his fingers on the canvas, then pressed the surface of the canvas, partly covered in glue, onto the sand.

Bahman Mohassess left Iran after the fall of Mossadegh in 1954. He mostly lived in seclusion after the coup of 1953 and is said to have held on to the catastrophe of what came next. He struggled with the Westernism of modernity the same way he struggled with the difficult memory of "Iran's troubled dive into modernity."[13] After leaving Iran, he studied at the Academy of Fine Arts in Rome. Although he lived in Rome most of his life and died there in 2005, he was not interested in the Italian art movements of the time. Nor, though he was an admirer of the poet Nima Yushij, whose work had been featured in the first issue of *Fighting Rooster*, was he interested in creating a language from the traditional art of Iran. With an aesthetic interest in Pablo Picasso and Henry Moore, Mohassess found his own theatrical and mythological figures in blind vultures, owls and ominous semi-human creatures. He also translated the works of Italian writers such as Italo Calvino and Luigi Pirandello into Farsi, directed several plays and participated in numerous exhibitions, including the Venice Biennale in 1956 and the biennales of Paris and São Paulo in 1962. Although he started his career as a painter, Mohassess produced many sculptures. Because he decided to destroy most of them in the early 2000s, very few still exist. In Iran, he found patronage in public commissions and with collectors such as Queen Farah Pahlavi and the film director Ebrahim Golestan.

Mansour Ghandriz
Untitled, c. 1960
oil on burlap

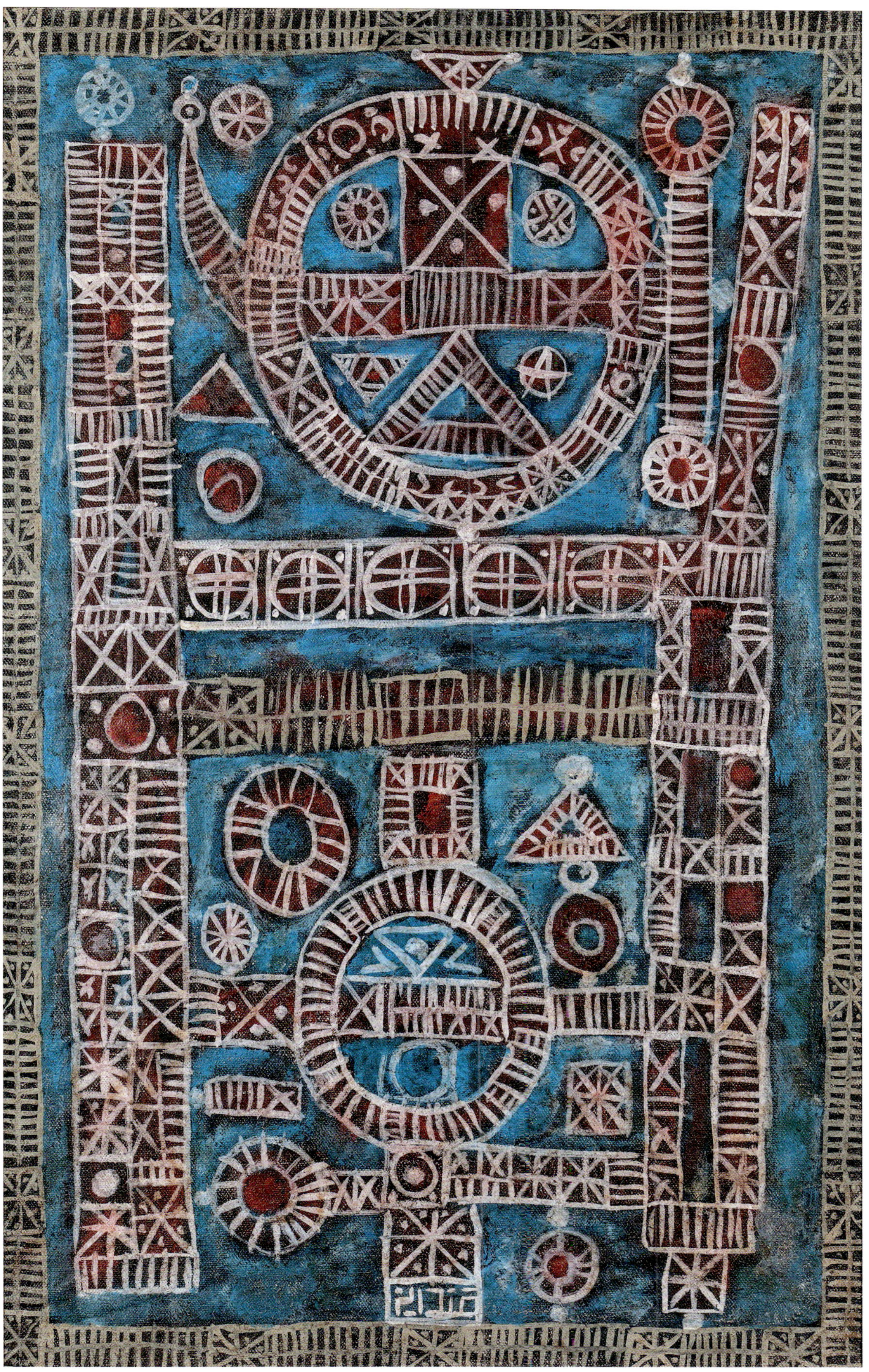

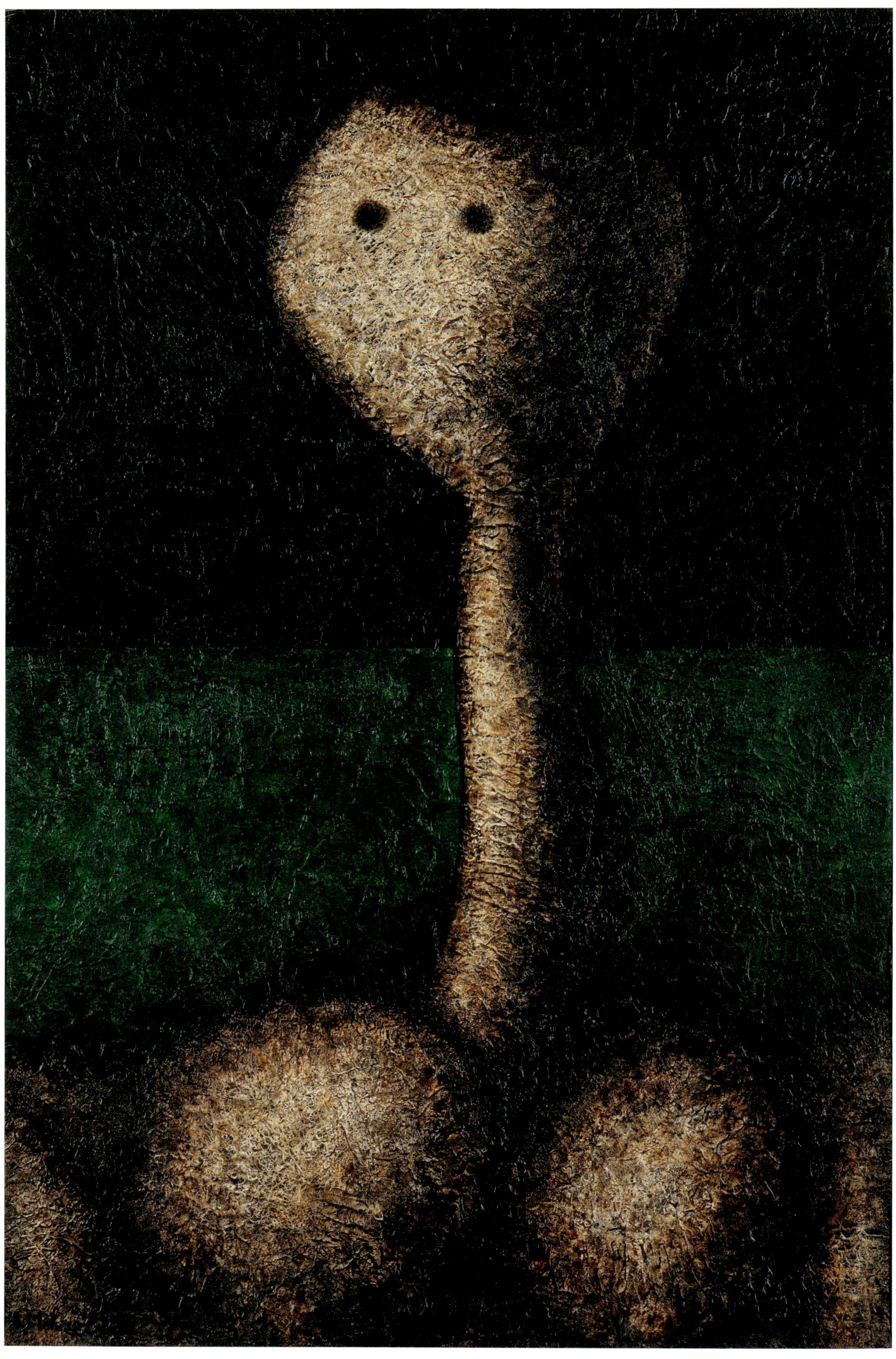

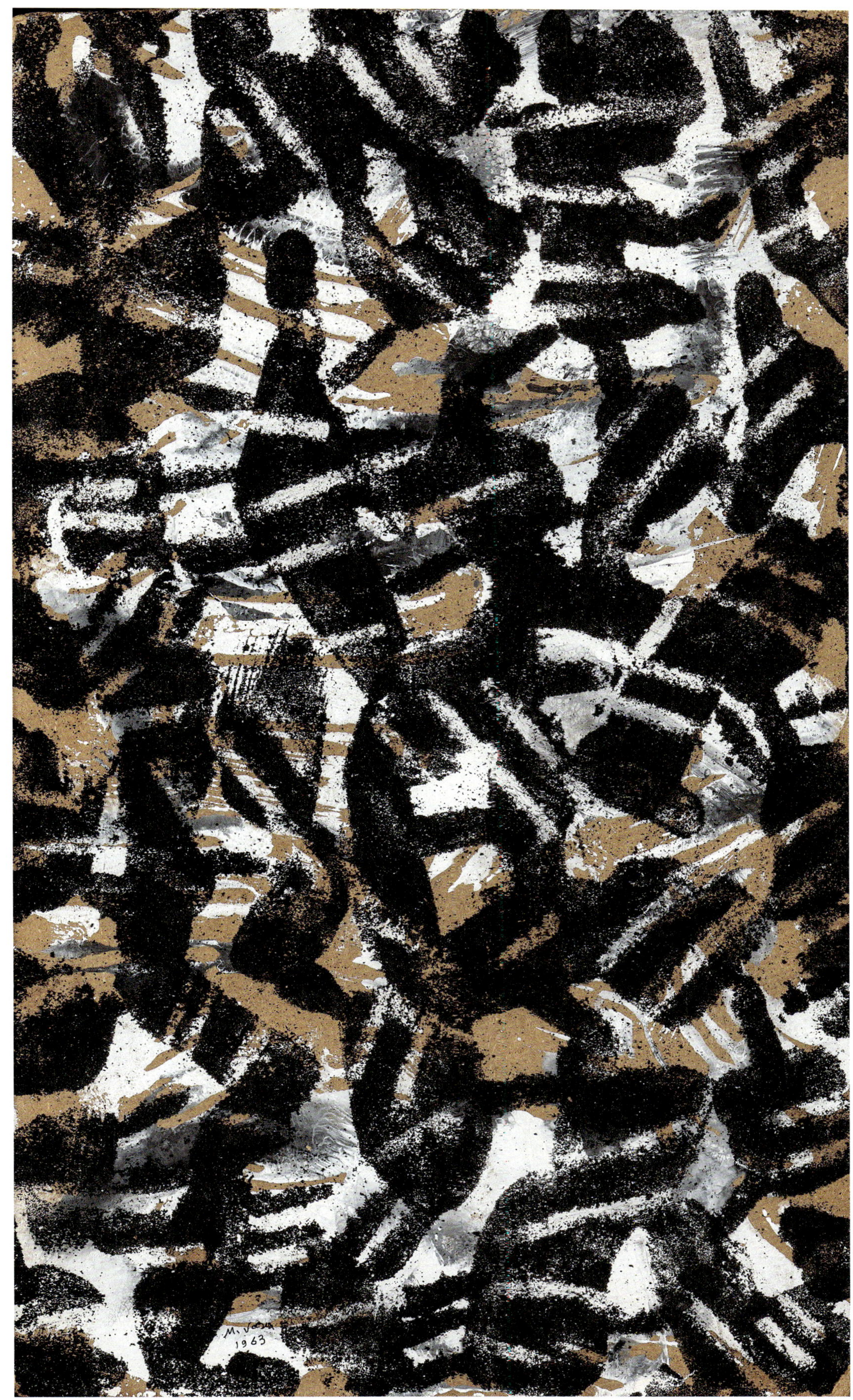

Opposite
Bahman Mohassess
Untitled, 1960
oil on canvas

Right
Mohsen Vaziri-Moghaddam
Ritmo Continuo
(Harkat-e modām), 1963
mixed media

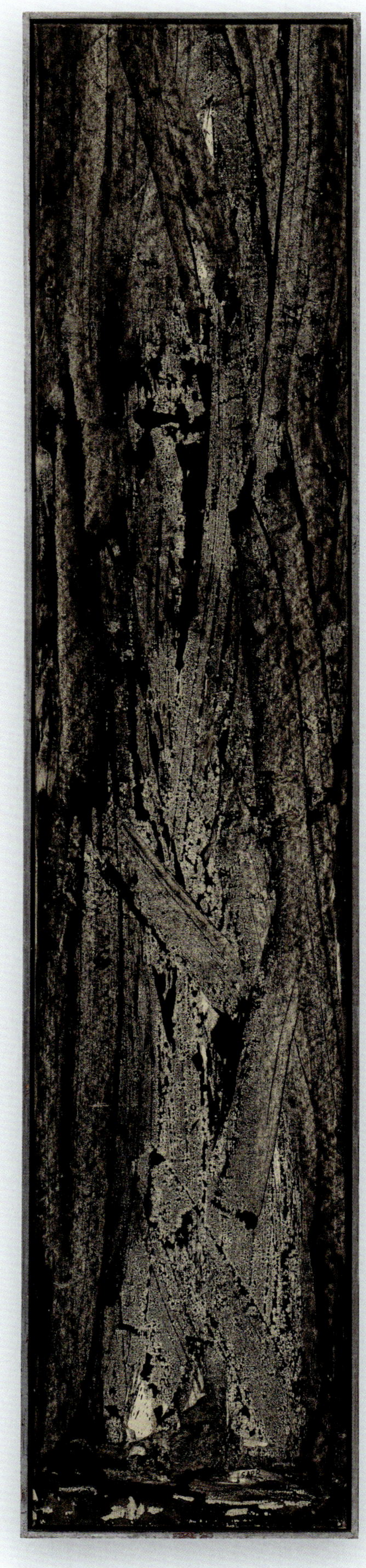

Like Mohassess, Behjat Sadr arrived in Italy in the post-World War II era, when the Arte Informale movement was the avant-garde. Sadr's practice was filled with experimentation with material and gesture. Although classically trained in calligraphy, she fully abstracted her brushstrokes, bringing traditional technique into dialogue with Abstract Expressionism out of the US. Sadr is affiliated with an action called "negative painting," which is a process of removing paint from the surface of material, canvas, glass or paper.

As Daftari quotes Sadr: "[W]ith all the possibilities of communication, travelling, and exchanges we are not just influenced by our traditional cultures, but the globalized, multicultural environment too leaves its own impression on us."[14] These artists worked fluidly between Iranian and Western modes, some more influenced by their early education in Iran than others.

Likewise, Monir Shahroudy Farmanfarmaian's sculptures can be seen in relation to Western modern art, yet they reference distinct cultural legacies, such as mirror mosaics and geometry related to Islamic architecture. Farmanfarmaian was born in 1924 in Iran and spent most of her adult life in New York City. In the 1940s and 50s, she studied fashion illustration and collaborated on many commercial projects with the Pop artist Andy Warhol, who at the time was working as an advertising illustrator. In the late 50s, Farmanfarmaian returned to Iran, fascinated with mirror and mosaic works—the cut-out squares and hexagons of the shrines and mosques. Her encounters in Iran with architectural decoration and artistry resulted in her most famous body of work—her mirror-mosaic relief sculptures—which Daftari describes from an art historical perspective as "an attempt to create modernism with local iconography, materials, and techniques."[15] Representative of neither traditional nor modern art in Iran, Monir's practice is not related to Sufism or spirituality. Her works are each an illusion created by geometric shapes fragmenting the surface of reverse paintings.

Through new expressions of forms, these artists positioned their work between a fixed past and an open future, and for a few years experimental and interdisciplinary art flourished. At a time when their Western contemporaries often strove to break with the past, Iran's contemporary artists reimagined folk culture and populist themes and reconstructed traditional content within contemporary forms.

Other artists drew on traditional calligraphic motifs to pursue modern forms. Seyed Mohammad Ehsaey and Reza Mafi, for example, did not find their inspiration toward abstraction primarily in European art. Ehsaey, born in 1939, and Mafi, born in 1943, were still children at the time of the 1953 coup. Both were classically trained in calligraphic techniques, including Persian *nastaʿliq* and Arabic *muhaqqaq*. In the years following the coup, when Iranian cultural practices underwent a transformation and a bifurcation, they were pioneers of

Behjat Sadr
Siyāh o Sefid, c. 1961
oil on canvas

Top
Reza Mafi
Untitled, 1971
ink on paper

Bottom
Seyed Mohammad Ehsaey
Untitled, 1973
oil on canvas

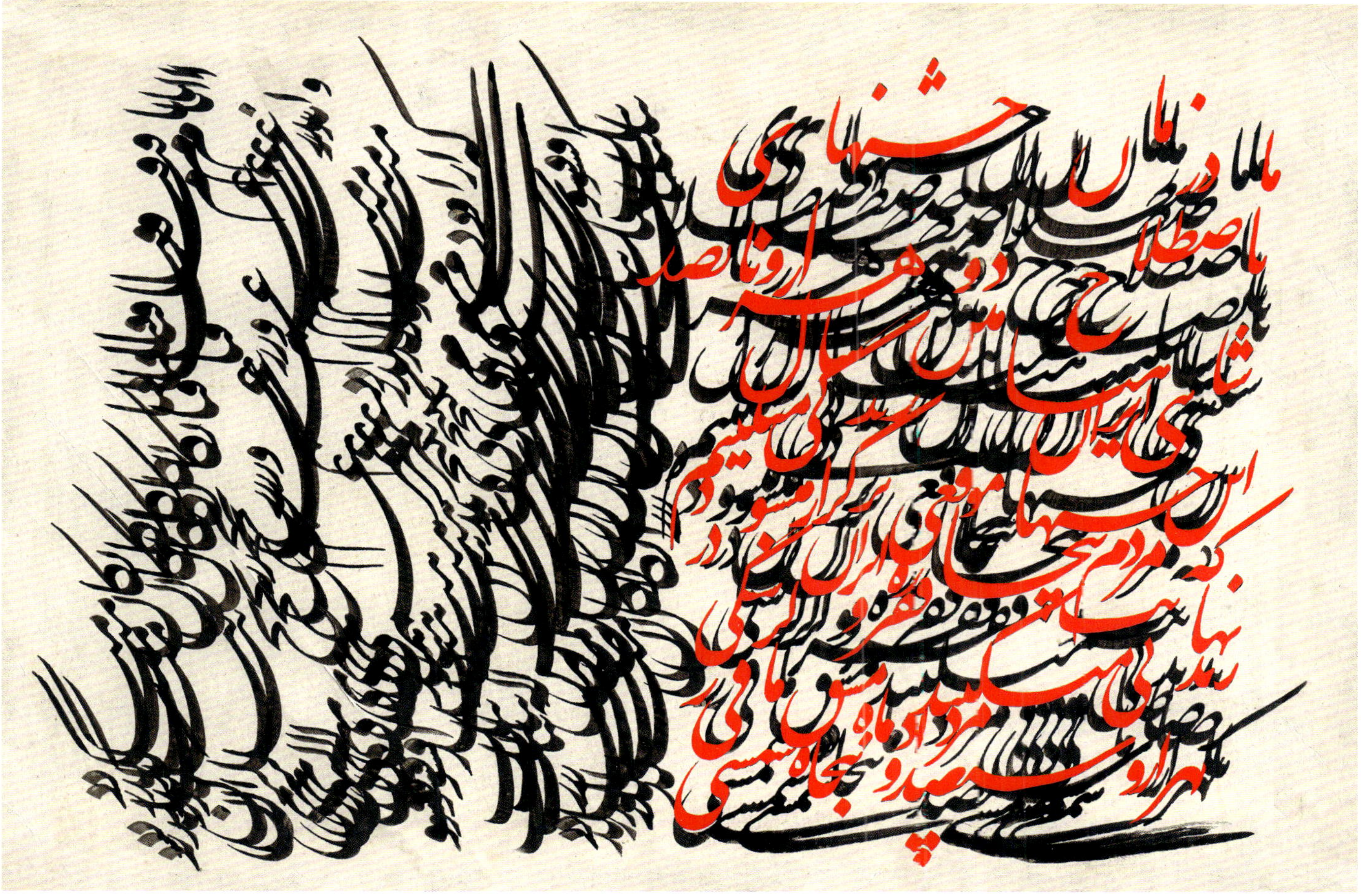

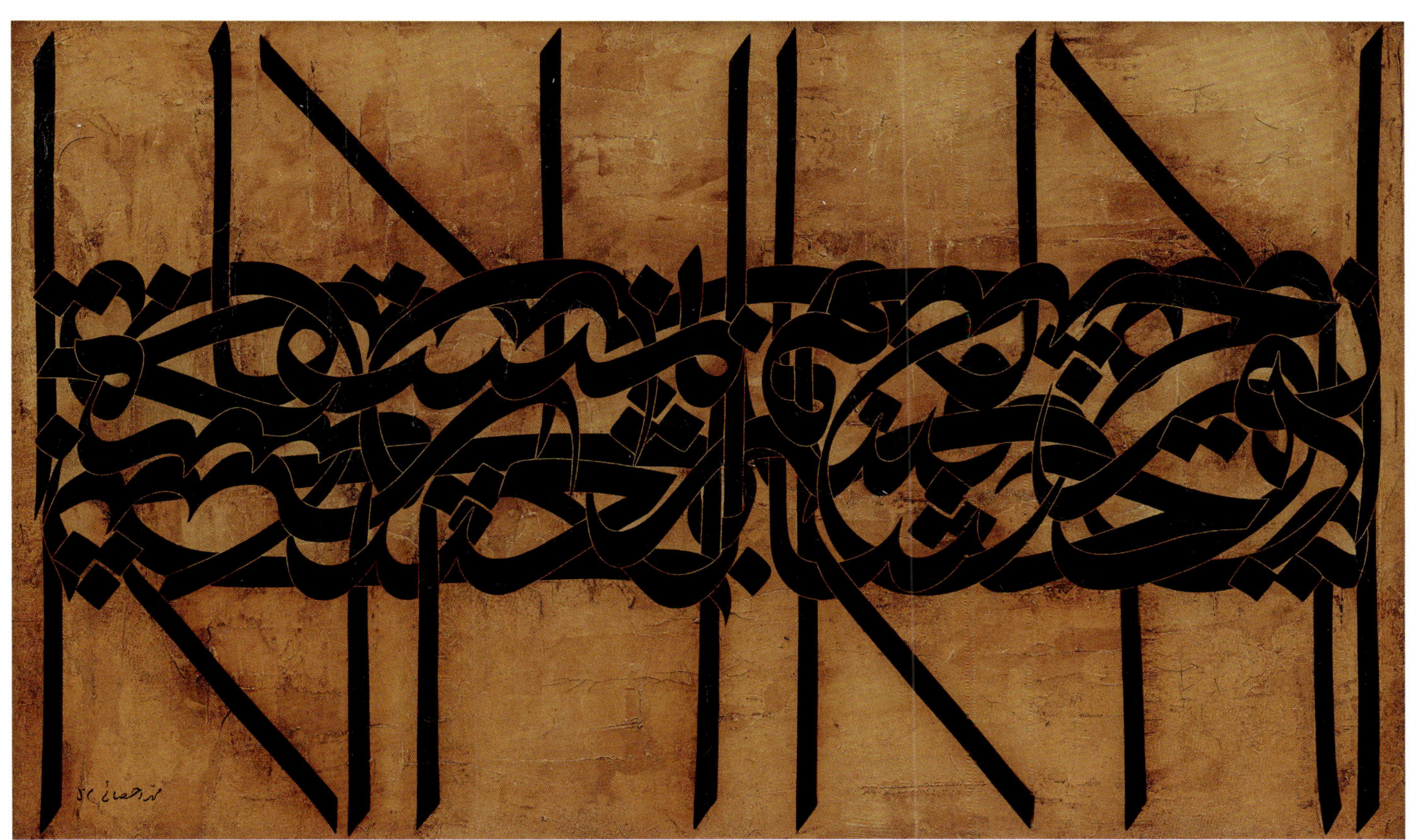

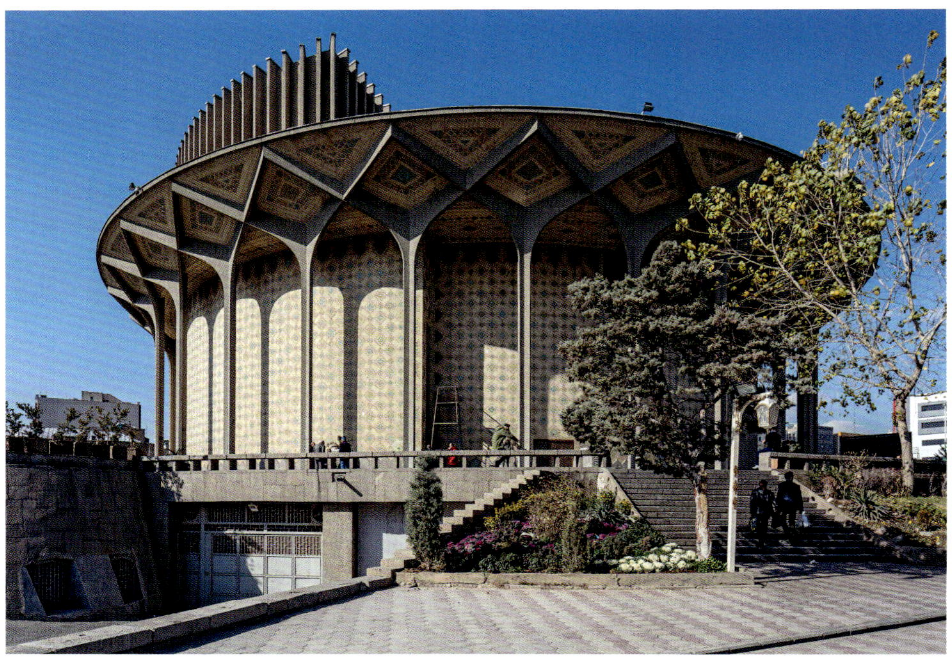

the neo-traditional approach, which drew heavily on calligraphy, iconography and ancient Persian motifs. At a time of increasing global consciousness and technological development, many artists reconceived folk culture and traditional craft to forge a link between heritage and progress. Along with others in the movement, Ehsaey and Mafi repurposed and extended the form and function of calligraphy into painting. Ehsaey in particular incorporated traditional script and Shi'i symbols into his artworks, interlacing texts to provide a contemplative space for language that does not rely on direct translation. Such calligraphic arts synthesized image and text, providing a rich medium through which history, literature and culture could be accessed and subverted.

Architecture in Iran during this period also reflected this confluence of national and international movements and references. The story of Iranian modern architecture from 1941 to 1960 is relatively unknown, but the nationalization of Iranian oil had an immense impact on the development of architecture in the country after 1960. During this era, the Pahlavi family as well as the academic and professional elites made key decisions regarding the nation's modernization process. After World War II, most engineers and architects were primarily educated in Europe, and they were given "a mandate by the hierarchy of the country to build a new identity for modern Iran."[16] Basic national infrastructure was the focus of construction after the war. However, beginning in 1960, several important architectural developments took place following the nationalization of oil in 1951. It was during the post-coup era that "[n]ationalization of oil awakened a civic pride that became a positive motivating force; national income saw a modest increase; master plans for most cities, along with national plans for development, were created; many foreign-trained Iranians returned home from abroad; and Iran became the site for major international architectural conferences."[17]

Ali Sardar Afkhami, The City Theater, Tehran, Iran, 1972 (photo 2018)

As described by architect and theorist Nader Ardalan, aesthetically, architectural design had two branches. One pursued the modernist International Style, as led by Ali Sardar Afkhami, Abdol-Aziz Farmanfarmaian and Jahangir Darvish. The other concept was mostly vernacular and drew on Iran's architectural history.[18] Practitioners of this style of design included Hossein Amanat, Kamran Diba and Houshang Seyhoun. This dual response to modernism mirrors the ways in which painters and sculptors approached their means of representation. On one side, they investigated traditional forms, and on the other, the progress of modernization in the West.

What makes Iranian modern visual art unique is its intertwined story with the specific politics of the time. Oil reserves in Iran were estimated to be the third largest in the world. Its production in Iran was the largest in the Middle East and fourth largest in the world. The political events that followed the nationalization of this oil industry had an immense impact on the cultural production of the time, and so it is important to recognize and study the effects of these events from the 1940s to the late 1970s on modernist art in Iran. It is the politics of the time that makes this an era of the vernacular and, as a result, of a modern art for Iran.

ENDNOTES

1 Katrin Nahidi, "Cubism in Iran: Jalil Ziapour and the Fighting Rooster Association," *Stedelijk Studies Journal*, no. 9 (2019): 9.

2 Fereshteh Daftari, "Iran Colloquium: Fereshteh Daftari, Independent Scholar and Curator," YouTube video, 1:32:52, posted February 19, 2021, by Middle Eastern Studies, Yale MacMillan Center, https://youtu.be/emG7LYJ_7NU.

3 Ervand Abrahamian, *The Coup: 1953, the CIA, and the Roots of Modern U.S.-Iranian Relations* (New York: New Press, 2013), 5.

4 Abrahamian, *The Coup*, 28.

5 Arta Khakpour, "A Divorce of Avant-Gardes: Surrealism and the Socialism in Post-Reza Shah Iran," *Middle Eastern Literatures* 19, no. 2 (2016): 132.

6 Hal Foster, *The Return of the Real: The Avant-Garde at the End of the Century* (Cambridge, MA: MIT Press), 29.

7 Raymond Williams, *The Politics of Modernism: Against the New Conformists* (London: Verso, 2007), 51.

8 Williams, *The Politics of Modernism*, 58.

9 Fereshteh Daftari, *Persia Reframed: Iranian Visions of Modern and Contemporary Art* (London: I.B. Tauris, 2019), 60.

10 David D. Galloway and James W. Allan, *Parviz Tanavoli: Sculptor, Writer, and Collector* (Tehran: Iranian Art Publishing, 2000), 25.

11 See Fereshteh Daftari, "Redefining Modernism," in *Iran Modern*, ed. Fereshteh Daftari and Layla S. Diba (New York: Yale University Press and Asia Society, 2013), 35.

12 Daftari, "Redefining Modernism," 35.

13 Morad Motazami, conversation with the author, Paris, 2016.

14 Sadr, quoted in Daftari, "Redefining Modernism," 35.

15 Daftari, *Persia Reframed*, 66.

16 Nader Ardalan, "Modern Iranian Architecture, 1941–79," in Daftari and Diba, *Iran Modern*, 73.

17 Ardalan, "Modern Iranian Architecture," 73.

18 Ardalan, "Modern Iranian Architecture," 74.

Massoumeh Seyhoun
Composition #13, 1967
enamel and lacquer
on canvas

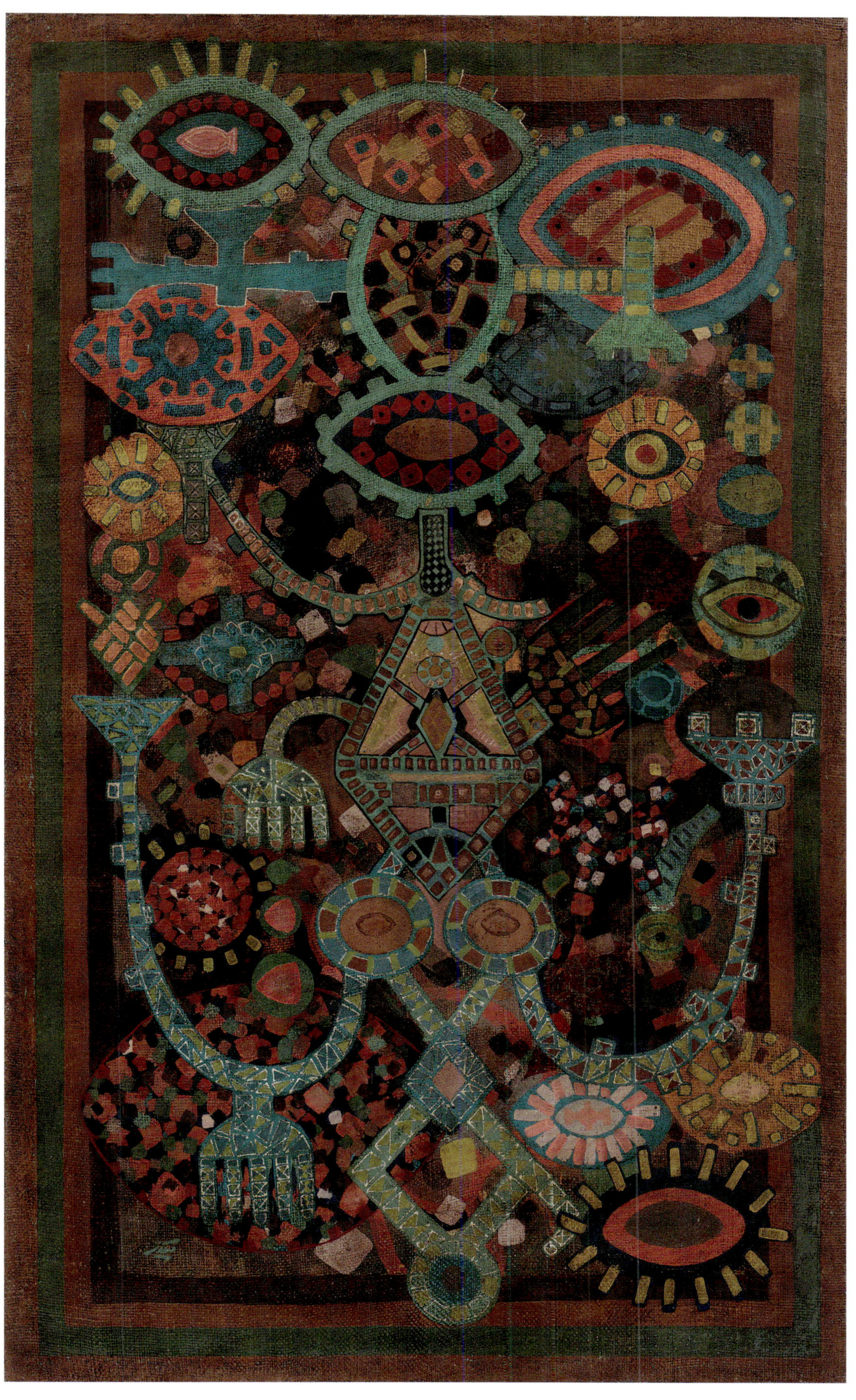

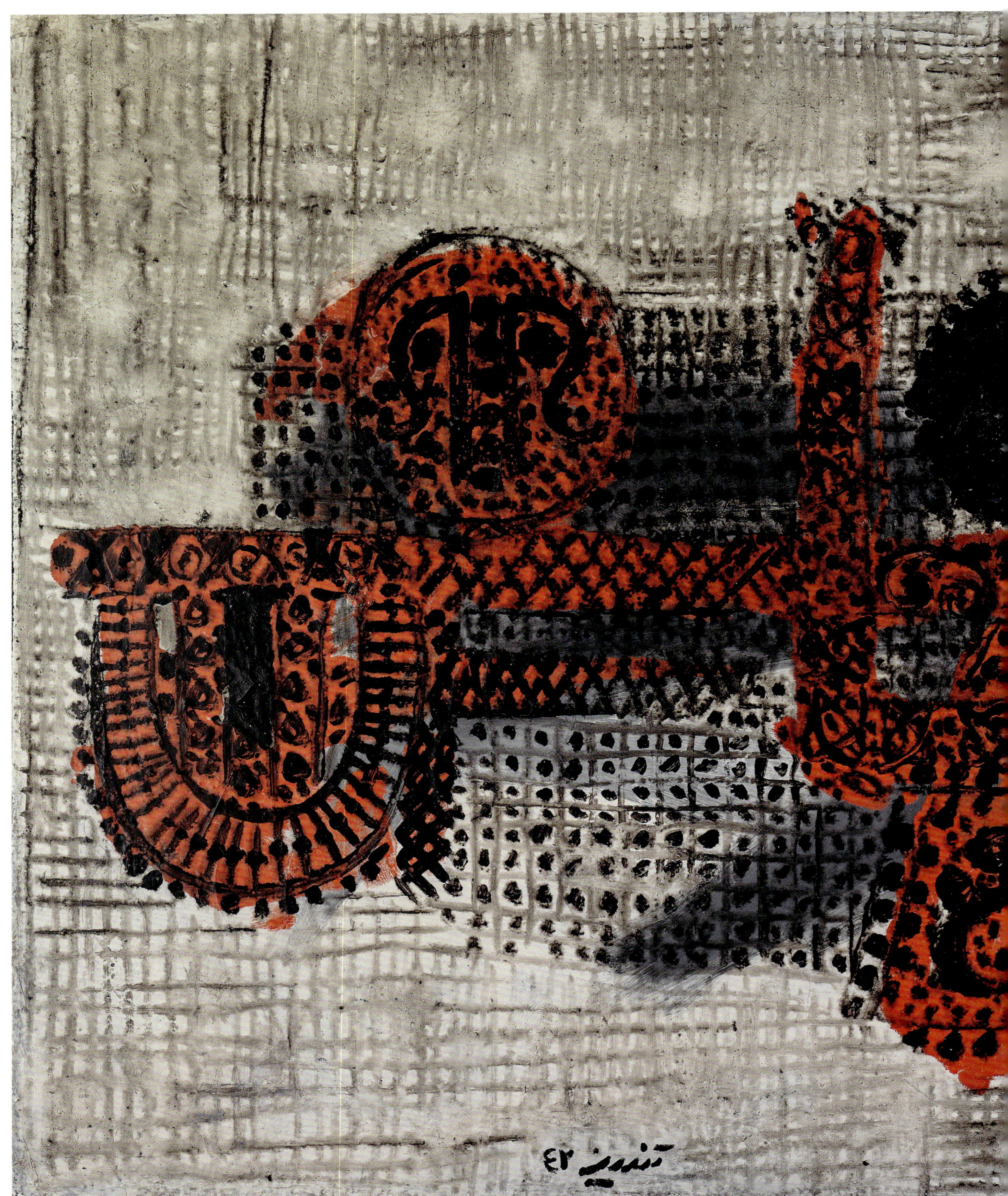

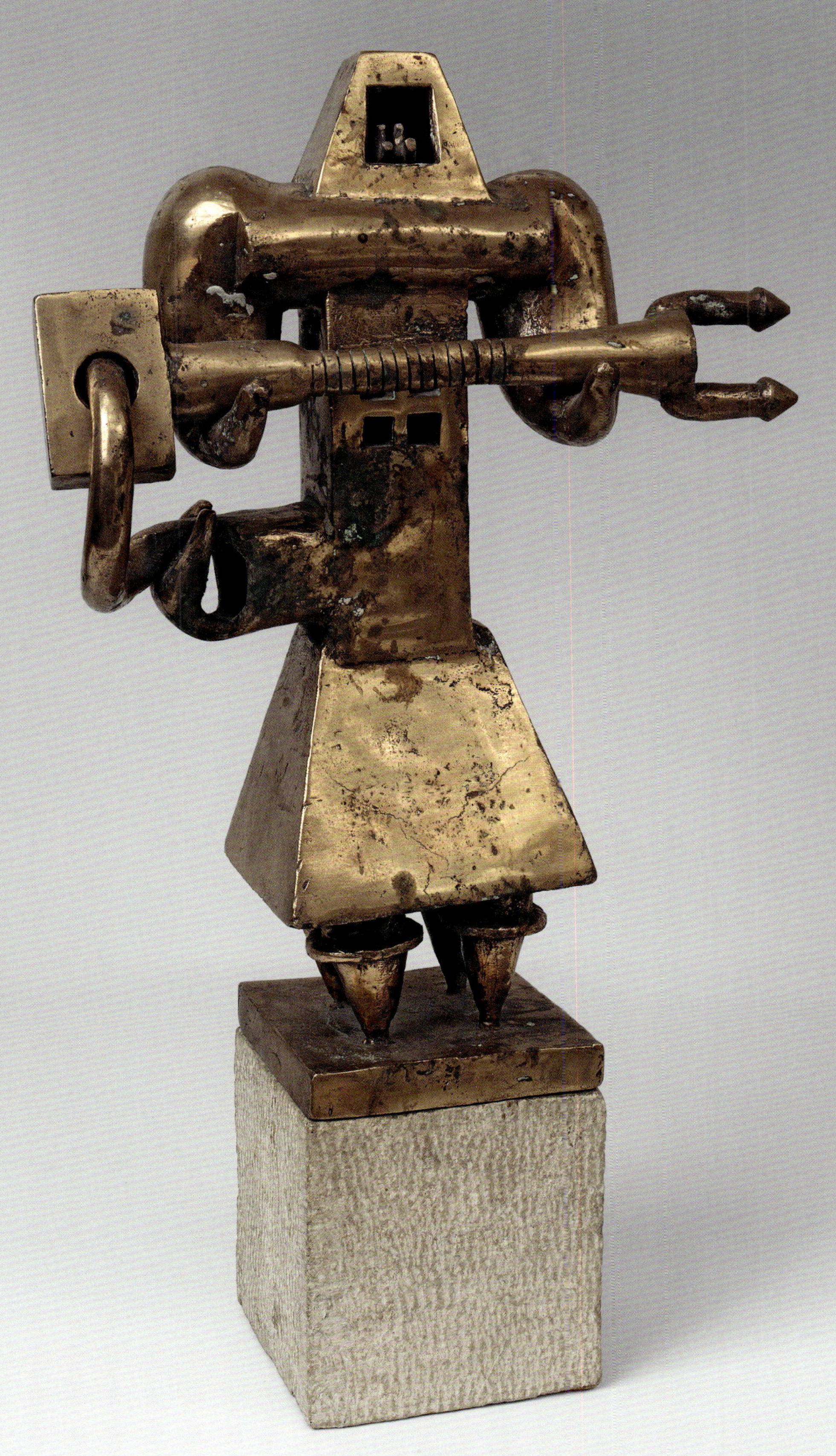

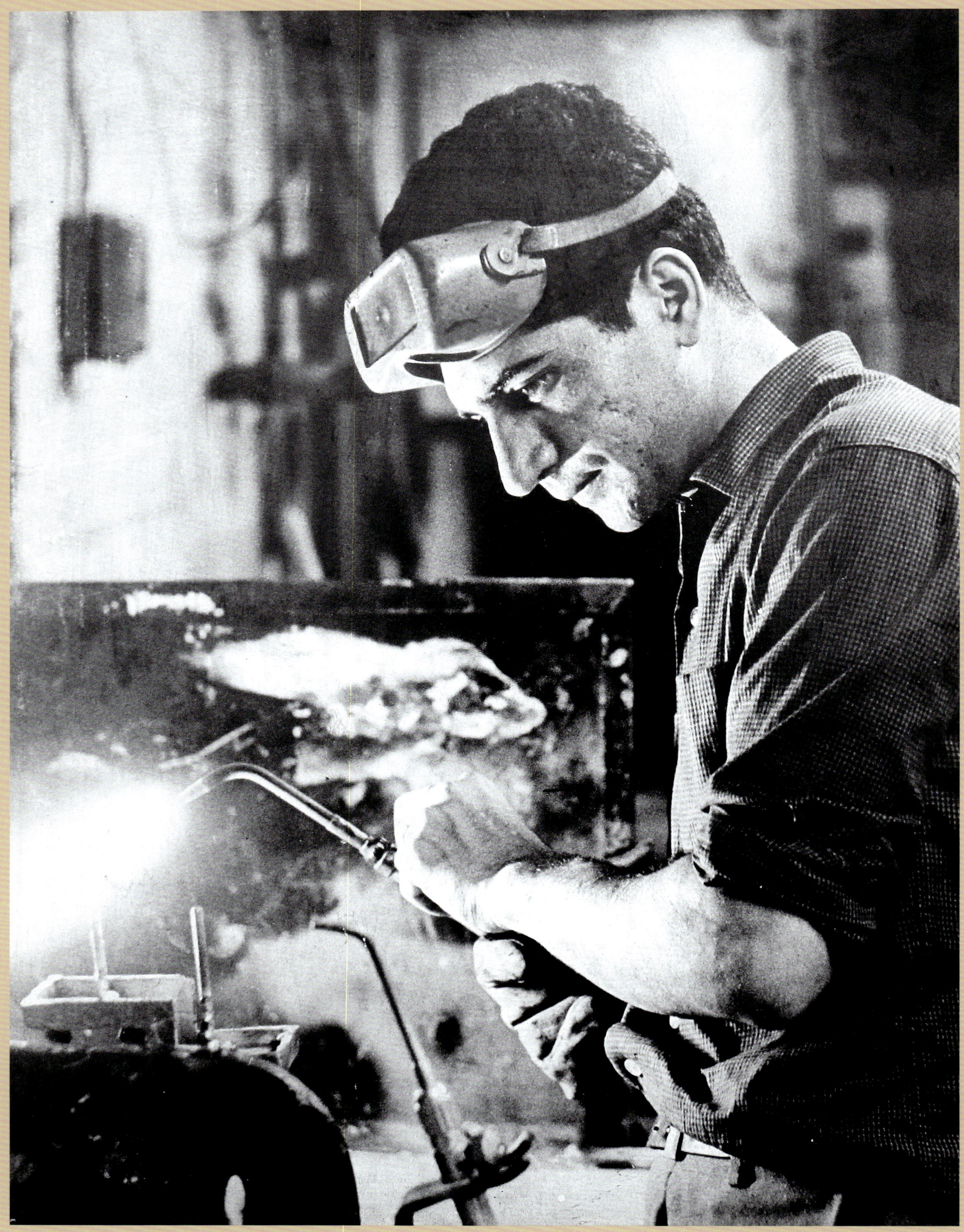

THREADS OF BRONZE AND VERSE: PARVIZ TANAVOLI IN CONVERSATION WITH DAVOOD MADADPOOR

Vancouver – Berlin, 2024

DAVOOD MADADPOOR Dear Maestro, I'd like to open our conversation with a personal question. With over sixty-five years of artistic creation and research, what moments in your journey inspired you to carve a path in art? What guided your hand to embrace such materials and themes?

PARVIZ TANAVOLI Apart from the early years when I worked with scrap metals—a relatively straightforward approach for anyone—my path evolved into something more unique. When my early works won awards at the Tehran Biennale, even the welder who assisted me in constructing those pieces soon began assembling similar animal figures from scrap metal and displaying them in front of his workshop. When I explained that this was not the correct way to approach art, he replied, "Why is it right for you but not for us when we want to earn a modest living?"

After that, I chose a path that could not be as easily imitated by others, whether in my bronze or copper works or in selecting materials and themes.

DM Upon returning to Iran after completing your studies abroad, you realized Iranian craftspeople's immense skill and expertise in creating forms and handcrafted works. This observation sparked your curiosity, prompting an interesting perspective toward these handmade objects and the architecture surrounding them. This process gradually evolved into an obsession for collecting and exploring these creations. Eventually, this obsession led you to believe that Iranian sculpture does not need inspiration from the West, as many sources of creativity and inspiration are already present within Iran. Could you elaborate further on this perspective and explain how you arrived at this viewpoint?

PT When I returned to Iran, I observed that craftspeople were highly skilled in creating forms and shapes with remarkable creativity, whether in locks or other objects. I enjoyed their expertise but never wanted to replicate their designs with slight modifications. I did not want to be part of that emerging trend, such as creating simplified replicas of Persepolis reliefs. I didn't want to replicate what others were doing, but I was not indifferent to the idea of transforming these concepts.

Eventually, I found a way and expressed it in my monumental bronze sculpture *Oh Persepolis* (1975). I did not neglect calligraphy either, engaging extensively with calligraphers and experimenting with printing houses. Among the countless iterations, I adopted the most straightforward form: the letter aleph, resembling the number one. I did not simply let it remain in its basic form but integrated it into a wall commemorating Farhad the Mountain Carver.[1] This was not the end of my journey, however, as I continued to explore new directions, leading to works that, despite their complexity, carried a simplicity that made them distinctive and difficult to imitate.

Parviz Tanavoli at the Minneapolis College of Art and Design, 1963

For instance, I began using repetitive two-layered forms in some of my sculptures and walls, eventually developing a personal approach. This technique was applied, among other things, to a monumental wall featuring the body of a lion, which became one of the emblematic works of that era.[2]

DM In your book *Virus of Collecting*, published by Nazar Art Publication in 2020, you mention that your interest in collecting began in childhood and developed into a lifelong passion. Unlike many collectors, your focus has been on acquiring peculiar and rare objects, with a particular emphasis on traditional Iranian crafts. Could you explain how these items have inspired your artistic creations and influenced your art-making process in a practical way? How have these items impacted your choice of materials, techniques or artistic themes? How do you view the relationship between the objects you collect and the pieces you create? And what fate awaits these collected items after they have been used in your creative process?

PT Despite my appreciation for works from all my contemporaries, I have never been willing to simply use ornamental motifs of Qajar women's faces, for example, or any other historical elements, just because they were visually compelling. If a particular shape or object captivated me to the extent that I could not ignore it, I would sometimes choose to use it *as is*—like casting it directly into my work. This is evident in many of my pieces, where you may find traces of certain items such as Safavid period birds or ceremonial *ʿālams* incorporated into my sculptures.

Since childhood, I have been drawn to collecting small items, and whenever I encounter a beautiful object, as you have noted, I feel restless until I acquire it. My wife, Manijeh, aware of this obsession, often anticipates my reactions when I encounter a captivating artifact. In this way, these collected items have transcended mere inspiration, becoming integral to the very fabric of my process—shaping my material choices, influencing my visual language and often dictating the overall form of my works.

DM You mentioned in a previous interview that you consider yourself more a poet than a sculptor and that your sculptural works are deeply rooted in the poetic traditions of Rumi, Hafiz, and Nezami. Could you explain what it is in the essence of this literary heritage that keeps you closely connected to it, despite having encountered many unfamiliar cultures throughout your life and career that could have piqued your curiosity? Could you describe the process you go through to translate these specific poetic themes into a physical form, and discuss the challenges you face in preserving the essence of poetry in your sculptures?

PT From the beginning of my career, even as a student at the School of Fine Arts, I socialized more with poets than with painters. The time itself was also more favourable for poets than for painters. Poets like Esmail Shahroudi, Nosrat Rahmani and Yadollah Royale were people I encountered almost daily. There was a lively discourse on poetry in the cafés, and it was not uncommon to see pages dedicated to these discussions in the newspapers and magazines of the time. The poets' gatherings at Café Firouzeh, on the corner of Mokhberoddoleh Square,

Parviz Tanavoli
Heech, 1972
bronze on wood base

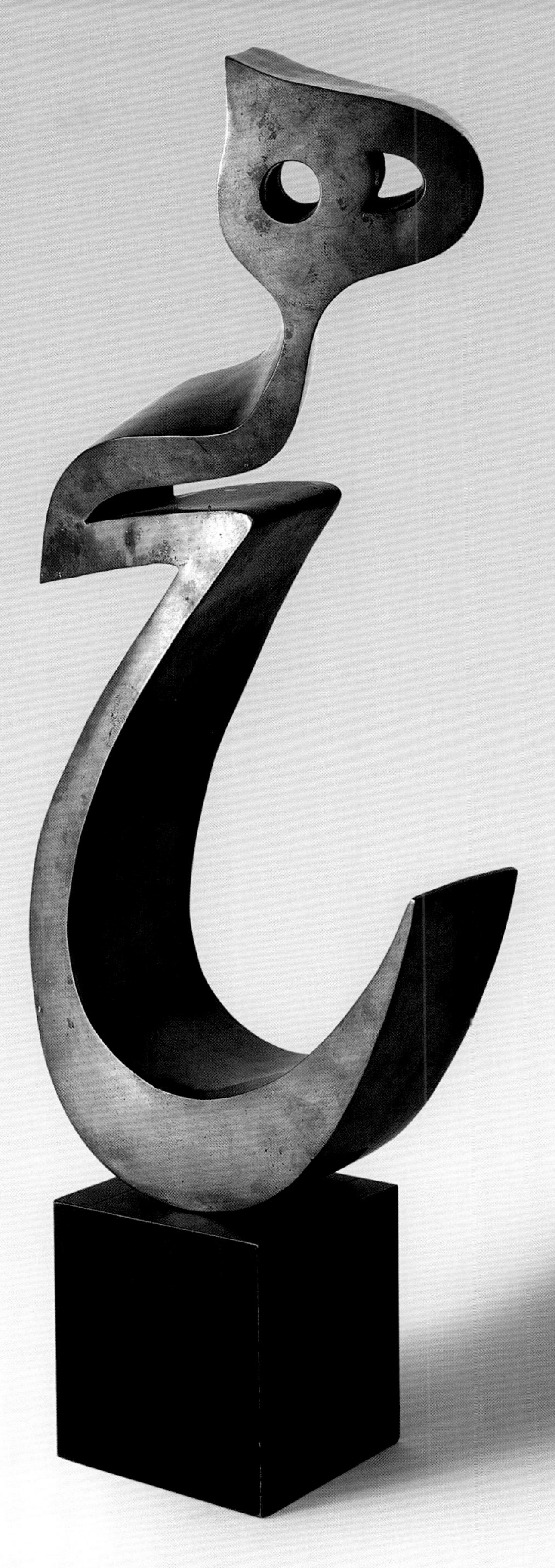

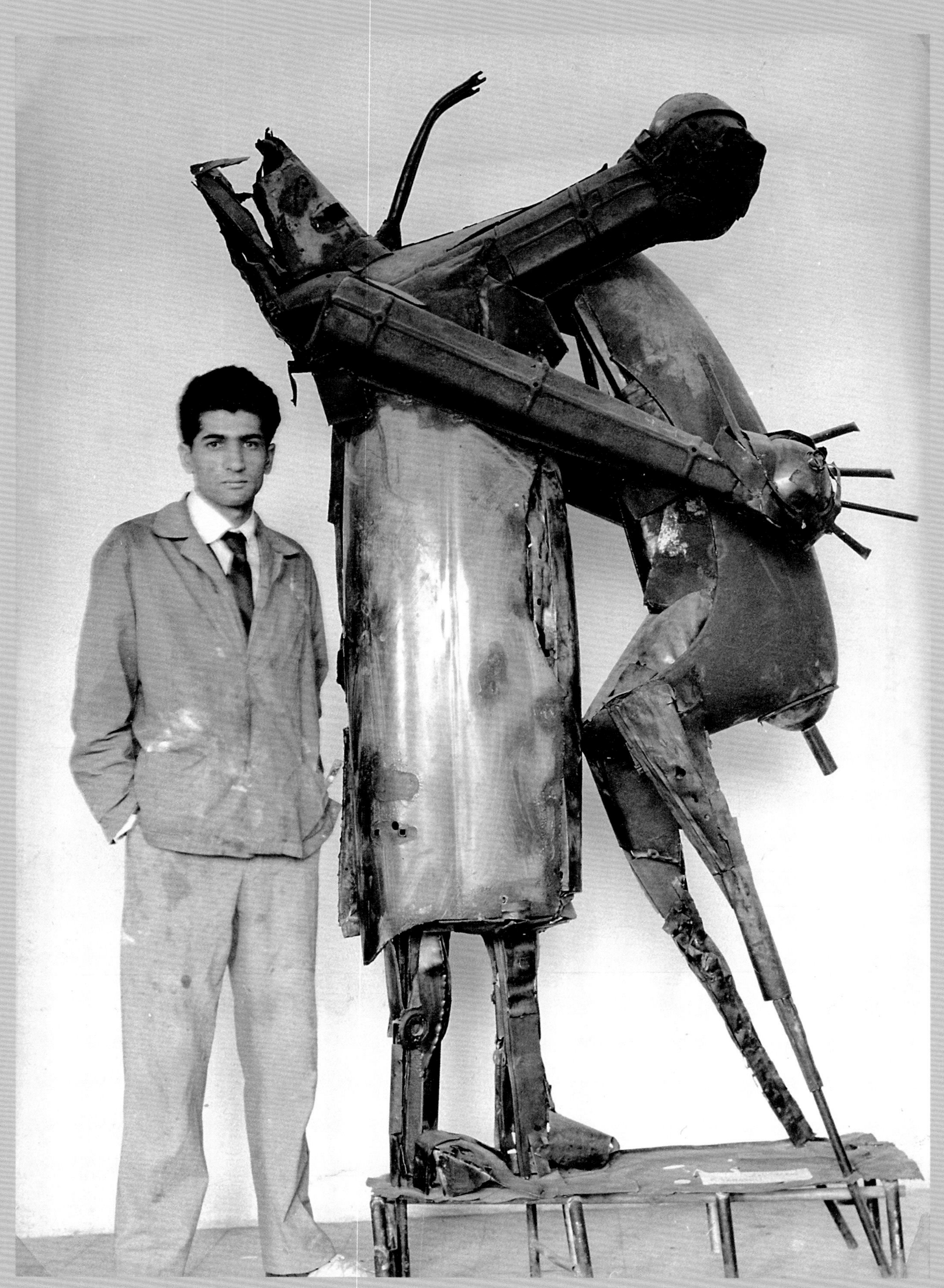

were prominent, while the Europe-returned poets frequented Café Naderi, a few hundred metres away. These spaces were the epicenter of cultural debates, such as the serious discussions on new poetry between Ahmad Shamlou and Reza Baraheni, which I actively followed. Occasionally, I would also write poetry, but my works never found an audience and never got published.

When I moved to Minneapolis in 1961 and gained access to bronze casting, I started creating sculptures inspired by the figure of Farhad the Mountain Carver, a character from Persian literature. Yet, since no one recognized Farhad, I transformed him into a Poet in my sculptures. When he appeared alongside Shirin, he would become the Poet and Lover, always speaking in praise of her. Thus, the Poet took the place of Farhad, but I juxtaposed him against prophets and messengers, who, for me, embody a different, higher realm of expression. As a sacred symbol, water became a recurrent motif in my work, inspired by the water reservoirs and sails (water fountains) I had seen in dry desert regions around Yazd and Kashan. This symbolic approach to water was a form of artistic liberation, yet the challenge lay in maintaining the poetic essence within these forms, without letting them become mere visual representations.

DM Your works have a solid cultural and historical connection, and your activities as an artist, researcher and collector over the years have served various purposes. One of these purposes is undoubtedly preserving the traditions and history of Iran. To what extent have you been motivated to protect, present and disseminate this history? How do you perceive the role of the artist as a historian, and to what extent does this responsibility influence your process?

PT The path I chose was inevitable, and I became an artist-researcher, consciously or unconsciously. The knowledge I gathered in the 1960s and 1970s was unique, as no one else knew these details. For instance, in 1974, I took an album of my collected *gabbeh* rugs to New York. Abby Weed Grey (1902–1983) helped arrange a meeting with Richard Ettinghausen (1906–1979), the head of the Islamic Art Department at the Metropolitan Museum of Art. I recall well that his secretary mentioned I would only have ten minutes to present my work. I had prepared myself, rehearsing various scenarios to ensure my presentation did not exceed the allotted time.

However, when Ettinghausen saw the lion-themed *gabbeh* rugs, he was astounded. He exclaimed, “I have travelled extensively through Iran, but I have never seen anything like these!” Jokingly, he even asked if they were of my own making. Our meeting, which was supposed to last just ten minutes, extended to over an hour. When I left his office, his secretary looked at me with surprise, curious how I had managed to captivate Ettinghausen for so long.

Afterward, Ettinghausen proposed exhibiting the collection at the Textile Museum in Washington, DC. It felt as if a blind person seeking treatment from a doctor had suddenly been offered a cure that restored not just sight but extraordinary vision. A few days later, I met with Anne Gossett from the Textile Museum, who explained all the arrangements that the museum would take care of, including the costs of packing, transportation and insurance, along with creating a catalogue featuring forty of the best photographs of my *gabbeh* rugs. She even invited me to

Parviz Tanavoli with *Farhad and the Deer*, Tehran, 1960

write the introductory essay for the catalogue. Initially, I hesitated, but she insisted that no one else had the expertise to write on this subject. Thus, I penned the foreword for *Lion Rugs from Fars*, marking the beginning of my scholarly journey.

Subsequently, when I wrote an article for *HALI* magazine, they invited me to join their editorial board for critiques and discussions related to Iranian handwoven textiles. My fascination with such cultural artifacts deepened, and whenever I encountered unfamiliar textiles—like the pictorial Bakhtiari *kilims*, *sejadeh* (ritual carpets) from Chaharmahal or *tacheh* (storage sacks) from rural communities—I felt compelled to share my findings. In 1977, I organized mobile exhibitions across several American cities, showcasing these rare Iranian artifacts through collaborations with the Smithsonian Institution. Over time, I received invitations from various rug societies and cultural institutions in the US to deliver lectures on tribal and village weavings, making each exhibition and lecture a journey of discovery for both myself and the audience.

Gradually, through publishing articles and books, I found myself financially stable, with my work supporting my family. Every closed door I encountered during my research journey only spurred me to find new paths forward. Returning to Iran after many years, I reconnected with old friends, reminiscing over simple chicken stew and bean soup dinners while continuing my work with a renewed passion.

Even as I delved into studying Iranian architectural techniques—building walls using traditional bricklaying methods—it was clear that my roots remained deeply intertwined with the vibrant culture of Iran's woven art. That period marked a pivotal chapter in my career as both a researcher and an artist, cementing my lifelong commitment to preserving and documenting the rich heritage of Iranian textiles.

DM Your works and research consistently reflect a steady and continuous artistic path, even as Iran has experienced significant political and social transformations. Given this stability in your work amid the country's constant changes, how have you managed to maintain a balance between the two? How have these changes influenced your artistic approach and the themes you choose to explore? And how have you navigated these fluctuations to remain true to your artistic journey?

PT The path I chose was consciously distanced from politics and its fluctuations. Even as the Revolution altered the landscape of rural Iran and its people, I realized that the essence of these communities remained unchanged. Their doors were still open to guests, and their Iranian spirit persisted, despite the shifts around them. This realization led me to focus on the nomadic tribes and rural areas of Iran.

When opportunities for sculpture were no longer available, I turned my attention to the diverse tribes of Iran in pursuit of deeper understanding and connection. Each journey was an effort to make up for the gaps in my life. I followed different nomadic groups across various terrains, dedicating myself to studying and documenting their lives and traditions.

One of my earliest undertakings was the study of the Shahsavan tribes of northwestern Iran, beginning with the nomadic clans from the Aras river, up to

Parviz Tanavoli with *Standing Poet*, Tehran, c. 1960s

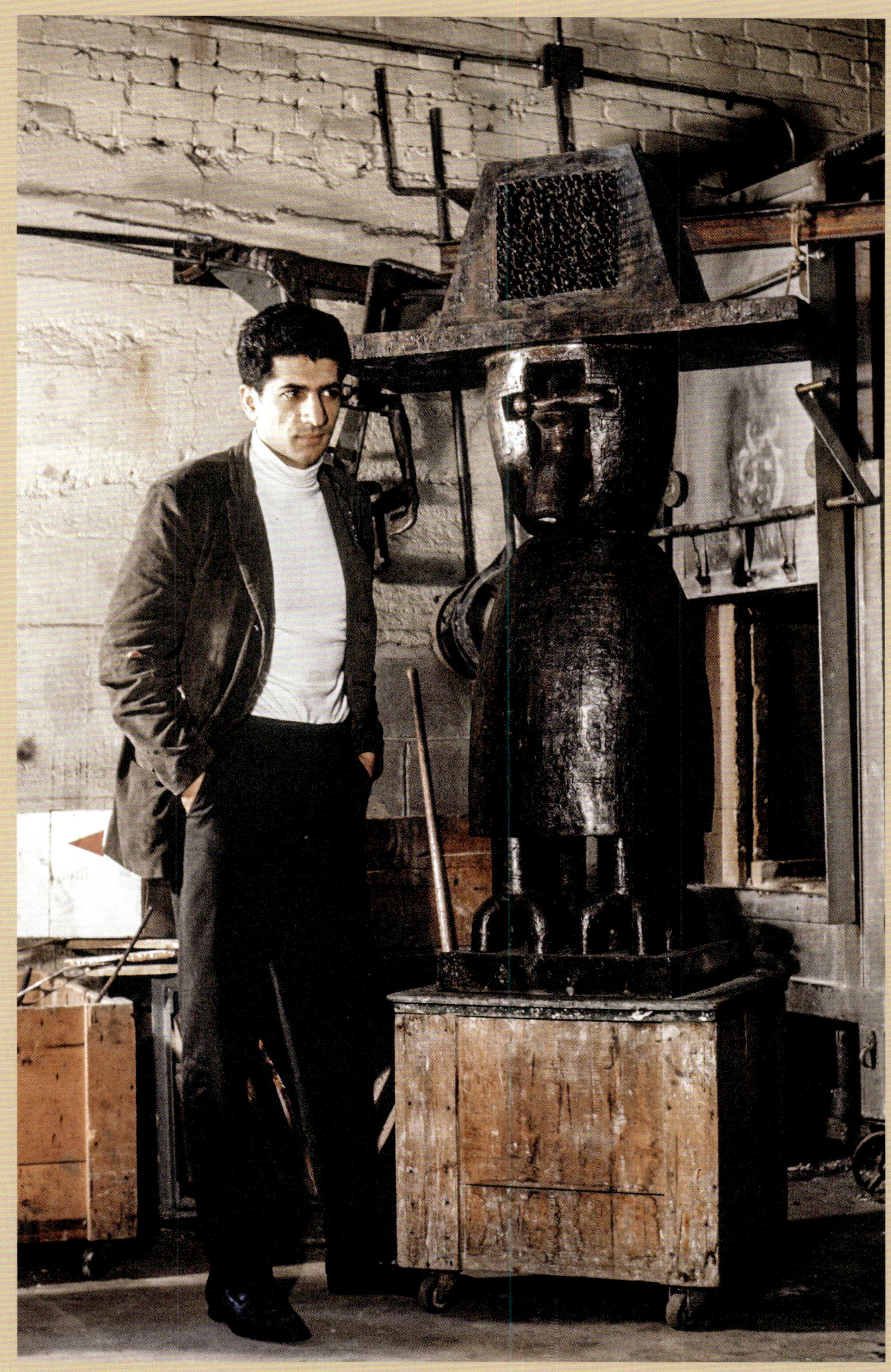

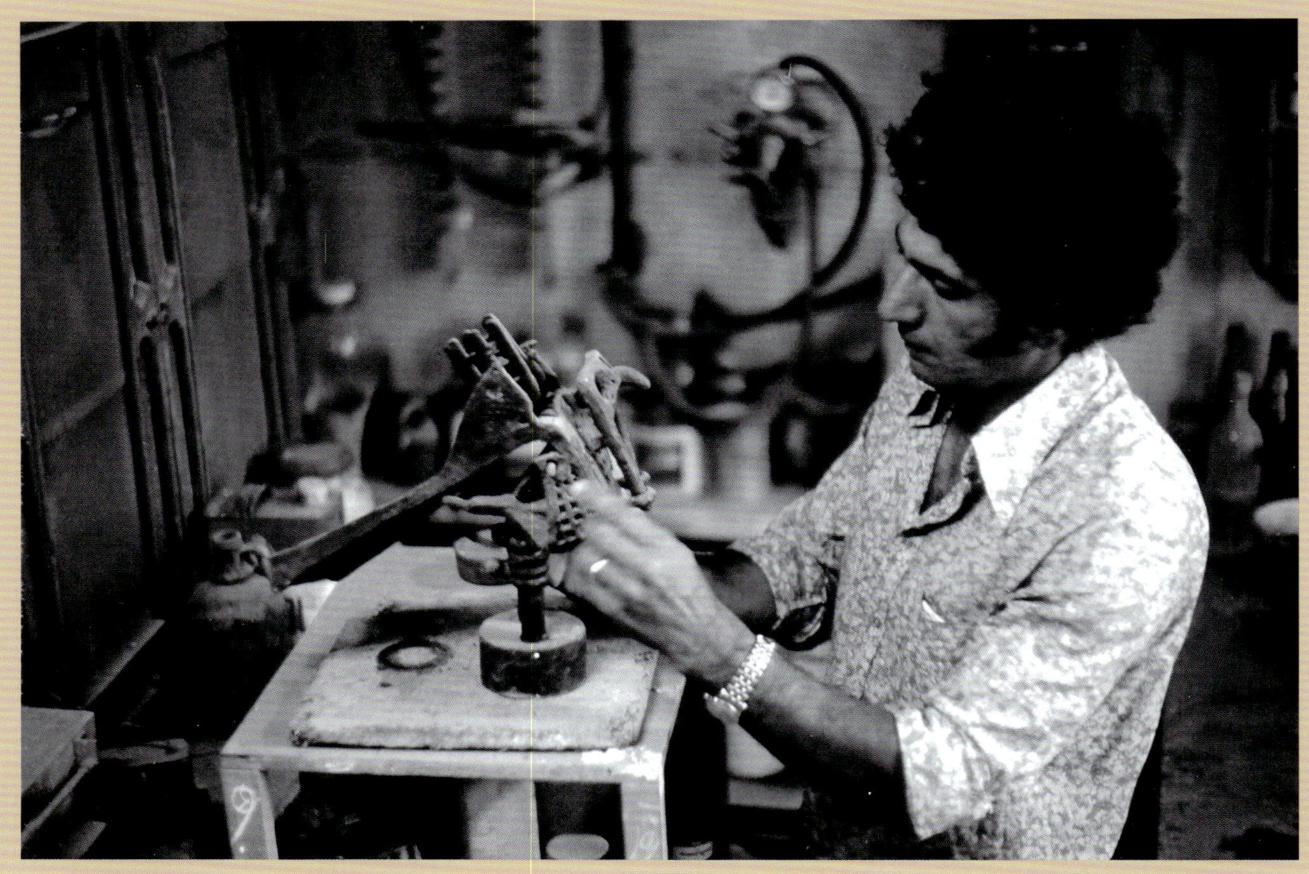

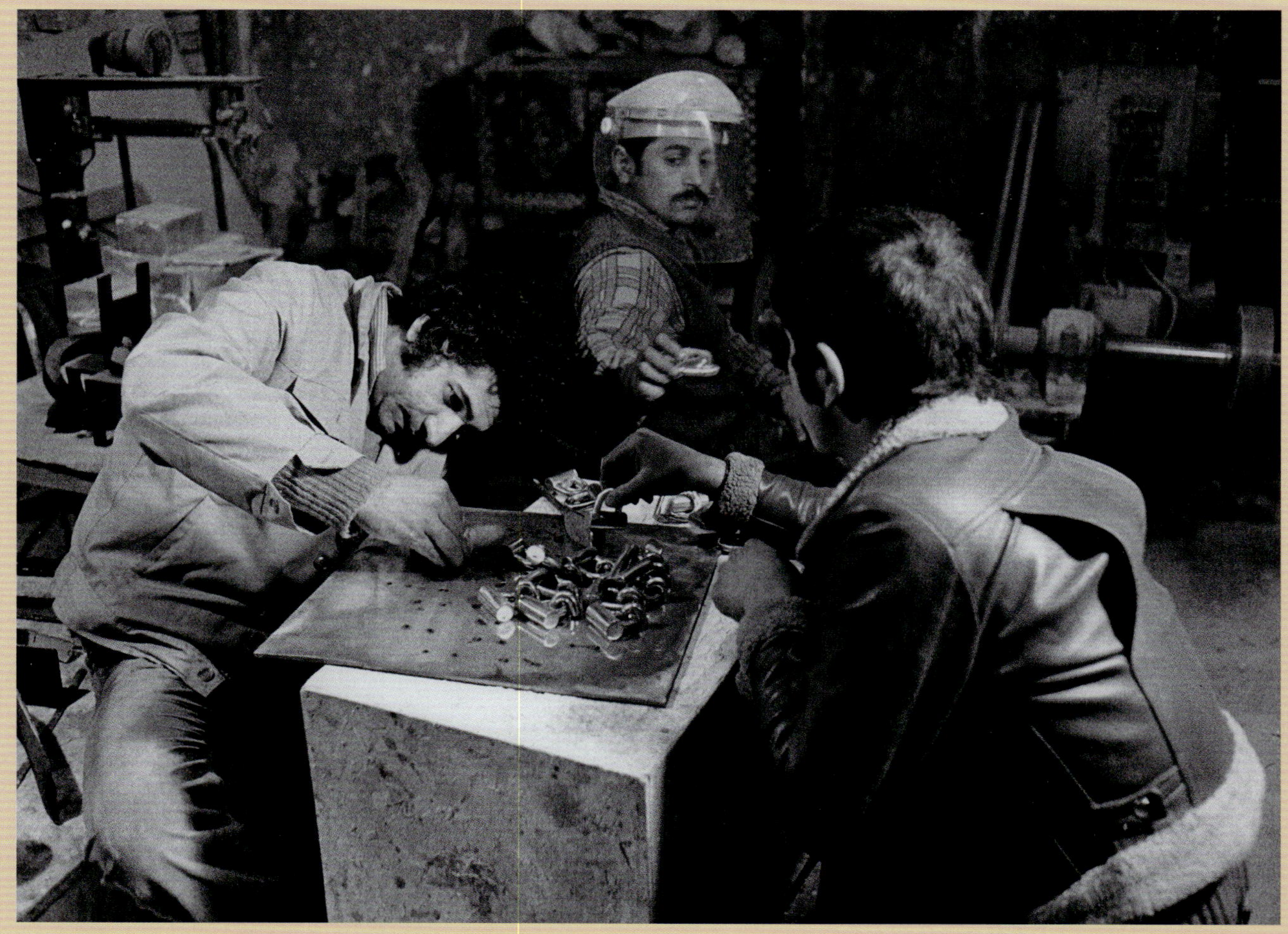

the highlands of Sabalan. This exploration resulted in my book *Shahsavan: Iranian Rugs and Textiles*, published by Rizzoli in 1985, in which I documented the cultural fabric and weaving traditions of these tribes. Through research, I gathered comprehensive information on their art, crafts and textiles, which had previously been little studied.

I visited many villages and small towns during my travels, observing their local customs. I acquired whatever artifacts seemed meaningful, from scales and weights to traditional locks and keys. I journeyed across Iran—from Tabriz and Zanjan to Isfahan, Shiraz and beyond, traversing the northern and western regions, and even reaching the heart of the Talysh areas in the south. Along the way, I documented the distinctive handwoven and craft items of various tribes, such as the Shahsavans and Afshars.

These journeys were more than mere expeditions—they were immersive experiences that shaped my artistic vision. With its vibrant culture and dynamic heritage, each place revealed new facets of Iranian life. As a collector and researcher, I sought to understand the rich tapestry of Iranian society, capturing its depth and resilience through the lenses of art and craftsmanship.

The art historian James W. Allan, who accompanied me on many of these trips, penned an article titled "Parviz Tanavoli, the Collector," detailing our explorations and my enthusiasm for the diverse nomadic cultures of Iran. In it, he writes:

> Travelling with Parviz is an experience. Over the years, in search of Iranian tribal and village rugs, he has travelled the length and breadth of Iran countless times. Field work and research have taken him to vast areas of north-west and western Iran, to the lands of the Shahsavan tribes and to the hills populated by the Talesh people, the central southern areas covered by the Afshar migrations, and to towns and villages too numerous to count, let alone record. Every grouping of huts or tents holds treasures for a man with such a breadth of interest, every bazaar is potentially a place of delight and surprise. And to travel with Parviz is to be infected by his enthusiasm for the rich diversity of his own Iranian culture.
>
> As a traveller, Parviz's energy is extraordinary. He drives vast distances without any apparent fatigue. While I, his passenger, all too often snooze beside him, affected by the heat of the sun and the strength of the light on the Iranian plateau.[3]

ENDNOTES

1 Parviz Tanavoli's 1976 bronze sculpture *Monument for Farhad, the Mountain Carver* stands at 196 cm in height and is housed in the Parviz Tanavoli Museum in Tehran. This iconic work draws inspiration from the Persian legend of Farhad, a master stone carver who, driven by love for the princess Shirin, was tasked with carving a path through a mountain.

2 *Fall of the Mountain Carver*, 1975, concrete and bronze.

3 James W. Allan, "Parviz Tanavoli, the Collector," in *Shahsavan: Iranian Rugs and Textiles*, Parviz Tanavoli (New York: Rizzoli, 1985), 33.

Top and bottom
Parviz Tanavoli in his Zal-e-Zar studio, Tehran, 1964

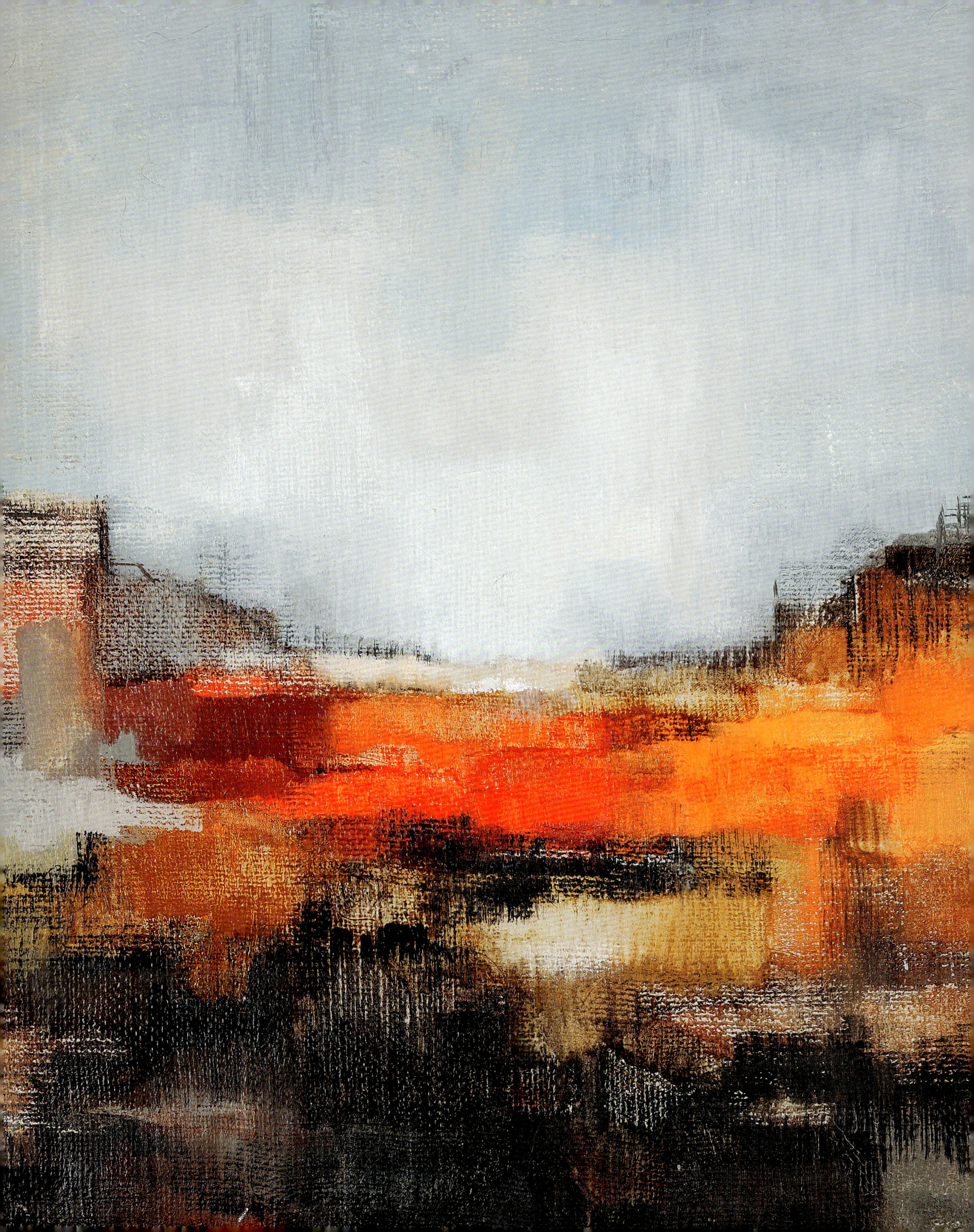

IRANIAN WOMEN: TACKLING MODERNISM ONE SENSIBILITY AT A TIME

Fereshteh Daftari

If the history of Iranian modernism is still in its infancy, then the literature on its women artists is in the prenatal phase. An early indication of this state of affairs is Akbar Tadjvidi's 1967 volume *L'Art moderne en Iran*, the first important book on the subject, which accounts for around ninety artists—of which only a dozen are women. Who were, for instance, Victoria Afshar, Shirin Akhavan, Soudabeh Ganjei and Fatemeh Sayah? Tadjvidi briefly mentions a few of them. While we cannot fill in all the historical gaps in this short essay, we have room at least to highlight ten eminent Iranian women artists active before the 1979 Revolution. Born between 1917 and 1947, most of these artists studied in the Faculty of Fine Arts at the University of Tehran, and as a group they were active from the 1950s on. They exhibited their works in galleries, cultural centres and biennials in Tehran (starting in 1958) and abroad (in Venice and São Paulo), and all of those who exhibited in Tehran were discussed by the highly influential art critic Karim Emami, who wrote for the English-language newspaper *Kayhan International* from 1962 to 1968.[1] The Armenian Iranian, then American, writer Janet Lazarian was the other prominent critic of the time. Among the artists, a few were noted teachers or owned a gallery of their own. On the surface, at least, no gender discrimination seems to have hampered their careers. Although many of these artists were concerned with matters of gender, these subjects are not, with one notable exception (Nahid Hagigat), revealed in the content or style of their work.[2] Such references are often found instead in their artist statements, when available, or in their biographies. Overall, the range of subject matter is as varied as the number of artists. As with male artists in this period, pluralism defined the landscape of women's art.

Following Reza Shah Pahlavi's abdication in 1941, he was succeeded by his son Mohammad Reza Shah Pahlavi, who ruled until the Revolution in 1978–79. In the annals of Iranian modern art, the year before Reza Shah's abdication is an

Iran Darroudi
Untitled, c. 1960 (detail)
oil on burlap

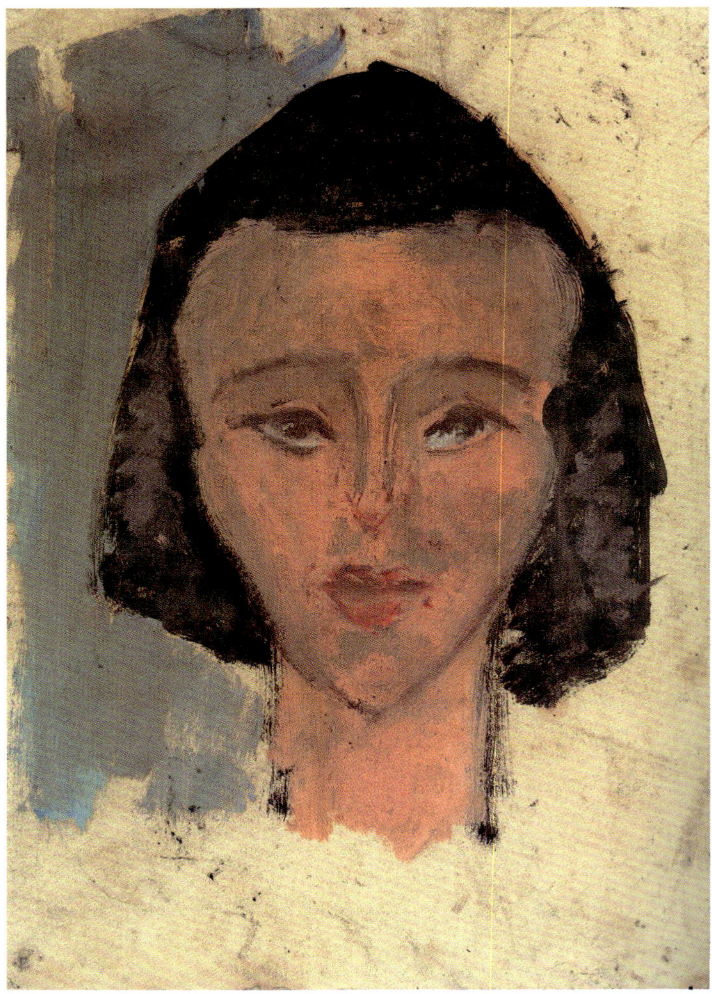

Fig. 1

important date. It was in 1940 that the Faculty of Fine Arts, a pseudo-Beaux-Arts institution, was created in Tehran. Its goal was the propagation of "the principles of modern art"[3] as differentiated from both traditional Persian painting and the imported academic naturalism that had prevailed for some fifty years. The Faculty of Fine Arts was probably the first official institution to admit women and to include them on its staff. Significantly, among the artists who were trained there, many (both men and women) attribute their first encounter with modernism to Marthe Célestine Eve, who was known as Madame Aminfar or Madame Ashoub. She was a French woman married to an Iranian, herself an artist trained at the École des Beaux-Arts in Paris. Her art still awaits discovery. Some of her colleagues, such as Ali Mohammad Heydarian, were still engaged with academic painting, a direction mostly attributable to the teacher and artist Mohammad Ghaffari, also known as Kamal al-Molk (1859–1940). Elsewhere I have termed this trend "Old Master modernism."[4] Madame Aminfar, however, was the only teacher who introduced her students, by means of illustrations, to Impressionist and Post-Impressionist artists such as Claude Monet, Paul Cézanne and Vincent van Gogh.

Shokouh Riazi (1917–1962) was one of Madame Aminfar's first students. As an artist, her name was forgotten until she was included in the 1998 publication

Shokuh Riazi
Portrait, n.d.
oil on paper

Pioneers of Contemporary Persian Painting, by Javad Mojabi, and her reputation was further resuscitated in Mehrnoush Ali Madadi's thoroughly researched monograph of 2022.[5] Until then, Riazi was better remembered by her students (mostly the illustrious, all-male Saqqakhaneh artists), who took her classes at the School of Fine Arts for Boys (*honarestan-e pessaran*) between 1956 and 1960, and then at the School of Decorative Arts, where she taught during the last two years of her life.

Riazi had spent her childhood in Paris, and later as a student at the Faculty of Fine Arts she acted as a translator for Madame Aminfar, who did not speak Persian. Later, following her return from her studies at the École des Beaux-Arts in Paris (1948–55), Riazi began her teaching career in Tehran. She encouraged her students to avoid copying Western art and to seek a personal vision.[6] Her own work, however, reveals the influence of Bernard Buffet and Amedeo Modigliani (fig. 1). Charles Hossein Zenderoudi, Riazi's student and a future Saqqakhaneh artist, reported that if you wanted a good grade in her class, you had to paint portraits with long necks.[7] His contribution to the publication *IIe Biennale de Teheran: Exposition de Peinture et de Sculpture* (1960) is a testament to this Riazi-Modigliani influence.[8]

While little of Riazi's artwork has survived, she continues to be remembered as a highly gifted teacher. New research by Ali Madadi indicates that she was equally engaged with social issues. She joined Mehrangiz Dowlatshahi's Anjoman-e jamiyat-e rah-e no, an activist association that fought for equal rights for women (Dowlatshahi was a close relation), and she also helped organize an international exhibition of women's art in Tehran in 1960. Art, Riazi believed, is an international language, its local ingredient being only one element of the whole.[9]

In addition to Paris, Italy was a mecca for Iranian art students in the 1950s, a period characterized by abstraction, and more specifically Art Informel, which was considered the most progressive artistic language of the time, aesthetically and politically. In 1958, a meeting took place in Rome between Mansoureh Hosseini (1926–2012), a young Iranian artist completing her studies at the Academy of Fine Arts, and Lionello Venturi, the prominent Italian art historian and critic. Hosseini, carrying her Cézannesque canvases and accompanied by the Iranian consul, was given a devastating critique by Venturi:

> If I had seen them [the canvases] fifty years ago, I would have said that the young painter is a genius. But, today I have to say that she is fifty years behind. Modernist artists have taken recourse to abstract art for thirty years now. The canvases of your young painter are in no way related to Cézanne. The fresh and lively colors and arabesque lines are more reminders of Iranian miniatures. In fact your Kufic calligraphy is abstract art in itself. Why don't you use that approach?[10]

This experience exemplifies the plight of so many artists engaged with a modernism defined and narrated in Europe and America. It persisted for many decades—in the 1980s, for example, the Egyptian artist Ghada Amer, while completing her studies in Nice, was encouraged by her art teacher to switch to Islamic calligraphy.[11] While Amer's critical rejection of that advice was the polar opposite of Hosseini's acquiescent reaction—which ultimately transformed her artistic direction—the experience was equally pivotal for both artists.

Should calligraphy or miniature painting provide the only models? With his comments, was Venturi, a European, telling the young Iranian artist to "stay in her lane," so to speak, despite the fact that European modern masters, such as Pablo Picasso and Henri Matisse, broke away from their own Renaissance tradition to draw from African and Persian art? Was there no path outside ethnic subservience for a West Asian (Middle Eastern) or North African artist? Hosseini's transition to her signature style, egged on by Venturi, is evident in a comparison of her "Cézannesque" painting *Roman Yard*, created in France and sent to the First Tehran Biennale in 1958, with *Abstraction*, exhibited at the Second Tehran Biennale in 1960.[12] Script progressively took centre stage, morphing into the elements: wind, water, fire (fig. 2). The liquid letters, billowing clouds and roaring flames, all swirling in a cosmic setting, allowed Hosseini to express her love of nature in the format Venturi had recommended.

Fig. 2

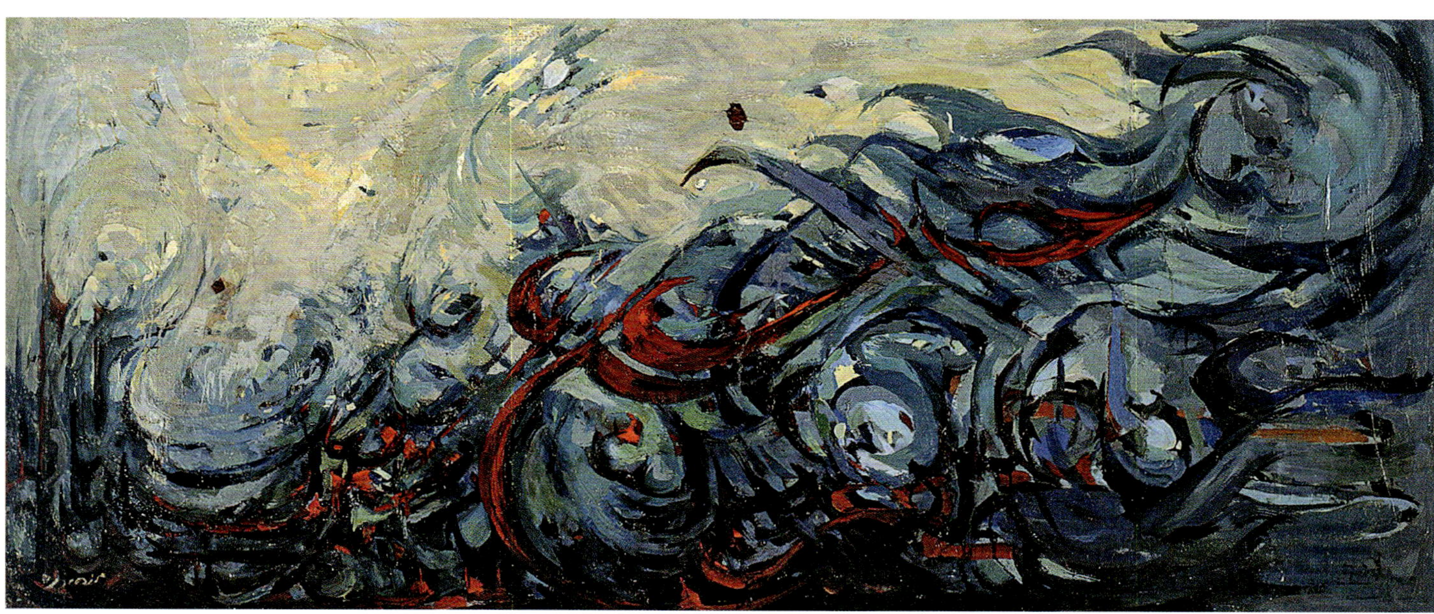

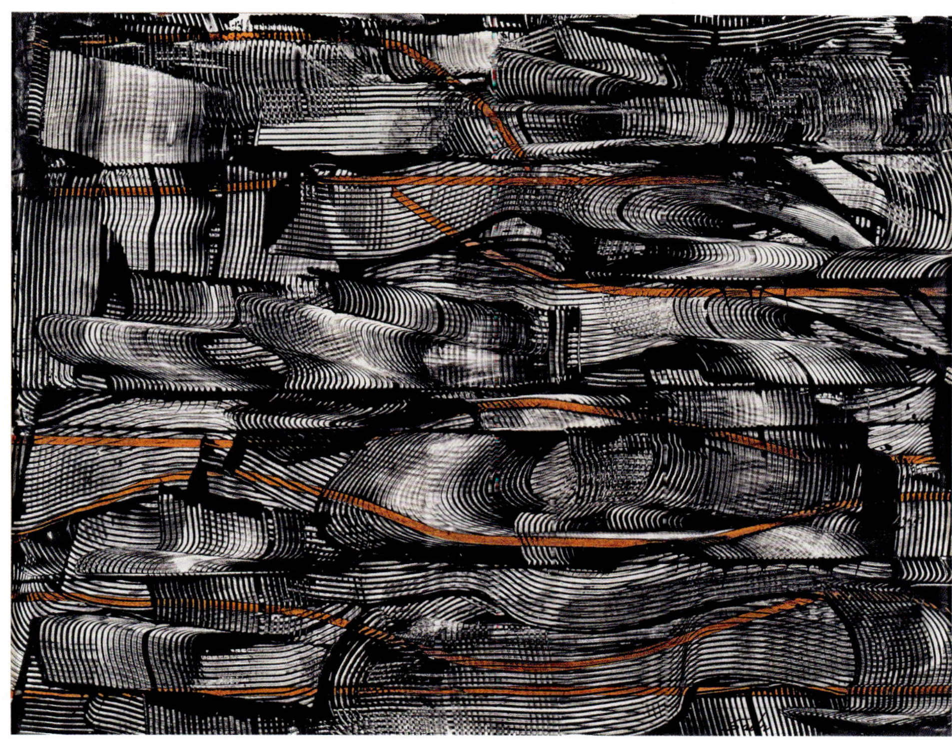

Fig. 3

At the time, traditional calligraphy was dominated by male practitioners. The use of text in modern Iranian art belongs to some extent to the Saqqakhaneh movement of the early 1960s and artists such as Zenderoudi and Faramarz Pilaram but mostly to the "calligraphic modernism" of the post-Saqqakhaneh period, in which text overtakes the entire canvas—a practice followed by an all-male group of artists. This style appeared first, however, in 1959—in Hosseini's paintings.

Not all artists experienced a binary choice between Art Informel and calligraphy. Behjat Sadr (1924–2009), who studied in Italy from 1955 to 1959 and often visited and lived in Paris, stumbled on abstraction through chance, a path that knows no ethnicity. In 1957, Roberto Melli, in the brochure of Sadr's exhibition at the Pincio Gallery, recounts a critical moment that the artist shared with him: "One day going home, at the moment of entering my room, I let a long piece of string fall to the ground. It drew a web of knots which coiled and recoiled creating such complex configuration that it made me decide to paint the interlaced forms."[13] While chance was fundamental to this discovery, the artist later rationalized her choice by claiming the legitimate inheritance of abstraction as a global and progressive idiom of her time. Given the level of "communication in the twentieth century," she declared, "it is not only our traditional culture that influences us, but also we are under the influence of a multicultural world."[14] Broadly speaking, she felt that abstraction belonged to no single culture.[15] As early as 1957, the artist wrote in her journal: "Today I really understood what I want. I want there to be in the history of world art the name of one woman at least." She added, "I'm prepared to place all I have, my comfort, my happiness [in] the bargain."[16] Her close friendship with the protofeminist poet Forough Farrokhzad and her various statements—including, "As a woman, I had the vigor of men"[17]—reveal her sentiments about the strength of liberated women.

Opposite
Mansoureh Hosseini
In Memory of an Epic, c. 1974
oil on canvas

Above
Behjat Sadr
Untitled, 1977
oil on board and adhesive bands

The complexity of Sadr's paintings, which she executed on supports ranging from canvas to venetian blinds, with tools including brushes, spatulas, razors and palette knifes, and in a wide array of themes, from nature to politics—resists a quick summary. In her paintings, a "tree" can signify desiccated bark or recall an oil refinery. The trace of her tool may be a reference to itself, a brushstroke in action or a representation of liquid in motion. More abstractly, it may give form to invisible, repetitive rhythms, a current of energy, a melody or even the viscosity of oil (a highly charged material, especially after the 1953 coup that ousted Prime Minister Mohammad Mossadegh, the man whose name is synonymous with the nationalization of the oil industry) (fig. 3). Sadr allows her gaze to roam in many directions, from the brickwork patterns of a mosque in Isfahan to the canvases of Pierre Soulages, not to narrate a grand epic but to tease out the multi-dimensional layers of any given sign. The local and the personal are contained within her global encyclopedia of references. "International art can turn into national art and the national into the personal," she declared.[18]

That abstraction was a Western model sheepishly followed by Iranians was a contention upheld even inside Iran. Abstraction, however, was not a Western invention. In Iran, canvas as a support was imported only in the mid-seventeenth century,[19] but abstraction appeared centuries before in media such as tiles, metalwork and carpets and later as mirrorworks adorning architecture.
The novelty in Europe was the migration of abstraction to canvas in the early twentieth century.

Criticism of Iranian artists' dependence on Western models falls apart if we look at the abstractions of Monir Shahroudy Farmanfarmaian (1922[20]–2019), whose inspiration came from the local craft of mirrorwork. She divorced this technique from its subservience to architecture and married it to elemental geometry (p. 81),[21] at times interlacing it with reverse-glass painting (p. 86). Blurring the boundary between painting and sculpture, she overcame the artistic bias against craft and privileged the decorative. The results are autonomous objects, unprecedented both in and outside Iran. She said, "I made classical mirrorwork modern."[22]

Like Hosseini and Sadr, Farmanfarmaian began her training at the Faculty of Fine Arts, where Madame Aminfar was one of her instructors.[23] Her itinerary, however, differs from those of the other two artists. The war raging in Europe prevented her from travelling to France; instead she and her future husband, Manoucher Yektai, travelled by boat to New York, where she studied at the Parsons School of Design and in the 1950s collaborated with Andy Warhol on layouts for advertisements. The pair's friendship continued, as attested by an exchange of gifts in Tehran in the 1970s, in which Farmanfarmaian gave Warhol one of her mirror balls (p. 80) and Warhol gifted a *Marilyn Monroe* silkscreen to his Iranian friend. In Europe and North America, widespread recognition of her work did not arrive until this millennium, but, when it did, her major exhibition at the Solomon R. Guggenheim Museum in New York in 2014 eclipsed the representation of all Iranian artists abroad up to that date.[24] The Guggenheim's investment in the project was likely due to the institution's foundational interest in abstraction and its increasing interest in West Asian art.

Massoumeh Seyhoun (1934–2010) also pursued abstraction, but unlike Riazi, Hosseini, Sadr and Farmanfarmaian, she did not travel abroad to study. Her education took place at the Faculty of Fine Arts, where Madame Aminfar and Ali Mohammad Heydarian were her teachers. She painted until late in her life and participated in exhibitions, but the literature on her art is quite meagre.[25] This may be because, like Riazi, Seyhoun was better known for her other activity: starting in 1960, she ran one of the most prestigious galleries in Tehran, an institution that remains in place to this day. Its operation was interrupted only once, in 1981–82, when she was charged with collaborating with the Pahlavi regime and incarcerated—the result of nothing more than the former queen's interest in the artists Seyhoun represented.

Seyhoun's paintings exhibit a high degree of abstraction; she preferred to leave their meaning to each viewer's interpretation. In 1967–68, she began using industrial paint and, according to her daughter, she tilted her canvases, allowing the medium to find its own path.[26] It would not be surprising to learn that she was acquainted with American Abstract Expressionist painters, as she and her husband, the architect, artist and scholar Houshang Seyhoun, were well informed about international art. The imagery, however, is unique to her. These centralized forms might be internal organs, cavities, cells seen under a microscope or something more macabre sourced from a childhood trauma:

> I remember from my childhood a horrible incidence when a Russian soldier [part of a Soviet force that invaded Northern Iran in 1941], whose crime we didn't know, was tied to and pulled by two trucks in opposite directions until he was in two pieces—a horrible scene which gave me nightmares for quite some time.[27]

New York's Grey Art Museum is the only institution in North America that owns a work by Seyhoun—an enamel-and-lacquer relief painting from 1967 with what may be a flower with potential sexual connotations (p. 31). The museum is named after its benefactor, Abby Weed Grey (1902–1983), whose collection of Iranian modern art is the largest held by any institution abroad.

The artist Leyly Matine-Daftary (1937–2007) was related to Prime Minister Mossadegh on both sides of her family. She did not engage in political subject

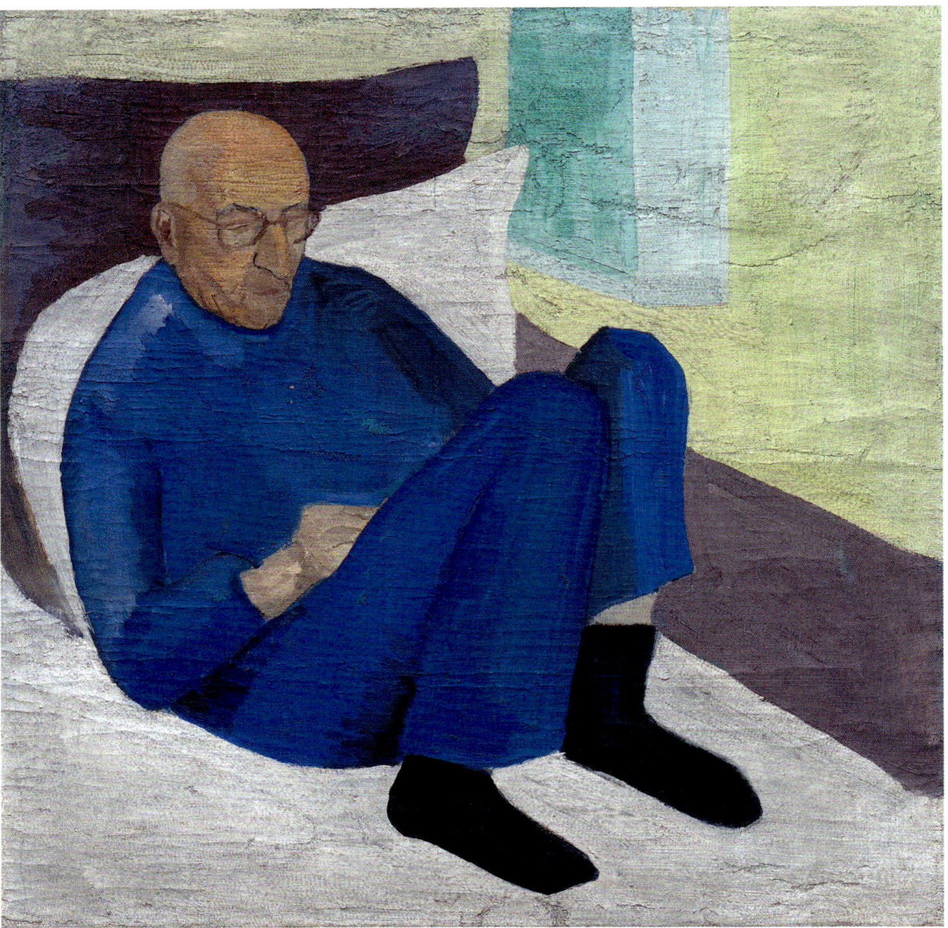

Fig. 4

matter, however—with one exception: an informal 1957 portrait of her grandfather, whose government was toppled in the 1953 coup engineered by Britain's MI6 and the US's CIA. The work speaks volumes about who this man was and where he ended up. With her idiosyncratic simplicity (not yet the flattened abstractions of her mature work), Matine-Daftary portrays this national hero reading in bed in his pajamas, conveying her subject's unadorned life, the last years of which were spent under house arrest in Ahmadabad (fig. 4). As his granddaughter, she was privy to this private moment in the life of an adulated, tragic hero.

From 1954 to 1959, Matine-Daftary studied in London at the Slade School of Fine Arts, where Lucian Freud was one of her instructors. For her, abstraction was a goal and figuration the means of achieving it, as exemplified in *Lydia*, a 1975 painting in the collection of the Centre Pompidou in Paris and, to a certain extent, in the portrait of the artist's uncle (p. 125). Freshness of colour, absence of volume and simplicity of line define a body of work that requires attention if its nuanced abstraction is to be unravelled. Fereydoun Ave, a multidisciplinary artist who was a friend of Matine-Daftary up to the very end of her life, when she was living in exile in Paris, defined her work best when he said that her main concern was the abstract division of space.[28]

Prime Minister Mossadegh also fired the imagination of younger artists such as

Above
Leyly Matine-Daftary
Untitled (Portrait of Dr. Mossadegh), 1957
oil on canvas

Opposite
Farideh Lashai
Untitled, 1967
oil on canvas

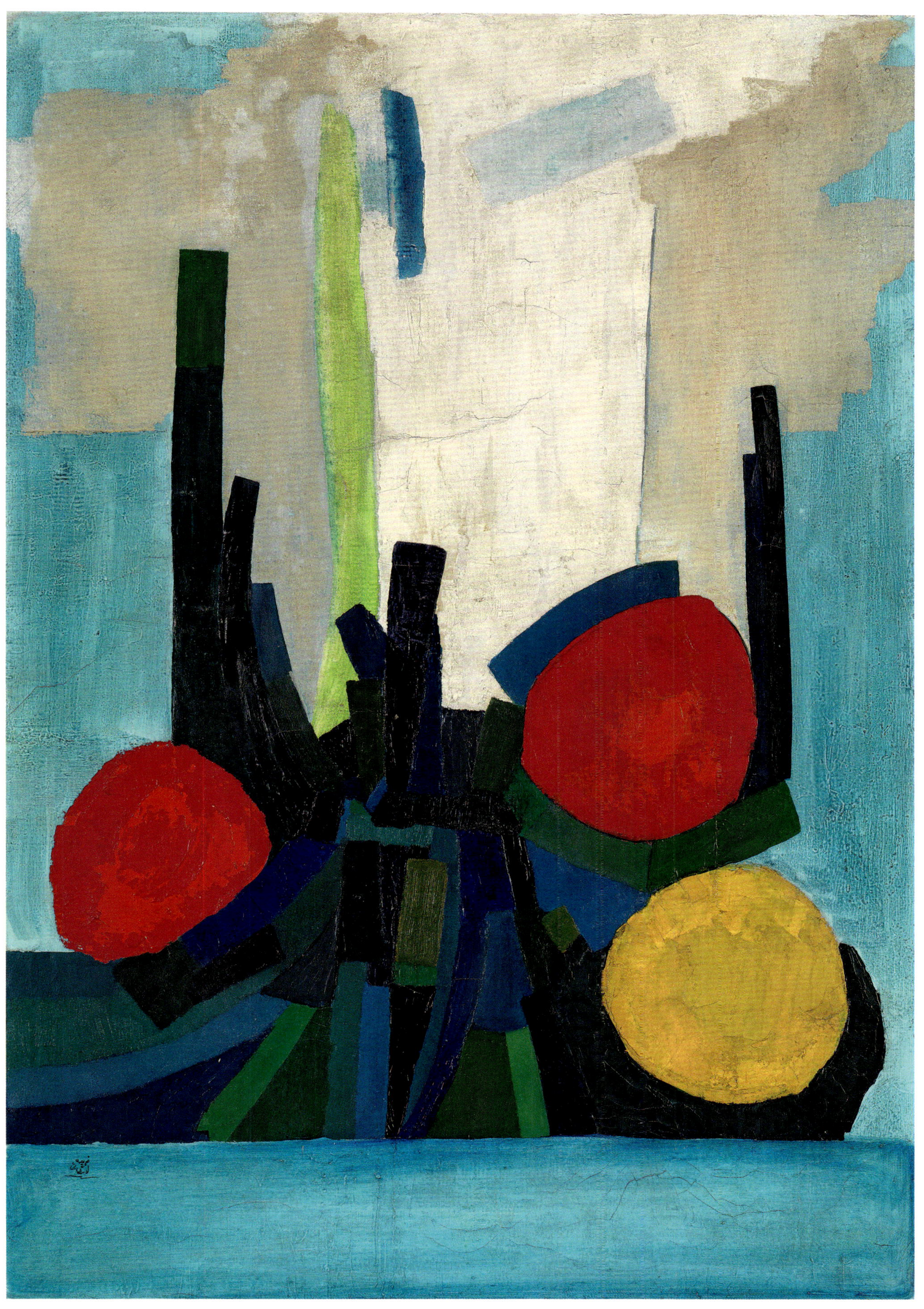

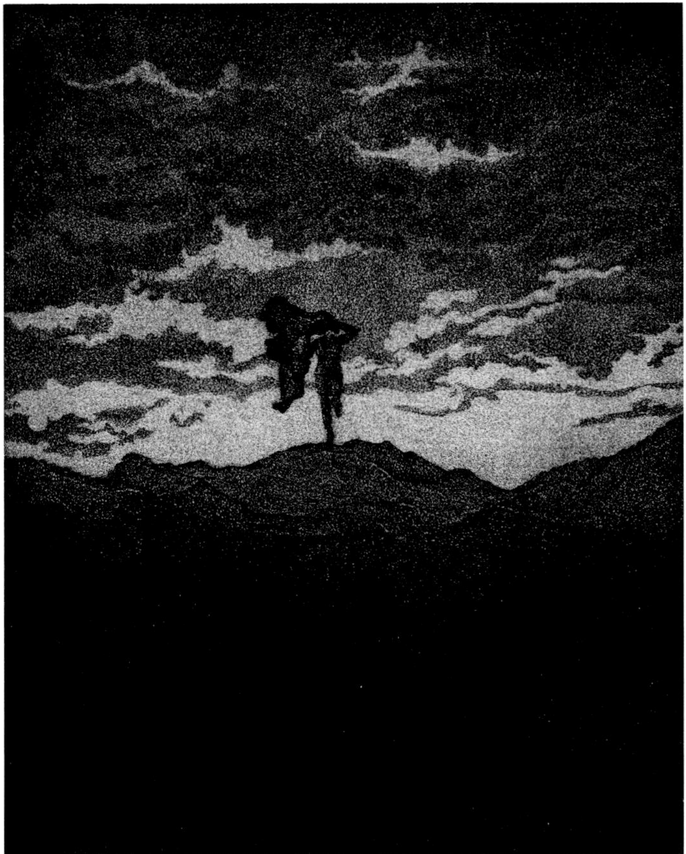

Fig. 6

Farideh Lashai (1944–2013), but he did not enter into her iconography until 1990. Lashai was rebellious from early childhood and an independent activist who was imprisoned in the 1970s. Her works made before the Revolution—abstractions in tribute to nature—are not explicitly political (fig. 5). However, after 1979, the same idiom took on a political meaning in its refusal to speak the figurative language of the propaganda extolled by the new regime.

In the early 1960s, Lashai followed her brother to Germany, where she studied literature and was deeply affected by the theatre of Bertolt Brecht. "Doubt and uncertainty" became her shield against dogma,[29] whether from the left or the right. She then moved to Austria, where she studied glass design at the studios of Riedel; later, she returned to Germany and worked for Rosenthal in Bavaria (pp. 76–77).[30] Her crystal vases are lesser-known objects in an oeuvre that includes a multiplicity of media, including video projections on abstract canvases—the products of Lashai's most inventive period, which postdates the Revolution. Among these are *Luncheon at the Mellat Park* (2010), a recontextualization of Edouard Manet's *Déjeuner sur l'herbe*; *Rabbit in Wonderland* (2010–12), a series inspired by Lewis Carroll's *Alice in Wonderland*; and her final masterpiece, *When I count, there are only you..., But when I look, there is only a shadow* (2013), inspired by Goya's *Disasters of War* (1810–20), exhibited posthumously at Museo Nacional del Prado in Madrid in 2017.

Nahid Hagigat
Escape, 1975
aquatint

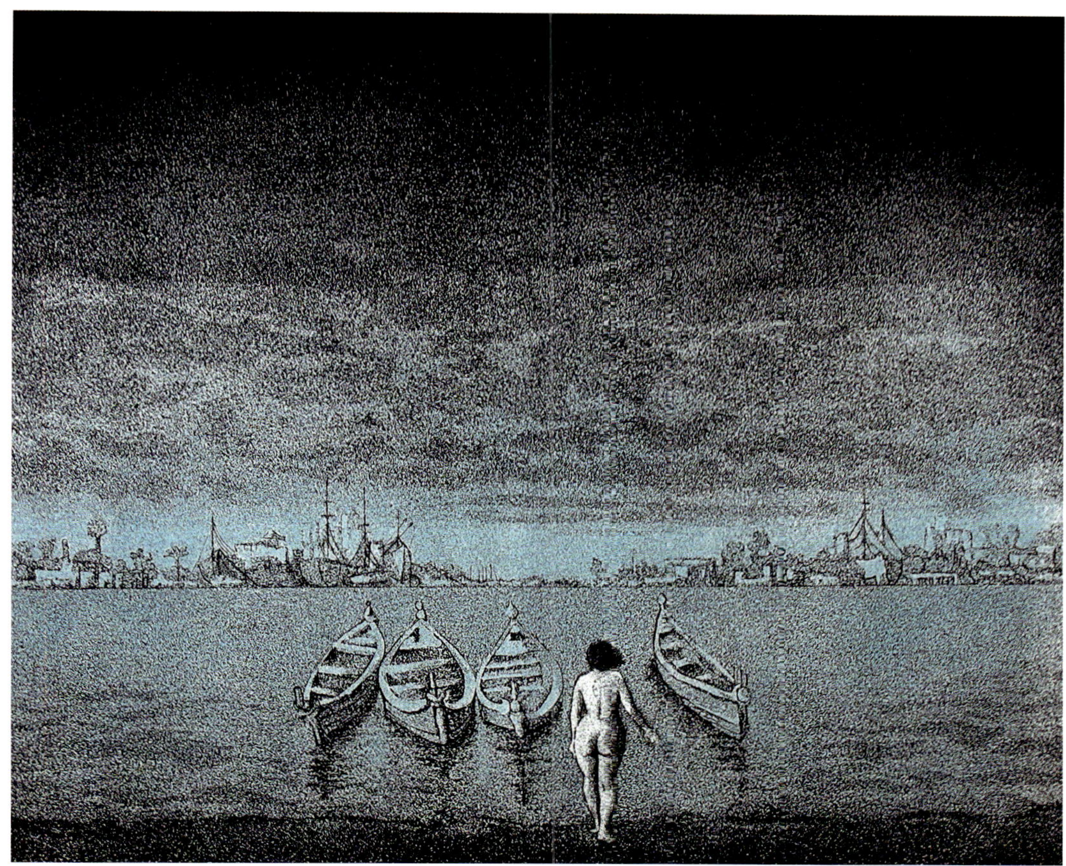

Fig. 7

In Iran Darroudi (1936–2021) we encounter a sensibility drastically different from those of the other artists discussed in this essay. Her visions belong to the irrational spaces of Surrealism. Her education in Paris, at the École des Beaux-Art and École du Louvre (where she studied art history), and then in Belgium, the birthplace of the Surrealists René Magritte and Paul Delvaux, provided her with plenty of opportunities to learn about the movement. In her memoir, she acknowledges these two artists, noting that Delvaux visited her 1963 exhibition in Brussels, the catalogue of which features a few words by poet and film director Jean Cocteau.[31] The following year, she interviewed Salvador Dalí at his home in Paris.[32] The novelist André Malraux and the poet Ahmad Shamlou were among the other luminaries who wrote prefaces for her publications.

In her memoir, Darroudi explains that one of her teachers in Paris criticized her work for lacking a sense of space, just like miniature painting.[33] She listened. As unpopulated as Italian Surrealist Giorgio de Chirico's desolate cities but closer to representations of ancient ruins, her paintings—whether depicting otherworldly vegetation, ghostly architecture (p. 58) or frozen walls melting into tears of pearls—are, above all, precariously floating stages concocted in ineffable dreamscapes. But at times the pipelines of an oil refinery, the dome of a mosque with its minarets or the columns of Persepolis ground these inventions back here on earth, in the land of miniature paintings.

Nahid Hagigat
Going Away, 1975
aquatint

After her graduation from the Faculty of Fine Arts in 1968, Nahid Hagigat (b. 1943) left Iran for the United States to pursue her studies at New York University.[34] Except for a visit in 1973, she never returned to Tehran. However, her prints were exhibited there yearly, from 1974 to 1978, at the Litho Gallery. While more research is needed, we might assert that Iranians had not seen one of their artists creating prints with techniques such as Hagigat's etching, aquatint and photoetching since Marcos Grigorian had taught linocut technique in the 1950s.

In a series of prints dating from the 1970s, Hagigat was the first Iranian female artist to address women's will to freedom and, by implication, to protest against patriarchal society. Regarding her imagery involving the veil, she has said, "Since a patriarchal society has deep roots in religion, my objection also is rooted in religion."[35] In an aquatint (fig. 6), a woman throws off her veil into the air; running, surging, almost flying, untethered over the mountains toward a dramatically lit sky. In another print, also executed in New York, titled *Going Away* (1975, fig. 7), a nude figure rushes toward the sea, where empty boats, docked and waiting at the shore, harbour the promise of freedom. Hagigat and Shirin Neshat, two diasporic artists from different generations both living and working in New York, seem to have resorted to the same metaphor: Hagigat in her print and Neshat in her 1999 video titled *Rapture.* A major difference is that Neshat presents her longing and fleeing women clad in chadors. Hagigat too has resorted to women covered in their veils. These include serialized single figures (a motif popularized by Warhol), to which she has assigned a process of evolution, of self-fulfillment, from (in one case) a dreary black-and-white to a flaming red that declares self-assertion. Hagigat's hardships and struggles in diaspora are subtly revealed in *A Revolution on Canvas* (2023), a film about the painter Nicky Nodjoumi, her former spouse, by their daughter, Sara Nodjoumi.

Parvaneh Etemadi (1947–2025), the youngest of the women artists discussed here, tackled a range of styles, from abstraction to representation, and a multiplicity of media, including cement painting and collage. At the Faculty of Fine Arts, where she was enrolled twice, she was taught by Behjat Sadr and Parviz Tanavoli (b. 1937); Hagigat was a fellow student. As early as 1968, Karim Emami alerted his readers to Etemadi: "Remember this name. She is here to conquer."[36] The artist is best known for her paintings of still lifes, empty chairs, portraits and highly stylized disembodied Persian fabrics dancing in midair, somewhat reminiscent of Qajar dancers and their acrobatic positions, a common subject a century before.

A series of pencil drawings by Etemadi belongs to the tumultuous days of the Revolution. Her subjects—scavenged from daily newspapers—are demonstrators against the Pahlavi regime in 1978 (p. 202) and troops of the Islamic regime suppressing the rebellion of the Kurdish minority in 1979 (p. 203). The anger

MONIR SHAHROUDY FARMANFARMAIAN

Hans Ulrich Obrist

Not only was Monir Shahroudy Farmanfarmaian (1922–2019) a pioneer of Iranian art, but through her visionary practice she was at the forefront of contemporary artistic models that have expanded into global dialogues. My journey with Monir's work is a journey through conversation, with many taking place between us over the years in different locations. Conversation changes people, and as Monir recounted her incredible saga over the time I knew her, I have been transformed. Monir was an active participant in what historian Eric Hobsbawm has called a "protest against forgetting." Her work serves to activate memory—a memory that is as multidimensional as the artist herself. She is a role model for the artist of the twenty-first century—a true artist's artist.

It was through other artists that I first came to Monir. In 2007, I visited Egypt for the Cairo Interview Project, an idea conceived with the artist Susan Hefuna. The contemporary art scene in Egypt was proving to be one of the most diverse in the region, stimulating both controversy and debate. Taking place at the Townhouse Gallery's Factory space in the heart of downtown Cairo, the project engaged audiences in a far-reaching set of conversations with young artists whose works had been internationally recognized. Participants, alongside Hefuna, included Lara Baladi, Amal Kenawy, Hassan Khan, Ahmed Khaled, Mona Marzouk, Bassam El Baroni, Mahmoud Khaled, Basim Magdy, Huda Lutfi, Rana El Nemr and Shady El Noshokaty. One of my favourite questions to ask during interviews is: Who are you inspired by? Many of the artists that I spoke with mentioned Hefuna, and many of them also mentioned Monir. It was this that led me to engage in deeper research on the artist's practice, with a desire to find out more.

Fast-forward to the following year, and Monir and I had our first conversation within the context of the Global Art Forum at Art Dubai, following my suggestion that she be invited. It was here that she began to tell me about her extraordinary life, from her studies at Cornell University in Upstate New York and Parsons School of Design and the rest of her time spent in New York City with artists such as Andy Warhol, Milton Avery, Frank Stella and Louise Nevelson, to her multiple exiles and returns to her native Iran. Arriving in New York after World War II, Monir quickly started to engage with the city's avant-garde art scene and associated

Monir Shahroudy Farmanfarmaian in her salon, Tehran, 1975

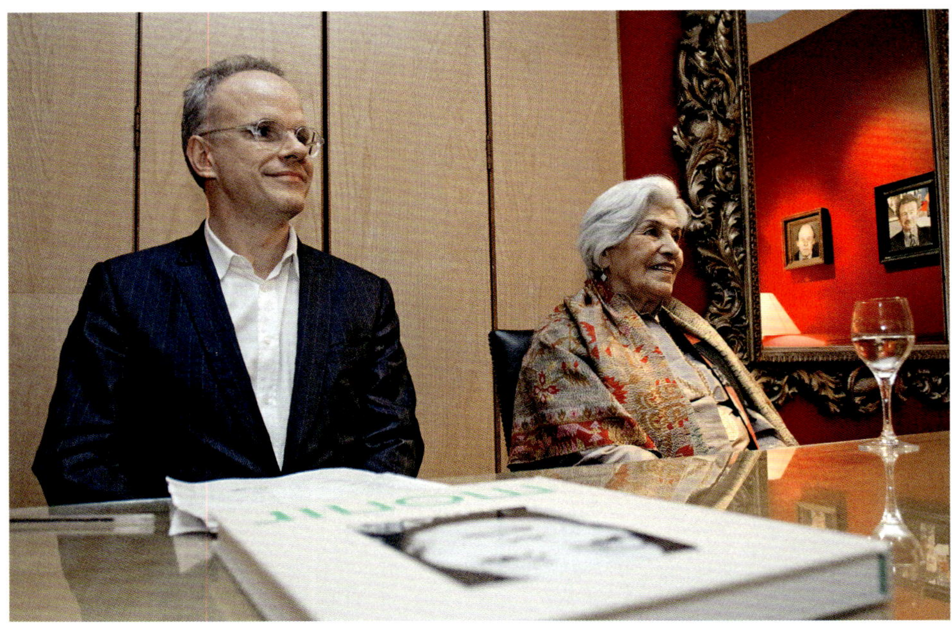

with various artists at its centre. Warhol was a particularly interesting encounter, who was her co-worker in the Bonwit Teller advertising department. As Monir told me in our first conversation:

> I was looking for a job and I used to do freelance fashion drawing. A friend of mine introduced me to the art director of a big department store and I got a full-time job. But before that I did some flower drawings, we call them Iranian violets, and I sold them for $150 to an agency. Later it became the design for the Bonwit Teller department store. It was all over the shopping bags, the negligees and shoes; that violet of mine was everywhere. When I was working at Bonwit Teller as an artist doing layouts, Andy was one of the artists that I used to make layouts for. He used to be very good at shoe drawings. I would make a big *New York Times* page with a layout of eight or ten shoes and I gave it to Andy to do. We used to see each other at the weekend and that was how I met Andy.

Moreover, Monir forged a deep connection with the painter Milton Avery, who was one of her closest neighbours in Woodstock, where Monir would go in the summertime. It was Avery who connected with her over her interest in drawing:

> He used to come to my cottage every day to do drawings. He was very good at drawing and I had a baby at that time, my first daughter. He said, "Never mind me Monir. I am sitting here." I said, "Do whatever you want," whenever I knew that he was following me doing some sketches. Later he taught me how to do monotypes. My first exhibition was with monotype flowers with Milton Avery's technique in Tehran in 1958.

Monir would continue to live and work in New York until 1957, at which point she returned to Iran, beginning an extensive process of research, collection and preservation of regional artistic, craft and architectural practices within the country. As she told me, this was a moment of bringing together everything experienced in the 1950s in the New York art scene with local research in Iran, reaching back to her childhood:

> I painted flowers and I travelled a lot in Iran because I became very interested in the past. I went to old cities and old ruins. I saw the Sassanid palaces, all the mosques in Isfahan and in small towns. I went to visit tribal people and my inspiration is always from the public art from the tribes and I like it. It is a pleasure seeing it. Somehow, I suppose I try and transfer it to my heart.

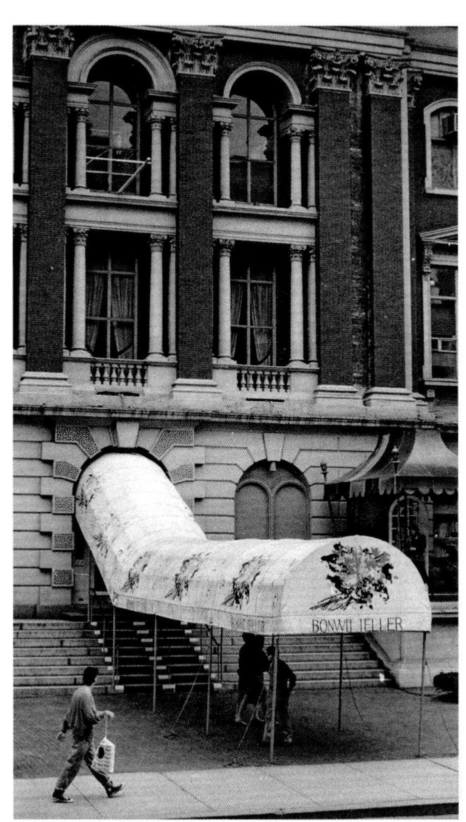

Opposite
Hans Ulrich Obrist and Monir Shahroudy Farmanfarmaian, London, 2010

Above
The exterior of Bonwit Teller on Berkeley Street, Boston, showing the violet logo designed by Farmanfarmaian, July 2, 1987

I've always felt that Monir's words have resonance with the Martinican novelist and poet Édouard Glissant's visionary concept of "mondialité," which proposes that if we resist the homogenizing forces of globalization, then we are able to take advantage of a great potential. As Glissant explains: "mondialité is the extraordinary adventure whereby we all live today in a world that, for the first time, in real and in immediate, sudden ways, without delay, is simultaneously multiple and unique."[1] Of course it is impossible to ignore global dialogues, but we can react to them and counter their universalizing tendency through negotiation, fostering plurality in the process. Monir's practice of interwoven politics and poetry is deeply resonant with Glissant's mondialité, which is evident in her desire to explore local tradition in her native Iran through the lens of a global dialogue.

In 1979, Monir and her husband, Abol-Bashar, travelled to New York to visit family, during which time the Islamic Revolution culminated. She thus found herself in a second exile from Iran, one that would last for over twenty years. Quite early on after returning to the United States, Monir expanded her work into collage and so-called memory boxes, work that, as she told me, "I call heartache, because it's very nostalgic... I miss Iran. I put a picture of it, I put a piece of jewellery, in those memory boxes." This desire to encapsulate the wonders of memory remind me of the boxes that defined the artistic career of Joseph Cornell, who collected and fashioned enclosed worlds out of found objects.

The yearning for her home country was only satisfied once again at the age of eighty, when in 2004 Monir returned once again to Iran to open her studio and workshop. Her return to Iran involved creating an incredible studio with craftspeople working there, many of whom were the last people to be familiar with local traditions and techniques that Monir was keen to nurture and support. After setting up this studio, she promptly set out in search of Haji Ostad Navid, with whom she had executed her early mirror mosaics, resulting in a reunion that would continue their collaboration. At the age of eighty-eight, Monir was overseeing a prolific workshop using centuries-old techniques, with a vision fixed on the future. The energy and willpower that she brought to this endeavour, during her ninth decade, is extraordinary.

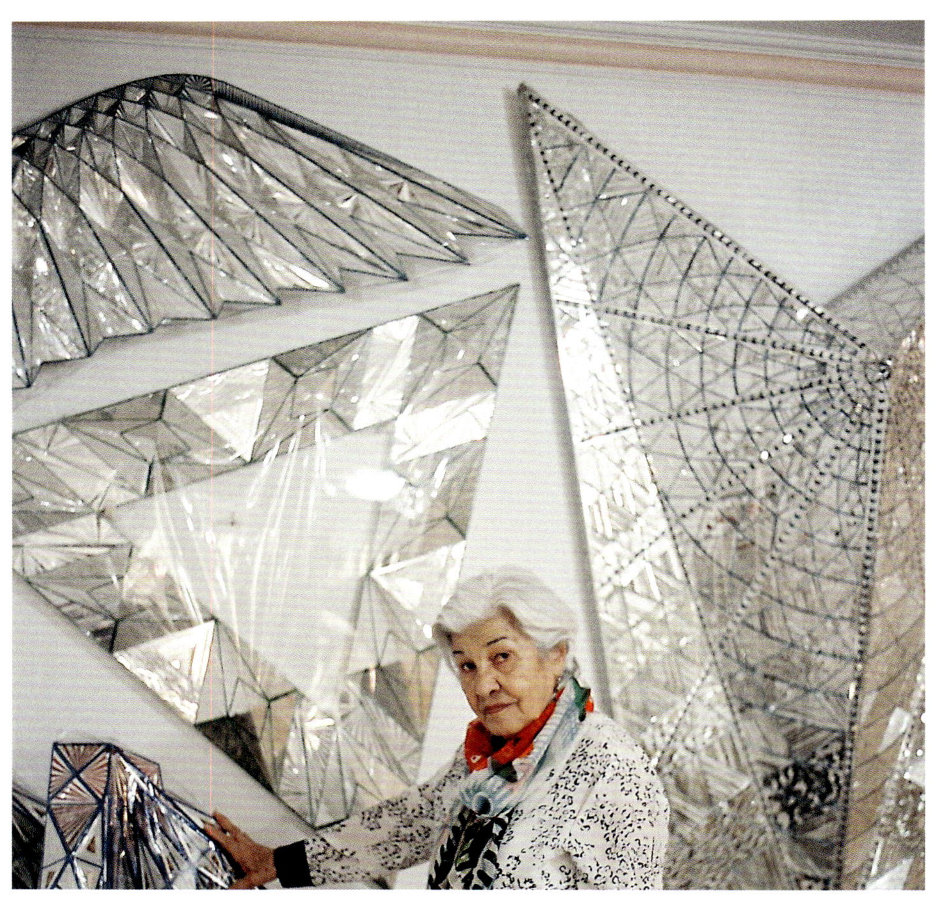

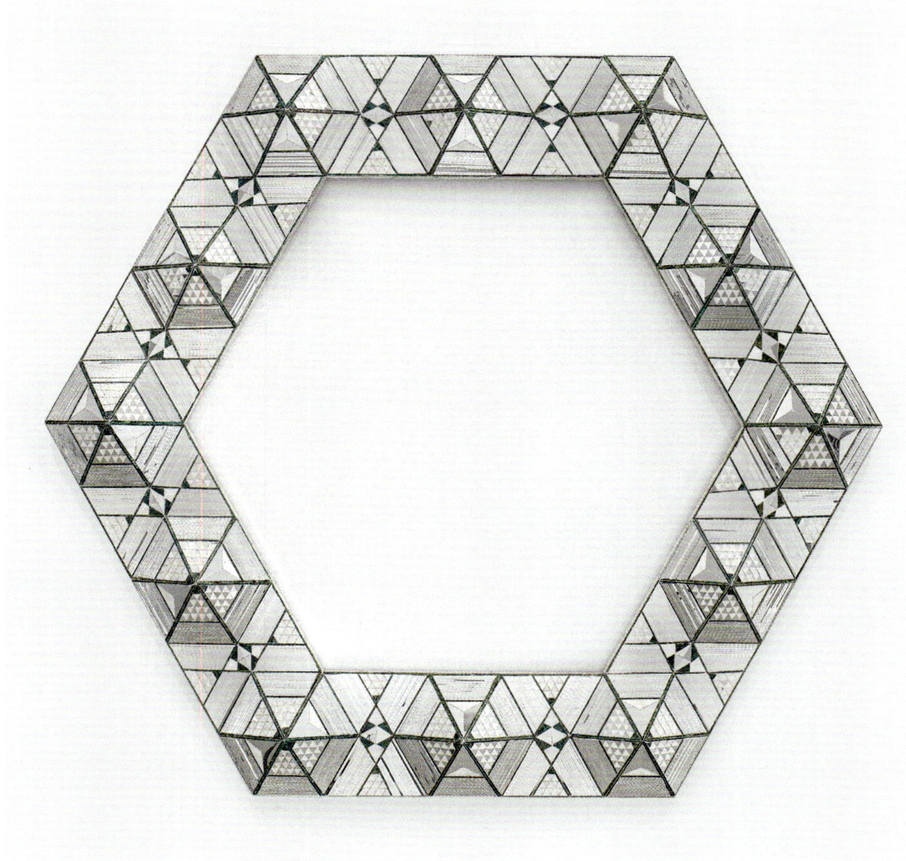

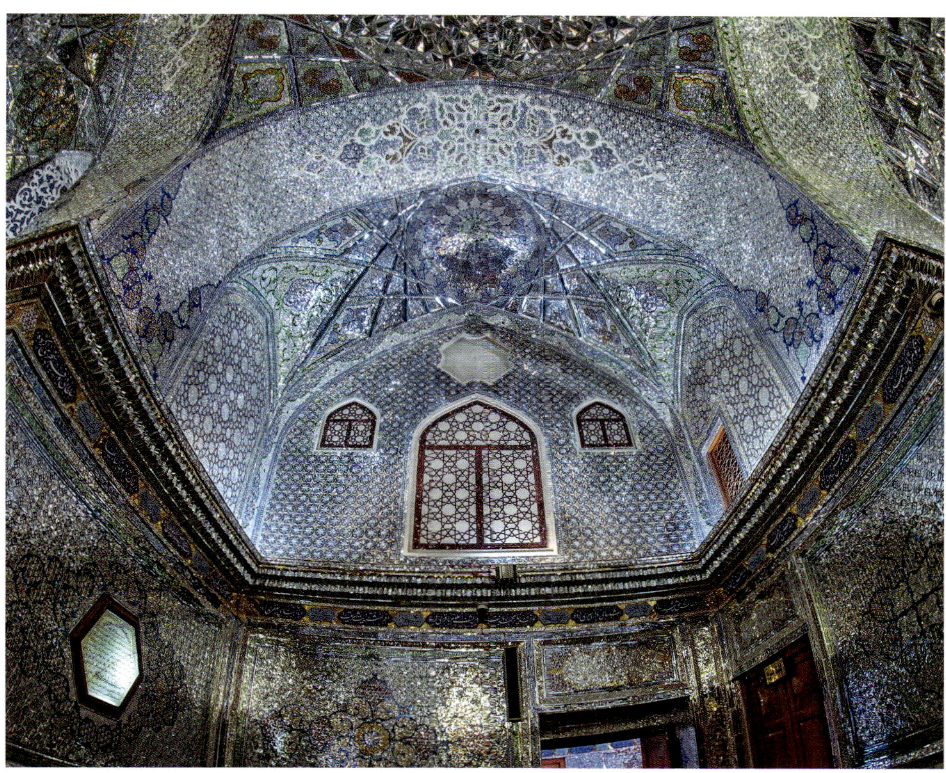

Above
Interior of Shah-e-Cheragh Mausoleum, Shiraz, Iran, 2015

Opposite, top
Monir Shahroudy Farmanfarmaian in her studio, Tehran, 2017

Opposite, bottom
Monir Shahroudy Farmanfarmaian
Fifth Family Hexagon, 2014
mirror and reverse-glass painting on plaster and wood

A fundamental thread throughout Monir's career was the mysticism and symbolism embedded within geometry. In 2015, curator Suzanne Cotter and I organized a conversation with Monir and her long-term friend, the artist Frank Stella. During this remarkable dialogue, Stella explained the significance of geometry for Monir:

> I think the thing is geometry. Monir grew up with it, and it was part of her world. I was a visitor to that world, and saw more or less the same things she grew up with and that she continued to see all of her life. For Monir, starting out, she was accustomed to it, but it didn't come until later that she immersed herself in it. It became a way of working that gave her confidence. In other words, coming to the West, and being familiarized with what was going on in the Western art world, she was able to go back, assimilate geometry, and come out on the other side, able to be completely free with her native geometry... Ultimately, everyone says, there is no art without geometry.[2]

As highlighted by Stella's words, geometry continued to resurface in Monir's work over the years. One of the most significant moments was early on in her career when, as she told me, she travelled to Shiraz with fellow artists Robert Morris and Marcia Hafif to visit the shrine Shah Cheragh: "It is beautiful. It has high ceilings, domes and mirror mosaics with fantastic reflections. I said, 'We have to sit in here for half an hour because it's a living theatre.' People were crying and begging for their wishes, and I was crying because of all the reflections in the ceiling." The inspiration from seeing these shrines enabled Monir to further the possibilities of geometric shapes within her work, notably the hexagon.

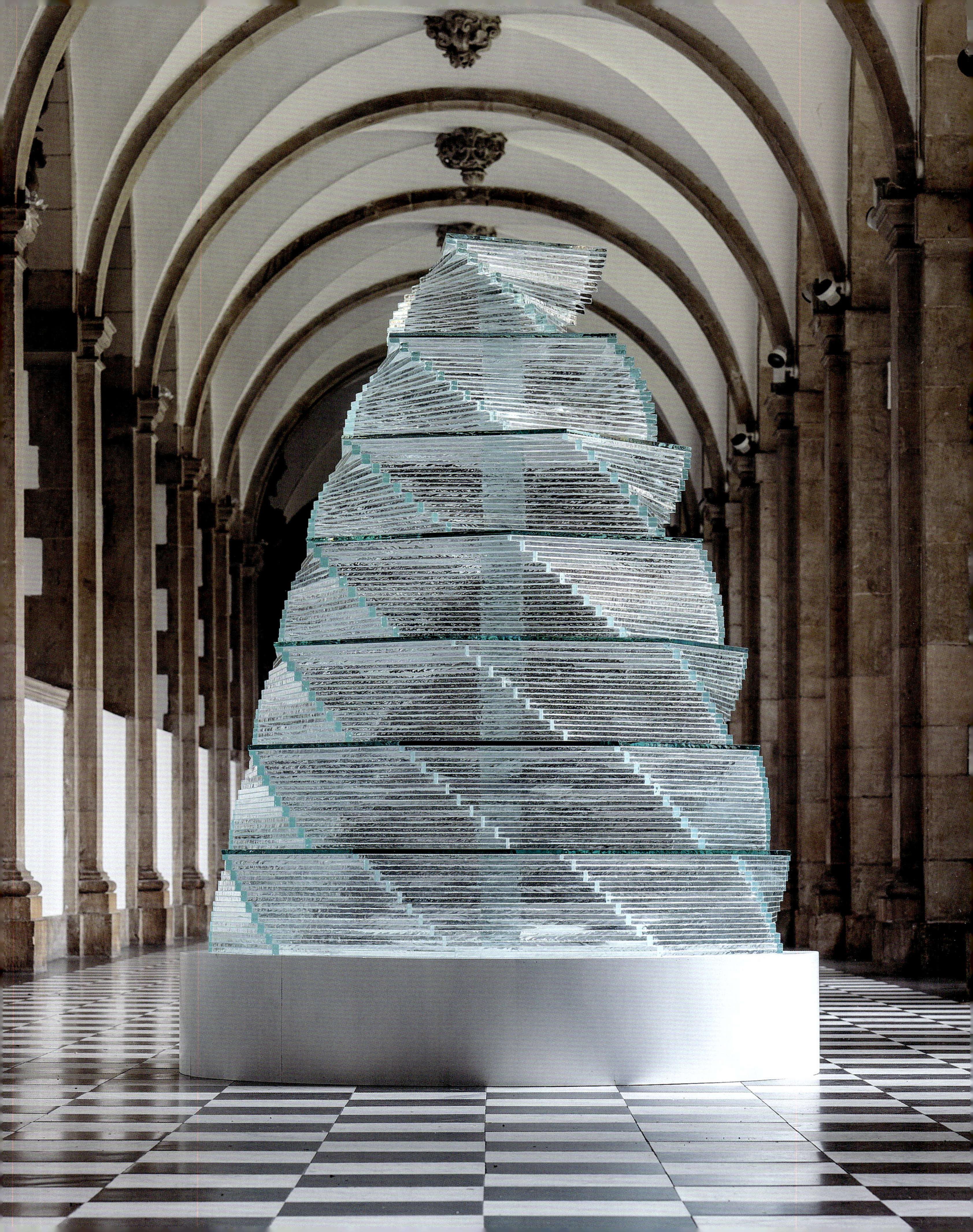

Moving from the basic drawing of the shape, she would start to add additional points, lines and shapes to this original form. Monir explained to me the symbolic meanings of these shapes: "the triangle is human consciousness; the square is the four directions: north, south, west and east. The pentagon is the five senses: hearing, smelling, seeing, taste and touch... The numbers go to twelve, and twelve is the zodiac, the twelve stars in the universe." Through her experimentation with geometry and its symbolic relationships, Monir transports us from the micro to the macro of what it means to interpret our environments and wider existence within the universe. Her work brings the mystic into the everyday lives of those who experience it.

Toward the end of her life, Monir was keen to move her practice into architecture and the public realm. This is evident in works such as her ambitious *Khayyam Fountain* (2018), comprising a series of triangular, pentagonal and hexagonal shapes that form a rotating tower, which interacts with the changing environment around it. Moreover, Monir's work found interrelations with architectural discourse, as elucidated by Stella in the same conversation that took place in 2015:

> Monir took geometry off the surface of architecture and made it into essentially its own surface. She hasn't put it back on the wall; it's come back as art. She's taking a geometry that is so tied to architecture, actually tied to a wall, and making it an independent surface.[3]

For Monir, geometry is an elemental part of architecture, and, by extension, of how we perceive the world around us. To engage with Monir's work is to engage with the universe, to unlock a mysticism that every surface, pattern or form is imbued with. Stella's words highlight the ongoing importance of Monir's work to contemporary art practice today. To return to the beginning, her role as an artist's artist continues as part of her enduring legacy.

ENDNOTES

1 Édouard Glissant, *La Cohée du Lamentin* (Paris: Gallimard, 2005), 27.

2 Hans Ulrich Obrist and Susan Cotter, "There Is No Art Without Geometry," *Mousse Magazine* 50 (2015): 36.

3 Obrist and Cotter, "There Is No Art Without Geometry," 36.

Monir Shahroudy Farmanfarmaian
Khayyam Fountain, 2018
glass

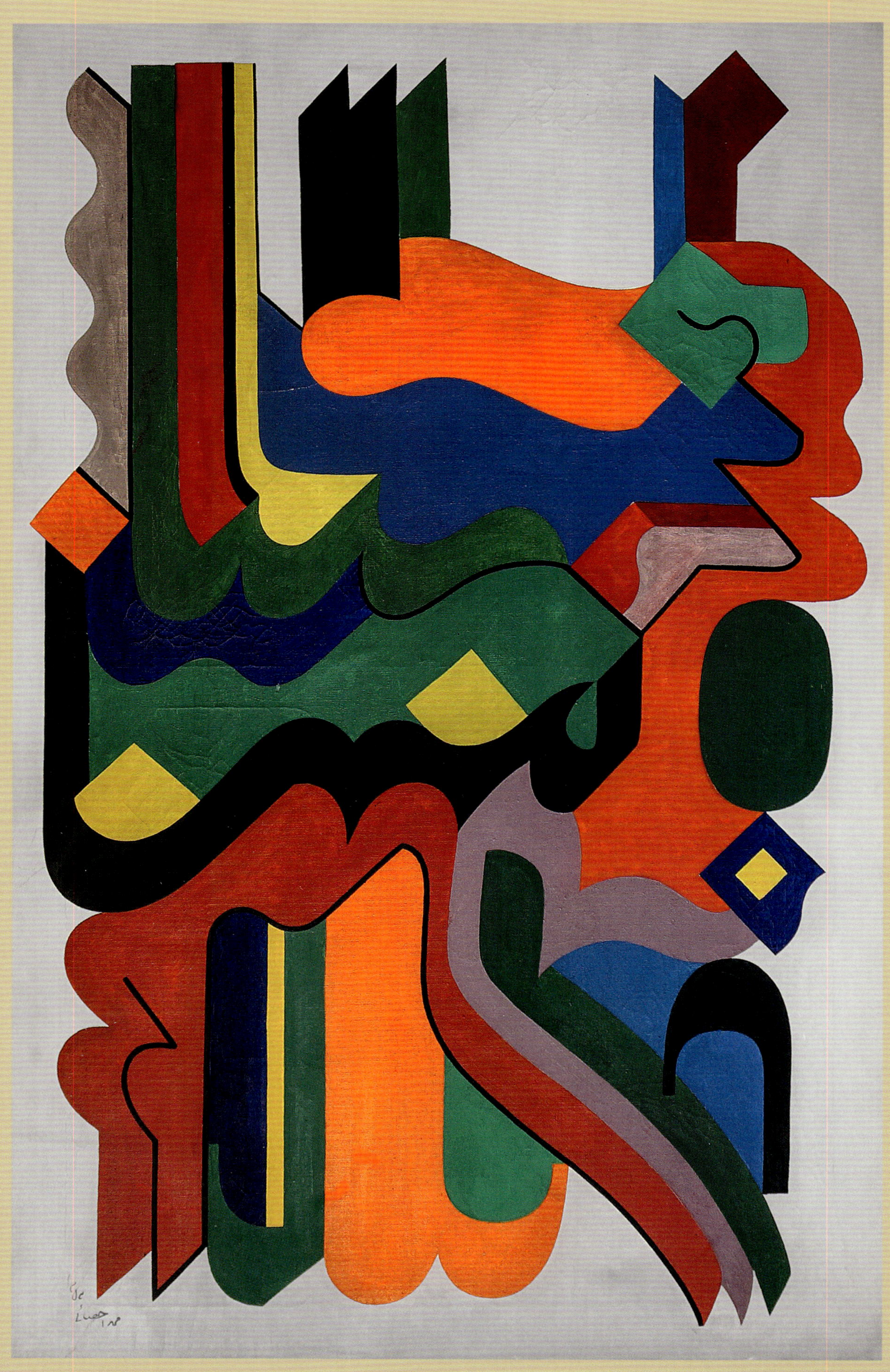

WHISPERING INKS, SILENT VERSES: SEYED MOHAMMAD EHSAEY IN CONVERSATION WITH DAVOOD MADADPOOR

Vancouver – Berlin, 2024

DAVOOD MADADPOOR The word and its deconstruction are crucial aspects of your work. This deconstruction and the interplay of familiar words create an unfamiliar experience for the audience. Naturally, those who resonate with these words follow this unfamiliar texture, generating new narratives. This aspect of your work—creating spaces to allow multiple narratives to emerge, intertwining the present with the past—holds a unique power. In my view, the audience no longer perceives a series of decorations on the canvas but instead enters into the spaces, worlds and philosophies of your thought. They read the words you have written and carry forth your message. Could you elaborate on the thought process behind creating these words and paintings, especially those based on *khat* (line calligraphy)?

SEYED MOHAMMAD EHSAEY Indeed, it is as you described. In this context, I must emphasize that the times dictate the approach. Human nature and the hidden essence of existence are shaped by past events that have transpired over the course of human history, leaving us in a state of powerlessness today.

In the early 1940s, we witnessed significant changes in Iranian society. How shall I put it? Society began to open itself to new horizons, most notably in literature. However, the visual arts were influenced by individuals' education in, and by certain people's growing familiarity with, European art. Gradually, following changes in government and later the 1953 Iranian coup d'état, along with the arrival of the Americans and the establishment of the Point Four Program,[1] a new perspective on various matters, including visual arts and architecture, began to take shape. The return of several artists from Europe, their initiation of new activities, the establishment of a few art galleries and the emergence of a deconstructionist movement or school can be observed in the collections of Tehran Museum of Contemporary Art and among private collectors.

Before my time, a few artists with a modernist perspective paid close attention to traditional sites such as *saqqakhanehs* (traditional water fountains)—authentic places deeply rooted in folk culture. These artists meticulously examined the objects within these spaces and presented new interpretations in their works, offering these thoughts to the public. The Point Four Program activated American involvement in Iran, and specialized teams brought structural changes to various fields.

The encouragement and purchase of such works and competition among prominent families fostered renewed interest in novel approaches to every phenomenon, which, I believe, had a political dimension at the time. Amid this atmosphere, with encouragement from the government (which itself was a pioneer of new art), I began experimenting with Persian script. By altering the composition of letters and words—breaking and reconnecting them, shifting and rearranging elements—I discovered a new structure in calligraphy.

Seyed Mohammad Ehsaey
Untitled, 1974
oil on canvas

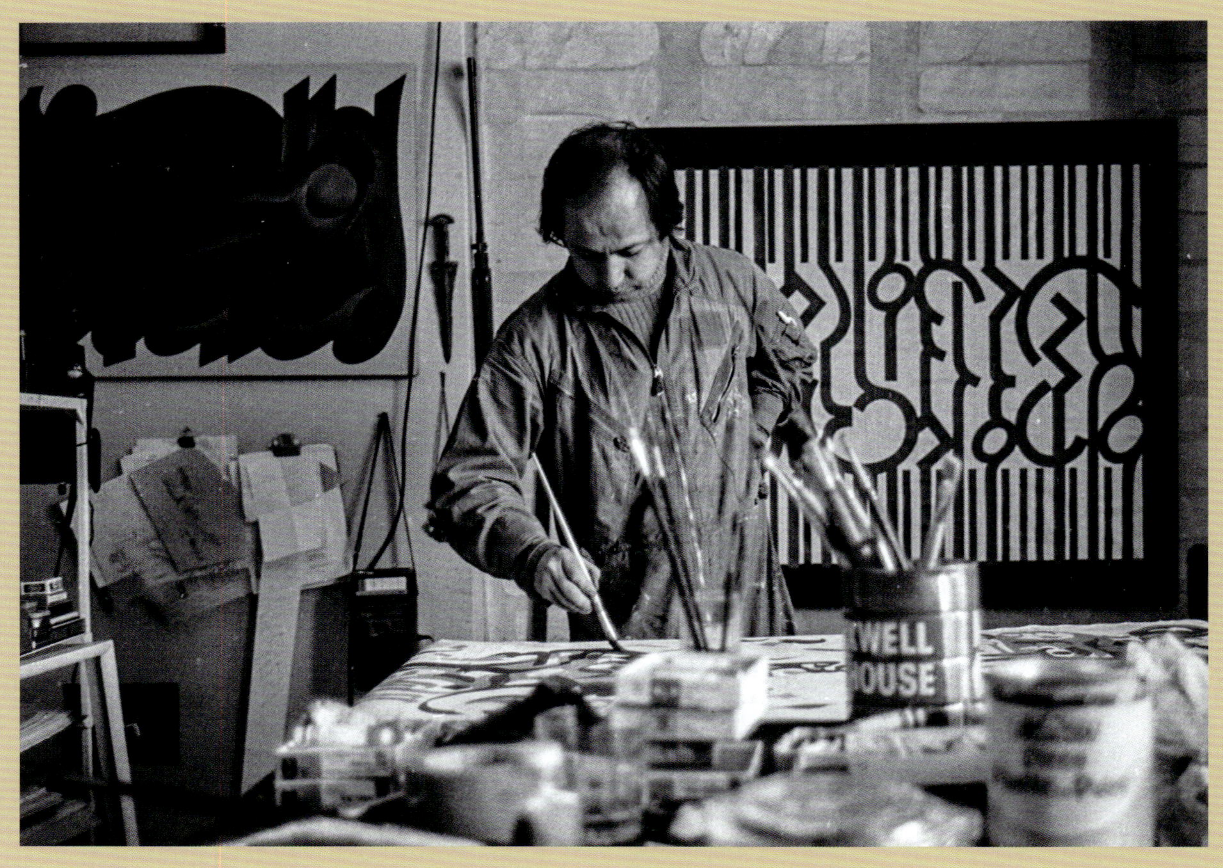
WELL
HOUSE

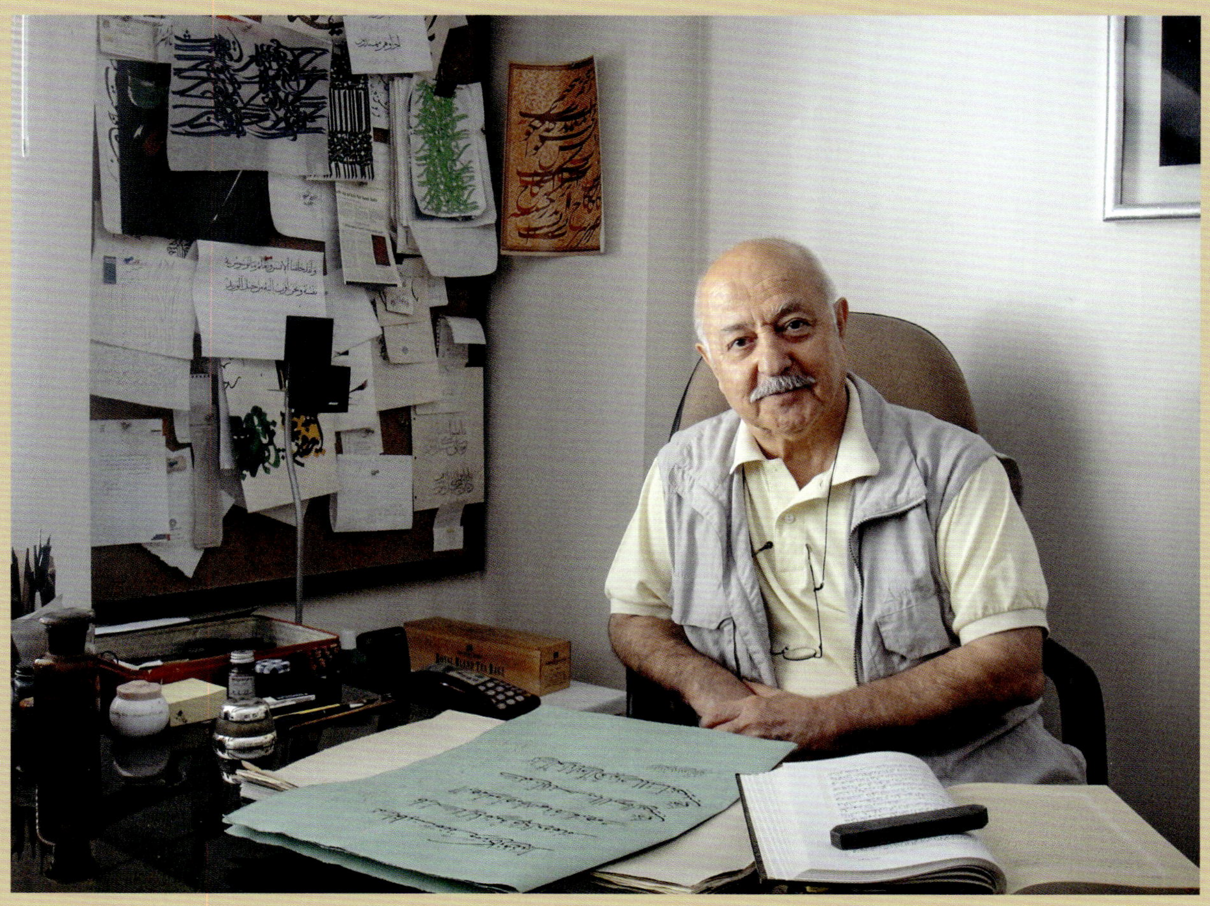

My artistic education in the Faculty of Fine Arts at the University of Tehran was in painting and graphic design. For years, I taught calligraphy and typography, emphasizing the latter significantly. During my painting studies, I became increasingly drawn to the essence of calligraphy. This connection to calligraphy became the foundation of my artistic expression, pulling me toward a diverse range of calligraphic experiences.

DM Combining traditional calligraphy with modern graphic elements marks a transformation in your work. Could you explain the motivations and influences that led you from classical calligraphy to this innovative merging? How did this transition develop over time, and does this perspective still persist in your work?

SME Through my teaching experiences, I realized that anyone who devotes great interest, practice and deep-rooted passion to any form of art can eventually produce work that is accepted by society. However, I still do not fully understand the factors that set someone apart, where their works garner special attention and endure.

Some may have no specific goal; they become entangled in situations they cannot escape. Over time, I noticed during exhibitions that viewers respond to or try to interpret various aspects of the works, depending on their backgrounds.

One contemporary writer, Sadeq Chubak (1916–1998), published a book in 1949—during the period I previously mentioned, when the Point Four Program was established—which included a story titled "The Monkey Whose Master Had Died." It is an allegory about a monkey who, after the death of its master, breaks free from its bonds but continues to wander, frightened, with a piece of the chain still hanging from its neck. This symbolizes intellectuals who cannot free themselves from the chains of their past—an umbilical cord. As a painter, I asked myself: What else could I use to express my inner self, and what better tool than the one I was known for and had mastery over?

Yes, I cannot separate myself from calligraphy. In whatever I create, calligraphy remains at the core of my work. However, in my works, my painterly side holds greater importance.

Rosalind E. Krauss (1941–), one of the founders of the journal *October*, speaks of this passion for a particular art form:

> I imagine that a person chooses this unique and mysterious form to express their feelings because they have had an original experience with it. Perhaps this original experience compels them to follow it, think about it, read about it, and write about it. But first, there must come a moment when they are enchanted and captivated by this form of expression and become one with it.

DM If we were to categorize your calligraphic paintings into two series, the first would be the *Eternal Alphabet*, which combines traditional calligraphy with modern abstract forms. Repeated texts such as "*Allah*" (God) and "*La ilaha illallah*" (There is no deity but God) create a mystical atmosphere, inviting viewers to reflect

Top
Seyed Mohammad Ehsaey
in his studio, Iran, 1954

Bottom
Seyed Mohammad Ehsaey
in his studio, n.d.

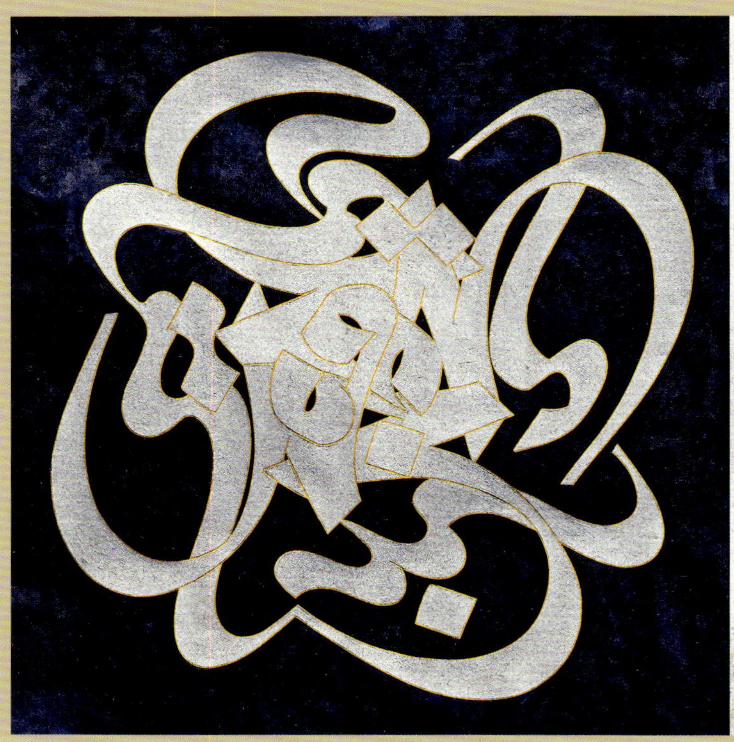

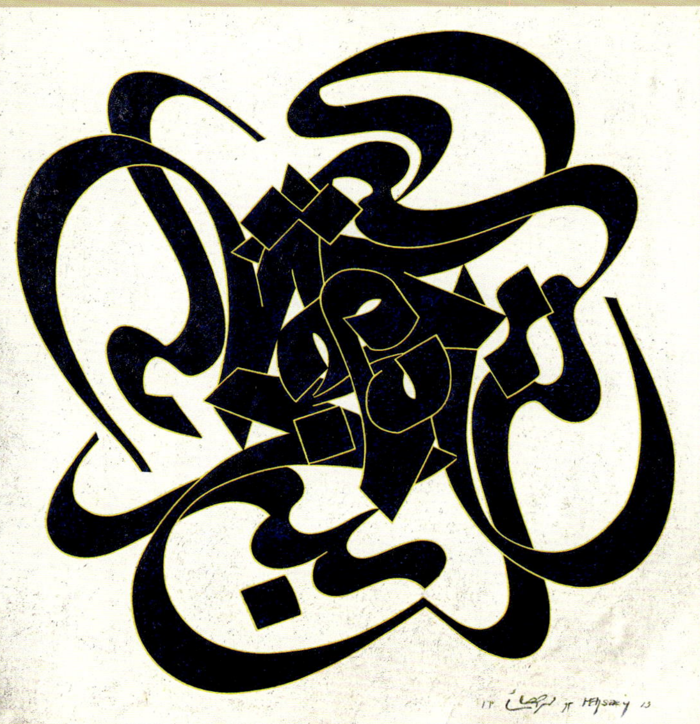

on spirituality. This series seems to reflect your mystical outlook. The other grouping, the *Knots* series, features intricate, intertwined forms that transcend readability, symbolizing the complexities of language and communication. How do these two approaches reflect your evolving artistic vision?

SME As you have correctly observed, another aspect of my work involves a mystical inclination and an attention to celestial themes, though this is a personal matter. In the *Knots* series, I find contemplative aspects in my work. Since writing about these collections is a laborious task, I leave their interpretation and critique to the viewer, allowing each to arrive at their own narrative. Let me just say that what is present within these works exists within them.

DM One of the most thoughtful statements I've heard from you is that you see yourself as an artist of the present—a view that is evident in your work. You've mentioned that if you had pursued pure calligraphy alone, you merely would have continued the path of earlier calligraphers. Instead, you have incorporated a contemporary perspective into your art. Today, "contemporary" is often tied to political and social contexts. How do you view the concept of the contemporary, and how does it relate to your work, which plays a role in Iranian art?

SME For me, as for others, the contemporary era in Iran began after World War II, around 1945, during the fourth year of the reign of the second Pahlavi dynasty. Between then and the 1953 coup, Iran's social and political structures seemed to change.

After the 1953 Iranian coup d'état, I entered high school, and political and social transformations accelerated, opening my eyes and ears to some extent. I became

Seyed Mohammad Ehsaey
Mohabbat (Affection), 2013
oil on canvas

intensely interested in calligraphy, and after high school, while teaching, I worked on calligraphy for various advertising agencies.

During these years, Iranian art took on a new flavour due to the demands of the time. Naturally, young people—influenced by observing various art movements and trends and the influx of new European theories—developed fresh mentalities.

As I mentioned earlier, I did not embrace the continuation of a stagnant tradition, which was weakening at the time. Collaborating with a group of fine arts graduates from the University of Tehran, their ideas and work impacted me, leading me to challenge traditional calligraphy—up until today, when contemporary artists' theories and works are studied, critiqued and interpreted.

I enrolled in painting and graphic design at the University of Tehran, in which the Faculty of Fine Arts is entirely devoted to painting and graphic arts. Thus, with a fresh perspective, calligraphic painting continued the calligraphic tradition in contemporary times.

DM Today's art often focuses on rituals, self-care and care for others, including nature and our surroundings. I feel that we now live in a cold, war-torn and harsh world—a world in which I, living in Berlin, and another person, living in Tehran, both experience a sense of alienation and disconnection from an unknown place. I would like to hear your thoughts on your work *mahabbat* (Affection, 2013), its formation and your internal need to create it. Is the *mahabbat* you have brought onto the canvas a cry born from necessity?

SME When someone presents large-scale works, such as two metres by four or five metres, containing text and intertwined, complex letters and words that seem devoid of meaning, one must wonder: why? The fact is, we have become so preoccupied these days that we are relatively indifferent to our surroundings. We no longer feel the pain of unfortunate events. We no longer notice the ugliness of lies and deceit or their destructive effects. We smile at someone's face while stabbing them in the back. Throughout the generations, humans have deliberately misused language. How many innocent people have been wrongfully hanged? How many rights have been falsely portrayed as wrong? And how many power-hungry governments have ruled societies for years, trampling the rights of honourable people and tarnishing their reputations with false accusations?

It seems that virtues in human communication have vanished, replaced by widespread and habitual opportunism. I strongly object to this abuse and misuse of words. I have voiced this objection in my works, where these concerns are subtly embedded as a third-person narrative. Perhaps this is my way of confronting unresolved inner conflicts, which have emerged as visual cries in my artworks. The works *mahabbat* (2013), *mahabbat va eshgh* (Affection and Passion, 2013) and their other iterations are, in reality, works that seem to express an outcry, as if someone has been shouting.

DM When I read your conversations with various members of the Iranian art community, I noticed your reference to how your works evoke a sense of empathy and connection in non-Iranian audiences. You also mentioned that, from a Western

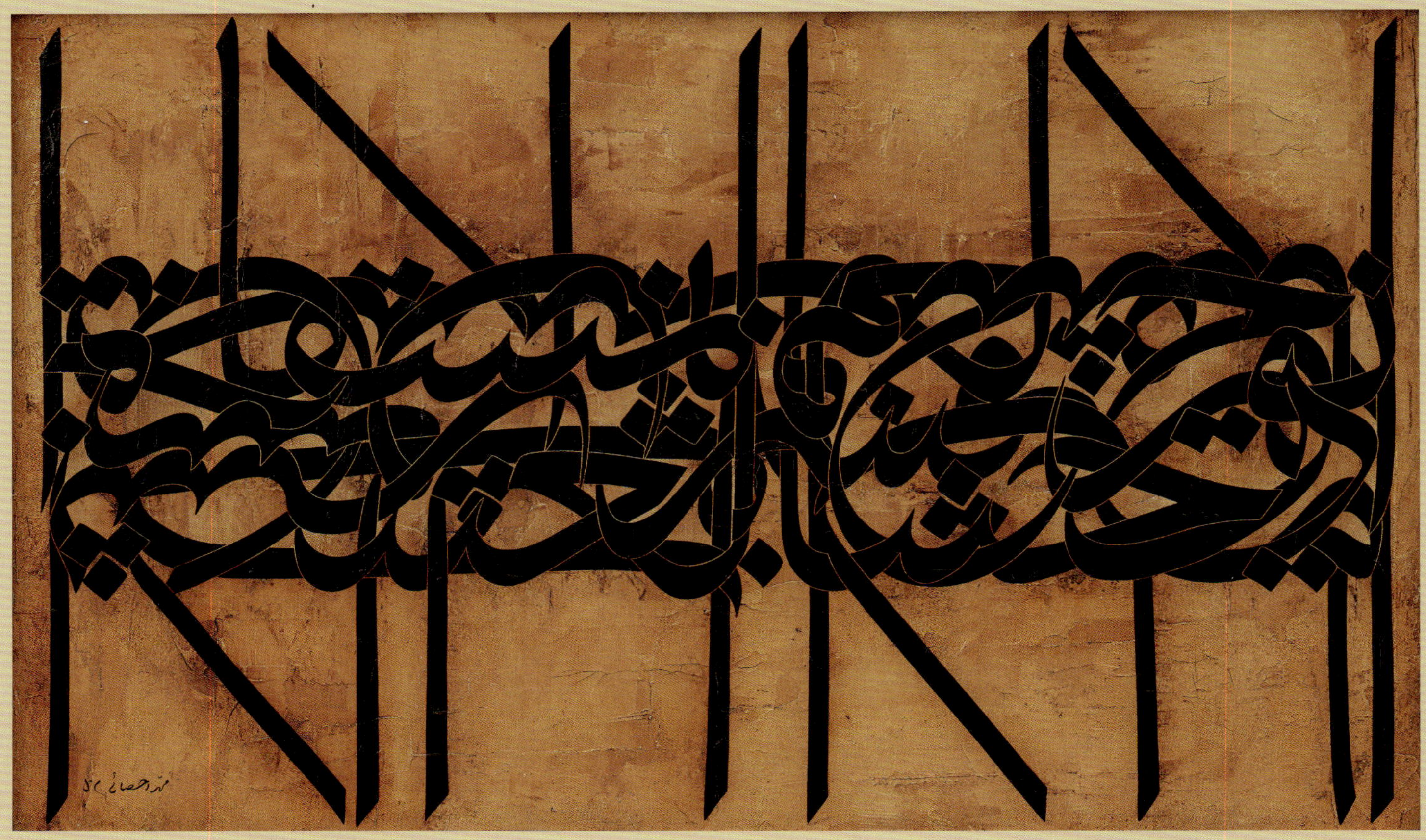

perspective, a sense of curiosity and exploration has profoundly influenced you. Based on your discussions about the importance of combining traditional calligraphy with modern design, it seems that *naqqashi-khat* (calligraphic painting) can serve as a reflection of Iranian culture and art on a global scale. Drawing from your international exhibitions and experiences, how do non-Iranian audiences receive your calligraphic paintings? Do you observe differences in how domestic and foreign viewers interpret and understand your works? What do you hope audiences take away from these works?

SME Exactly! The perspective you've presented in your question encapsulates the essence of the situation. So, let's allow your statement to serve as the answer to your question.

DM Before we delve into the distinction between artist and audience, I'd like to ask: What is your opinion of the role of the audience in art? I ask because, in contemporary art, the audience sometimes takes on different, even crucial, roles. For instance, the audience can become the artist, and, similarly, the artist can become the audience of their work.

SME With respect, I must say it's too late to dwell on such topics now. For years, critiques and articles have been written about artworks and their audiences, and various theories have been proposed.

Seyed Mohammad Ehsaey
Untitled, 1973
oil on canvas

Once, someone stood in front of one of my works and asked, "What are these writings? What have you written?" I replied, "Writing." They asked again, "Well, what does this mean?" Again, I said, "Writing." What else could I have said?

I eventually became both the viewer and the audience of my own works.

DM Given the cultural and social changes in Iran, how do you think calligraphic painting can reflect contemporary issues and concerns?

SME Allow me to conclude this conversation with a beautiful and wise reflection from the mystic and sage Rumi:

> No calligrapher writes a script merely for the letters,
> But for the essence of the script, not for reading.
> The outer form is for the hidden meaning,
> And that is closed for another hidden essence.
> Count this, second and third, and up to ten,
> These benefits are all according to one's perspective.
> Like chess games, my dear,
> The purpose of each move is revealed in the next.
> This was established for the hidden game,
> And that for this, and this for the next ...

Ultimately, I have another interpretation of my works, just as the calligrapher wrote three types of scripts:

> One that only he could read,
> Another that could be read by both him and others,
> And one that neither he nor anyone else could read.

That third script is me, who speaks,

> But neither I know nor others know! (Shams Tabrizi)

ENDNOTES

1 The Point Four Program, initiated by the United States in 1949, extended its technical assistance to Iran, focusing primarily on agriculture, health and education. While the program mainly emphasized these areas, its influence indirectly touched upon cultural aspects by promoting modernization and development.

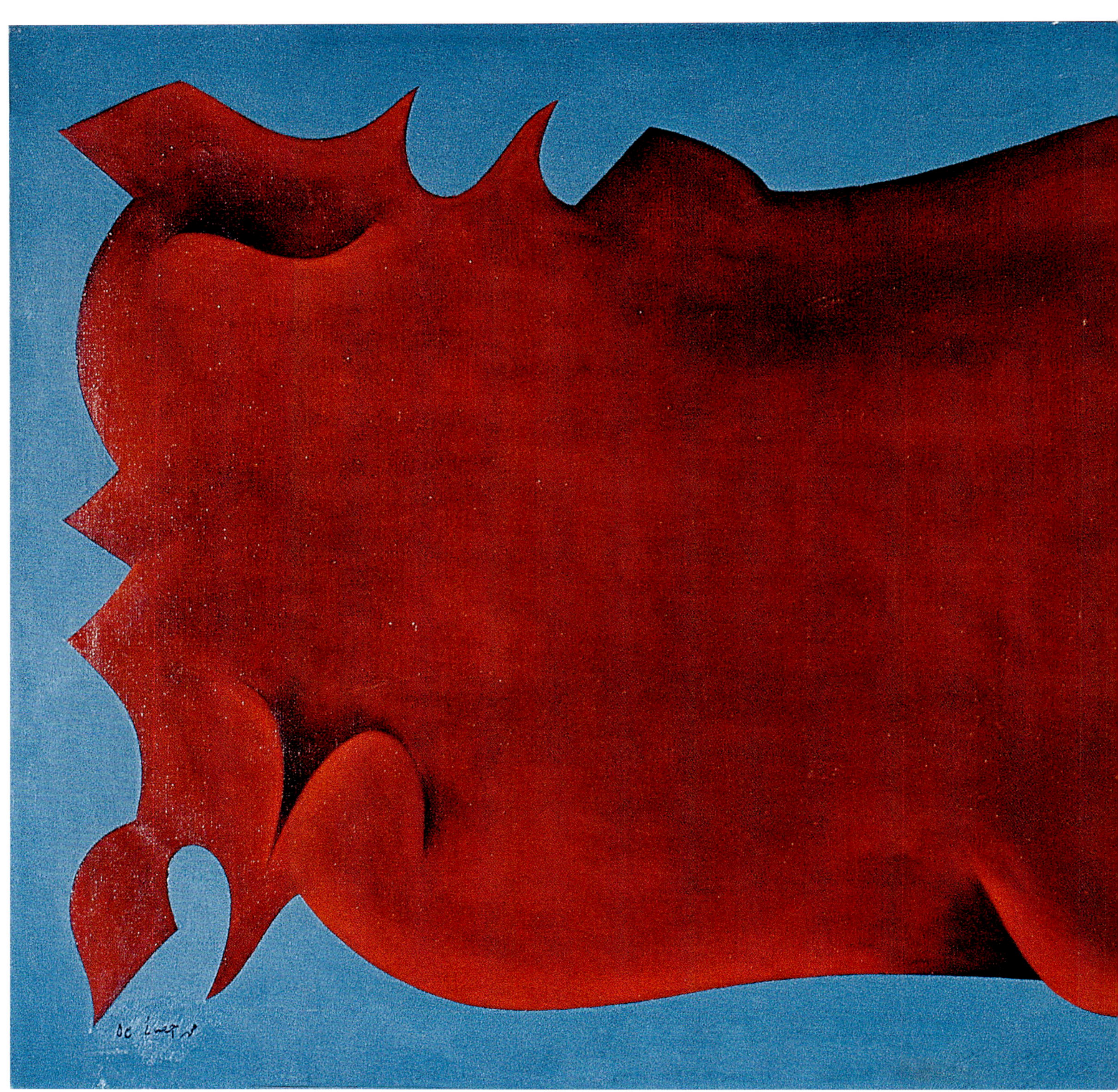

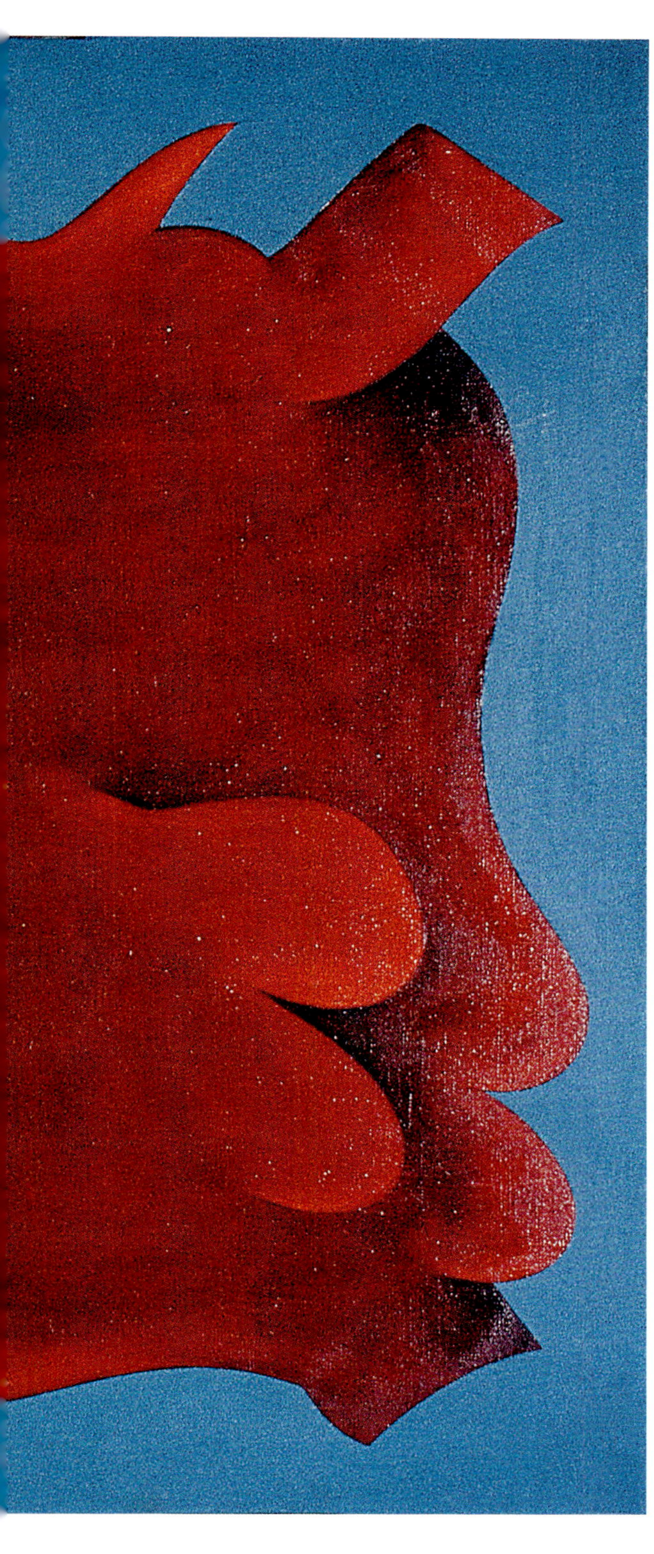

Seyed Mohammad Ehsaey
Untitled, 1974
oil on canvas

Reza Mafi
Untitled, late 1970s
ink on paper

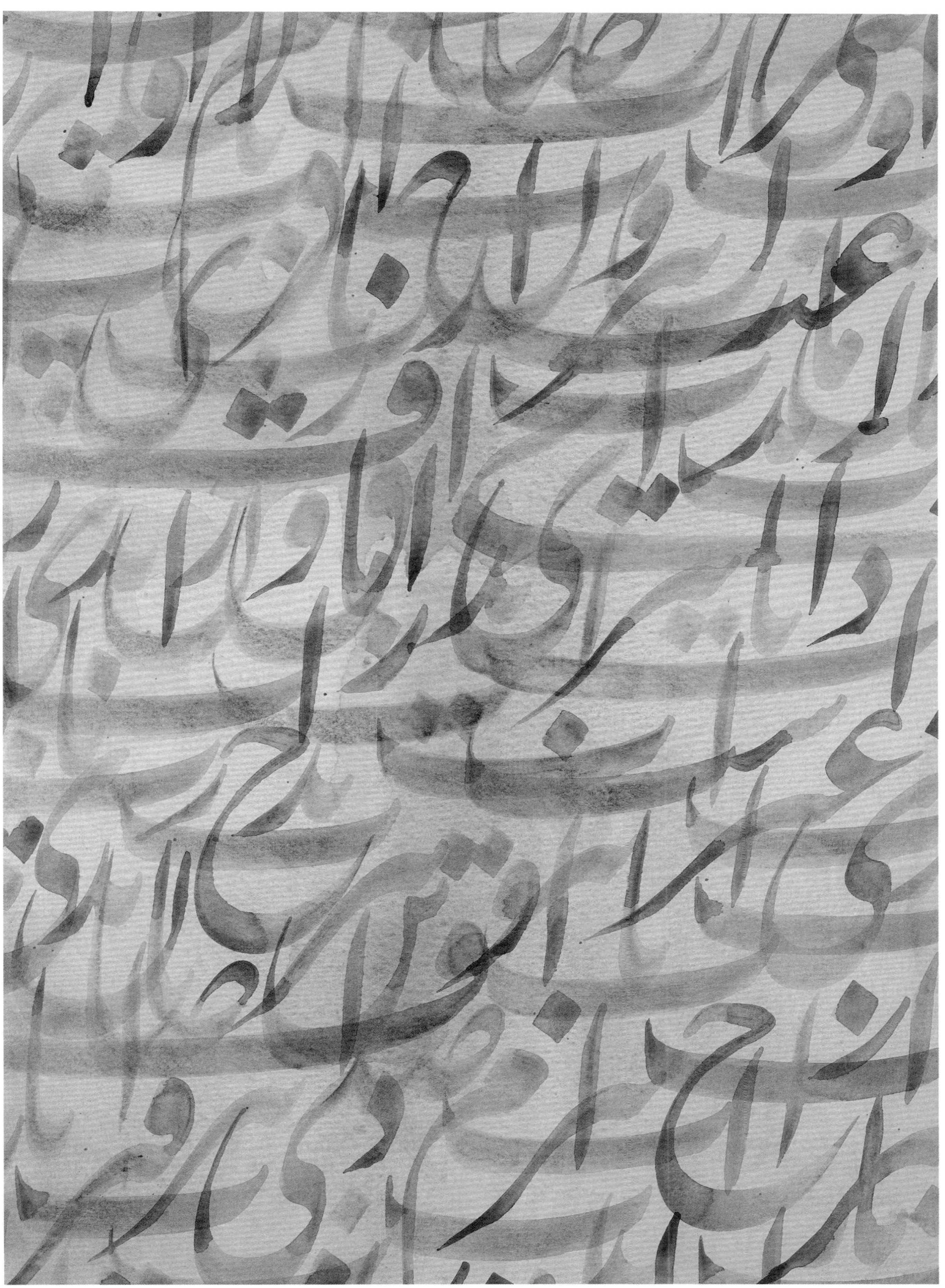

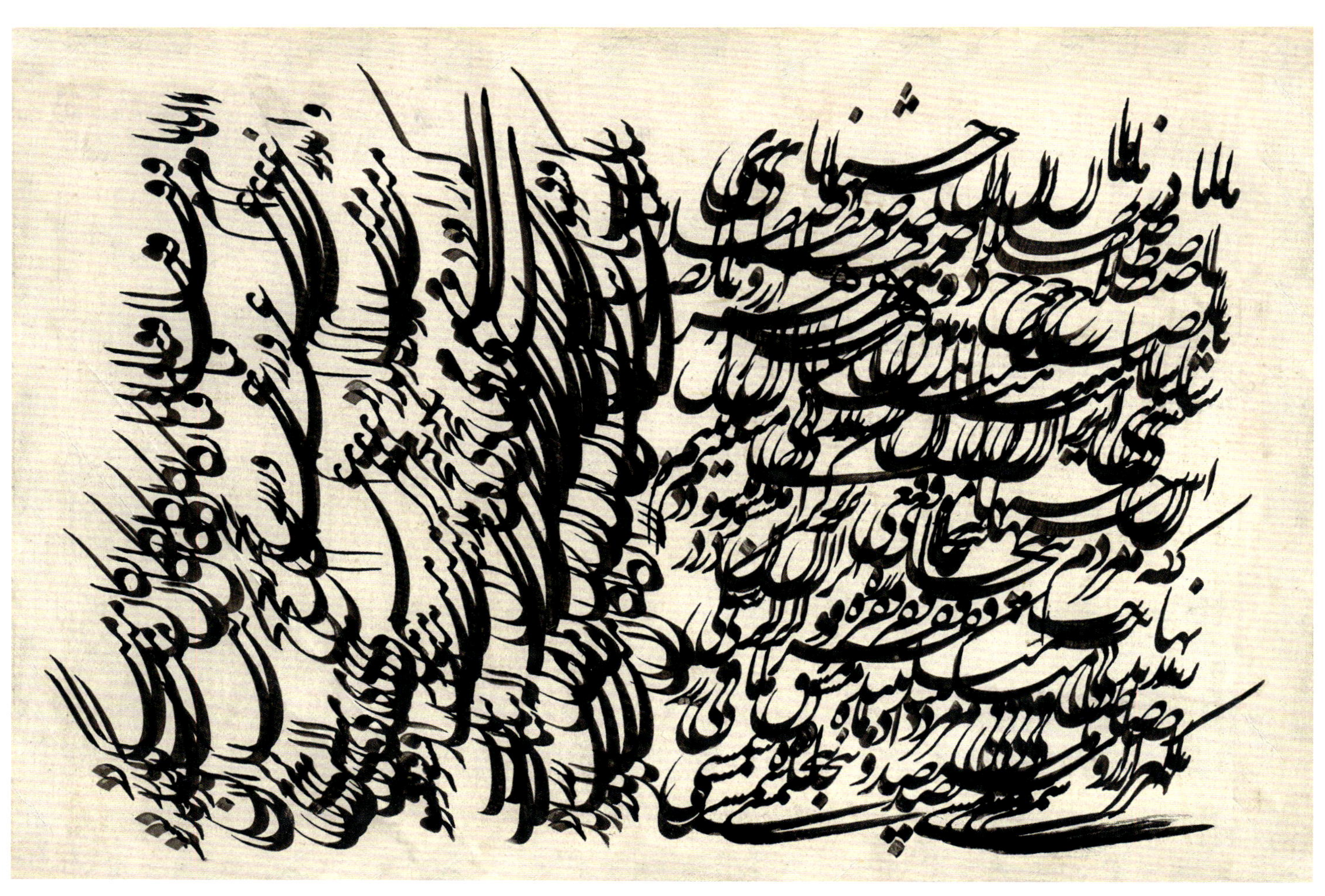

Above
Reza Mafi
Untitled, 1971
ink on paper

Opposite
Reza Mafi
Untitled, 1975
ink on paper

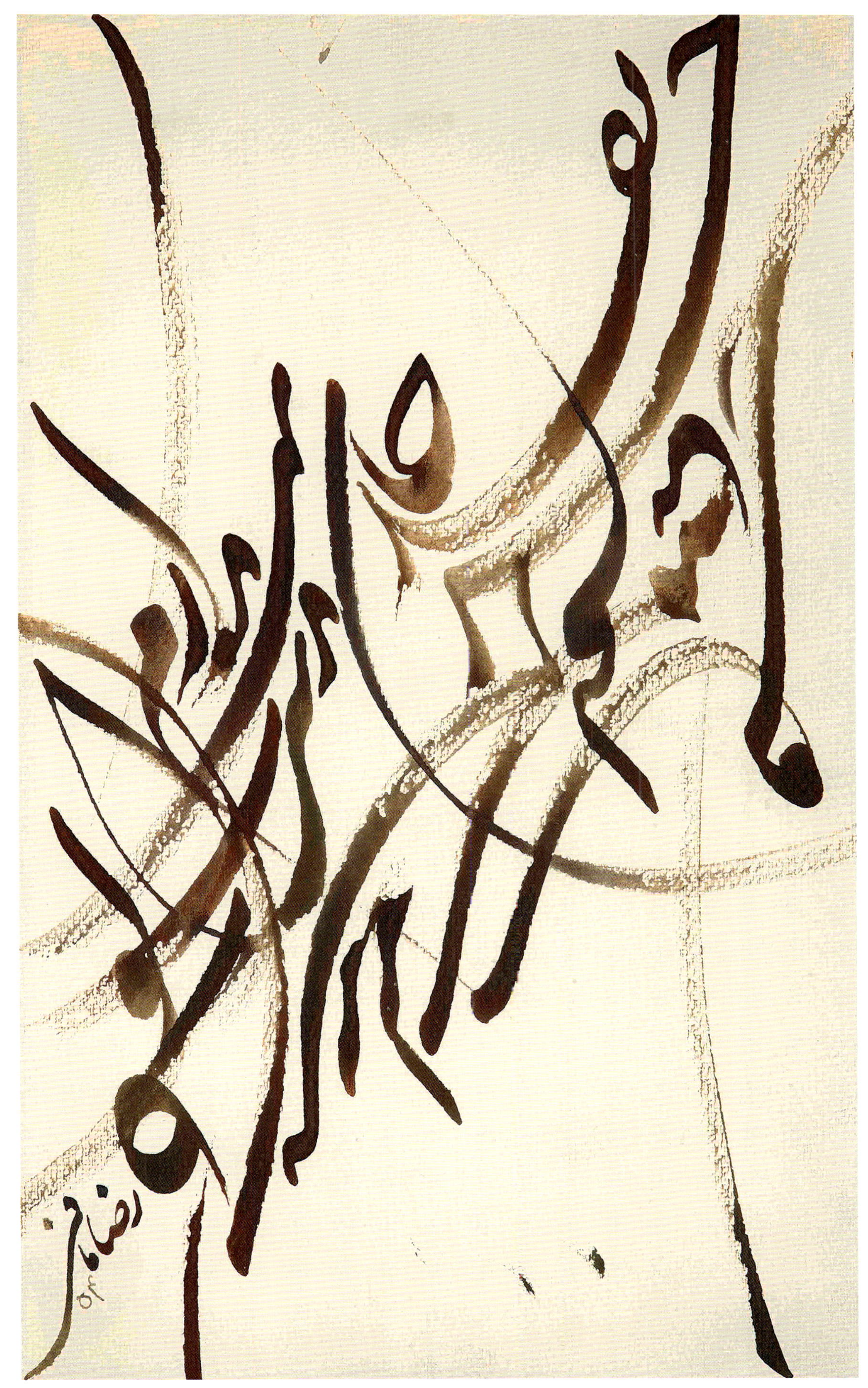

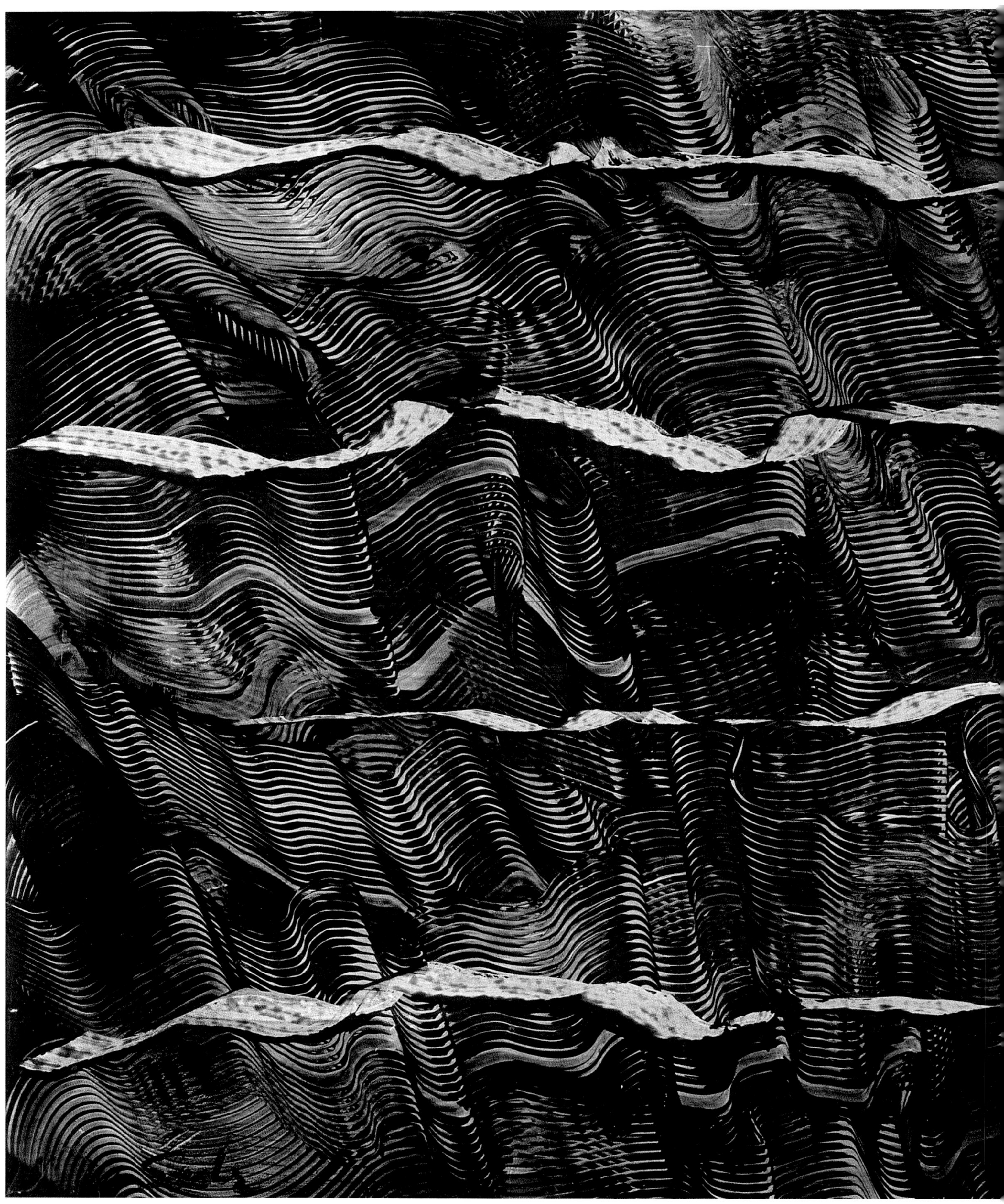

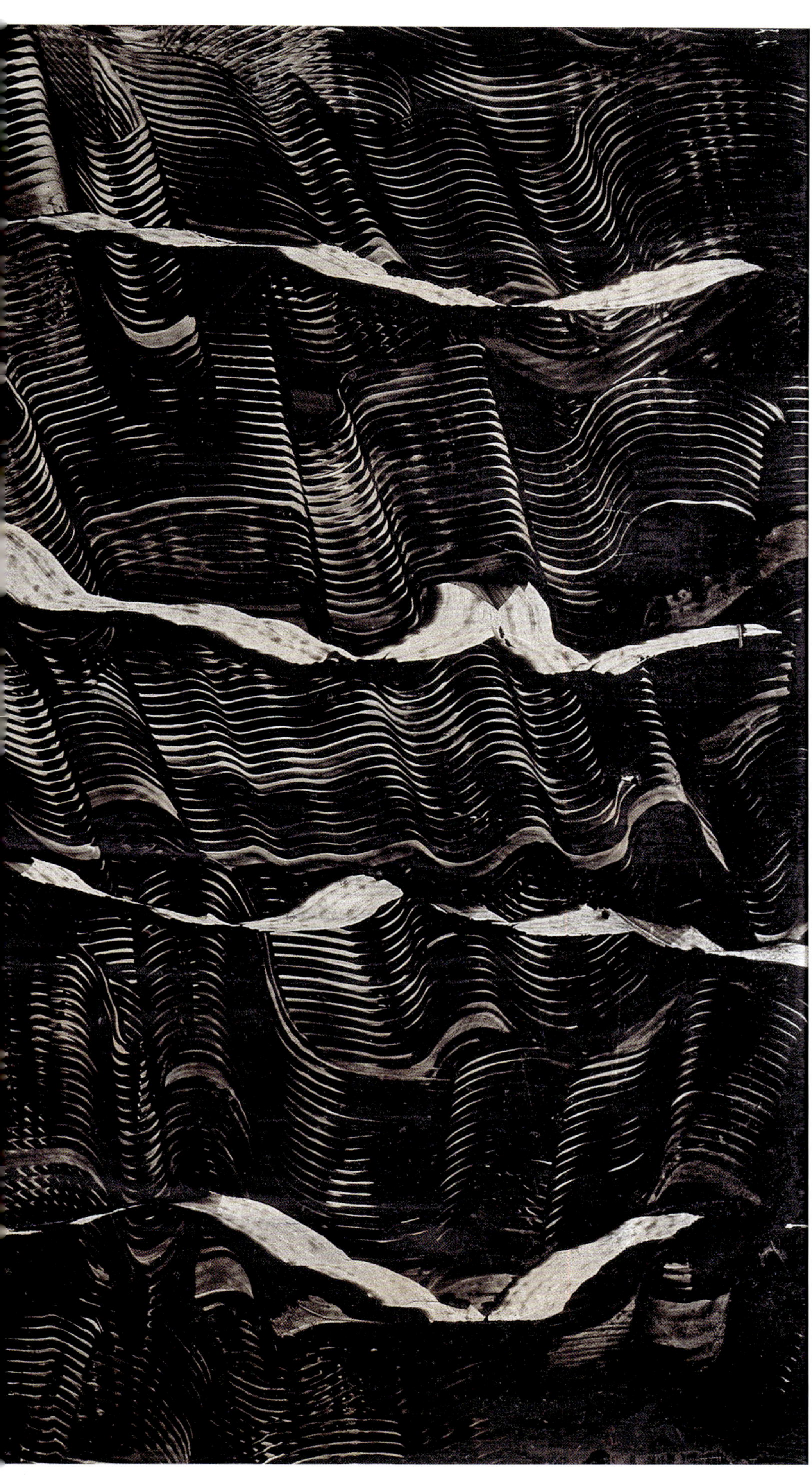

Behjat Sadr
Untitled, 1974
oil on metal

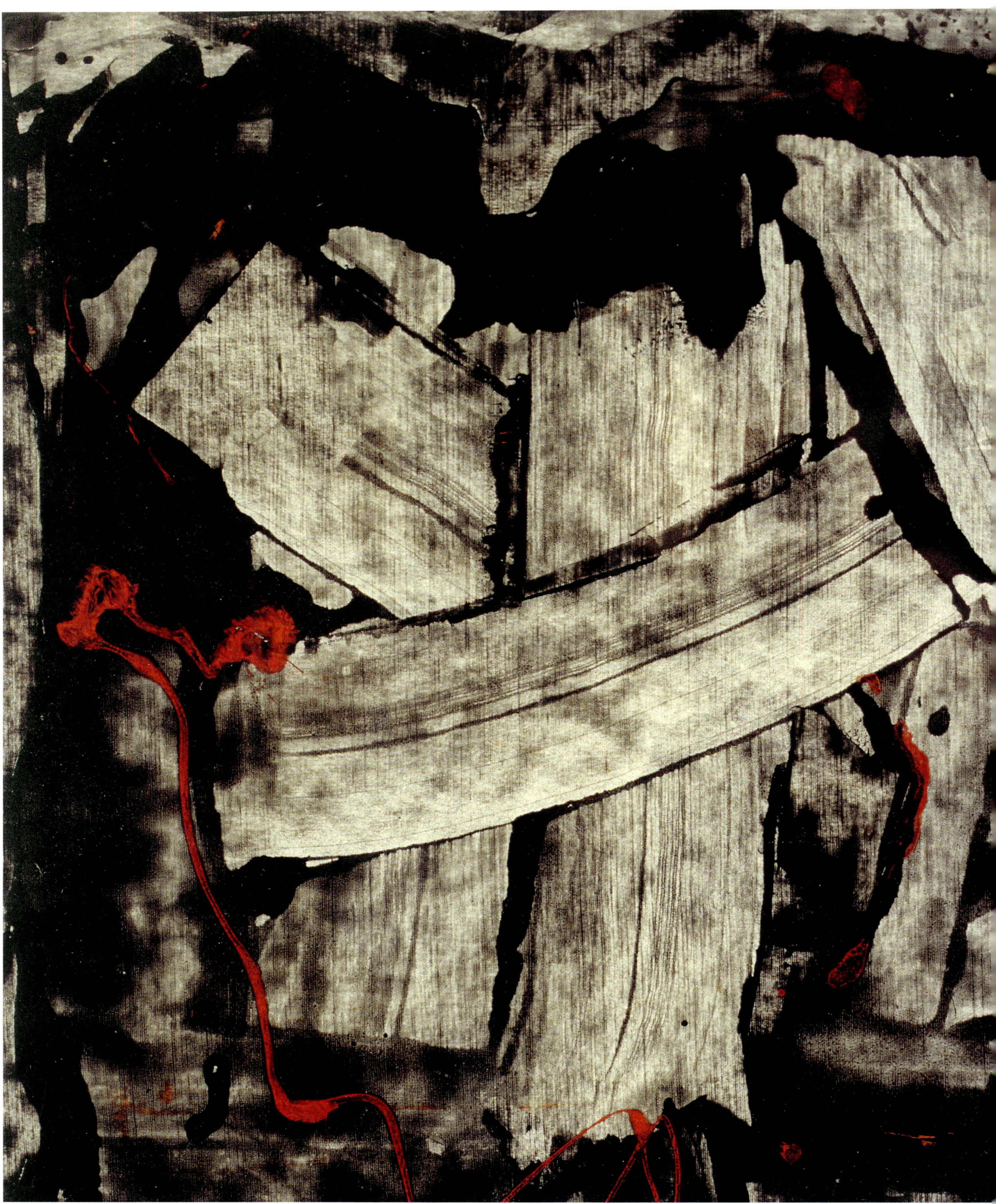

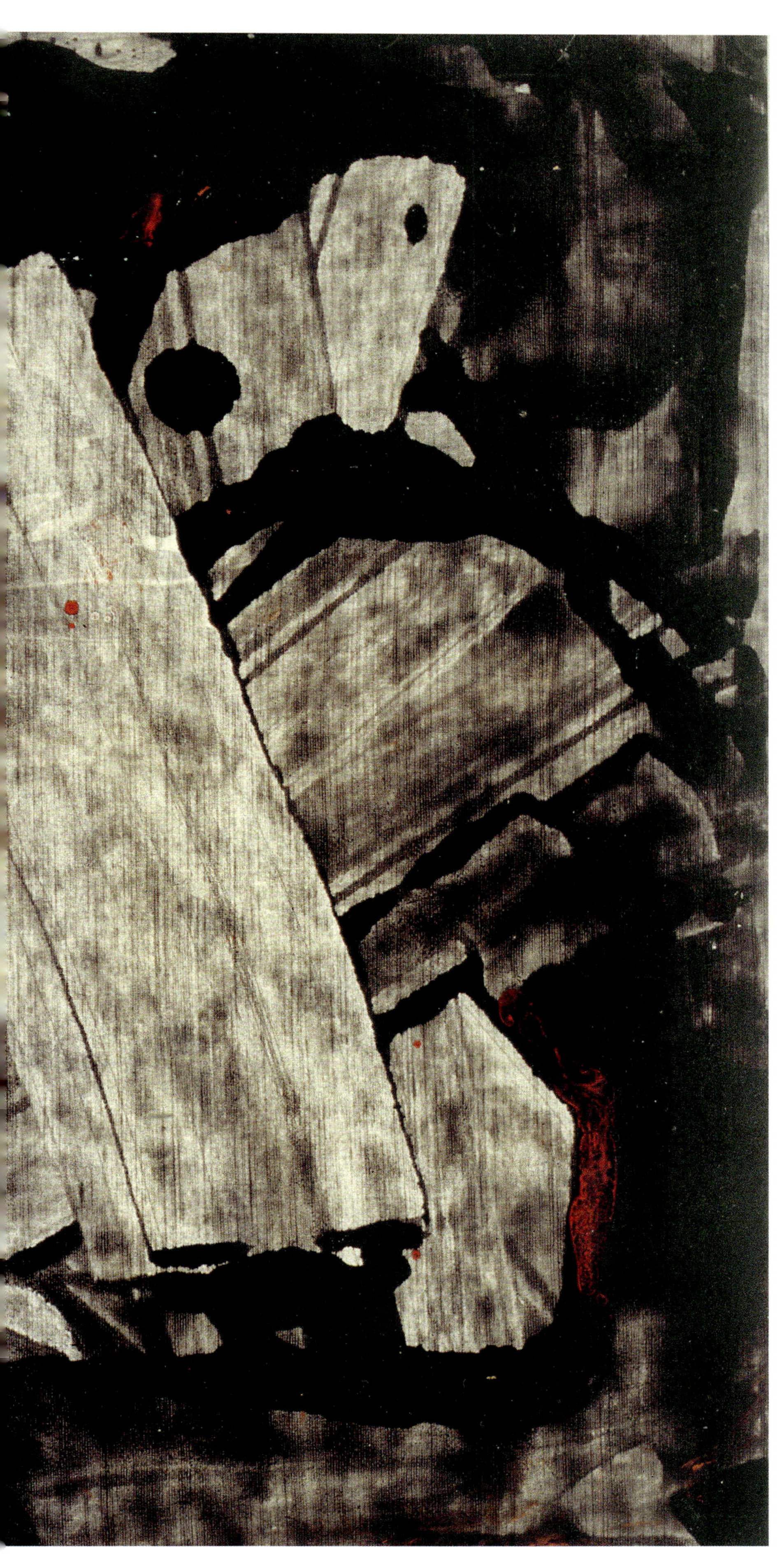

Behjat Sadr
Abstract IV, 1961
oil on paper

Following
Behjat Sadr
Untitled, 1975
oil on canvas

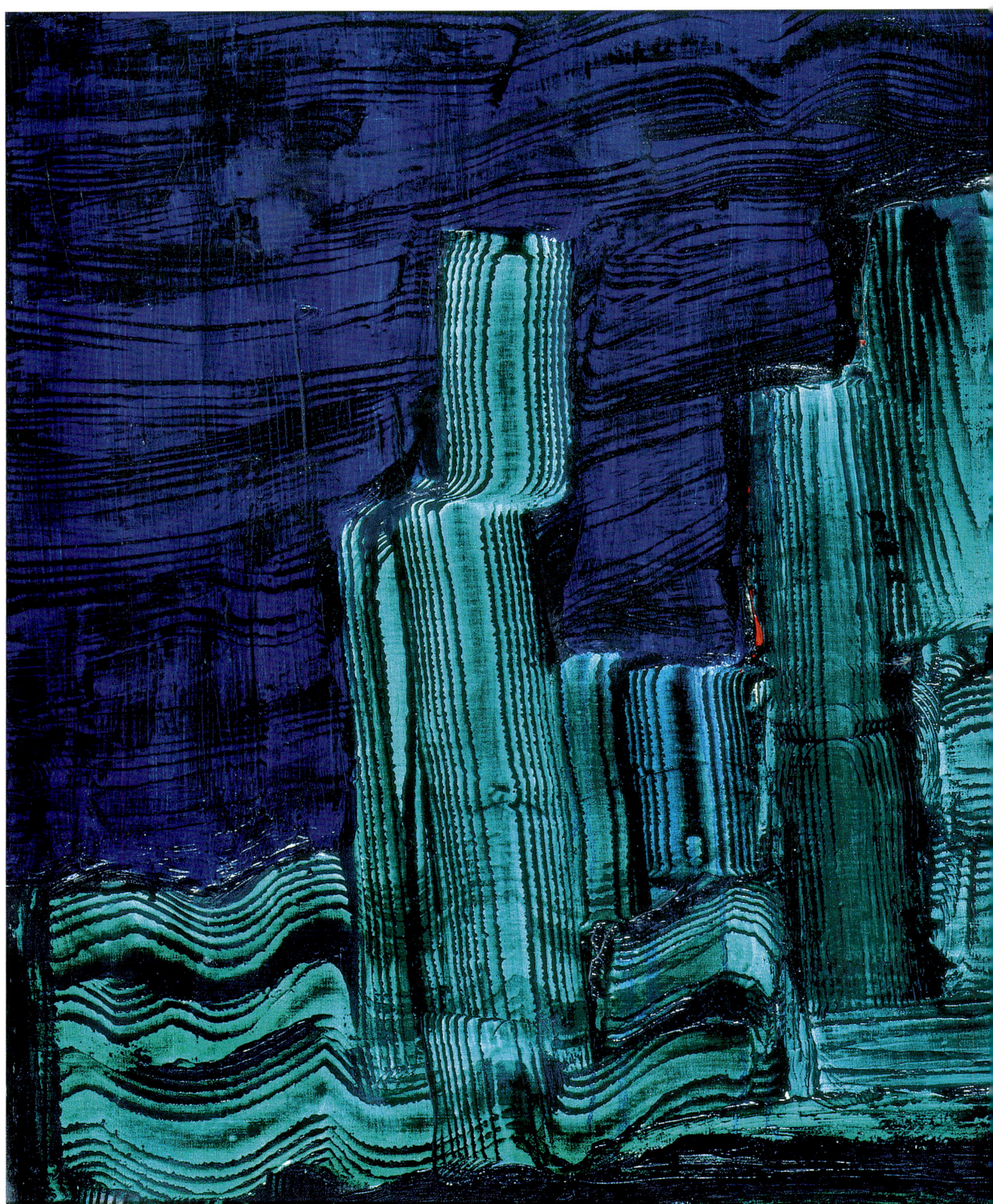

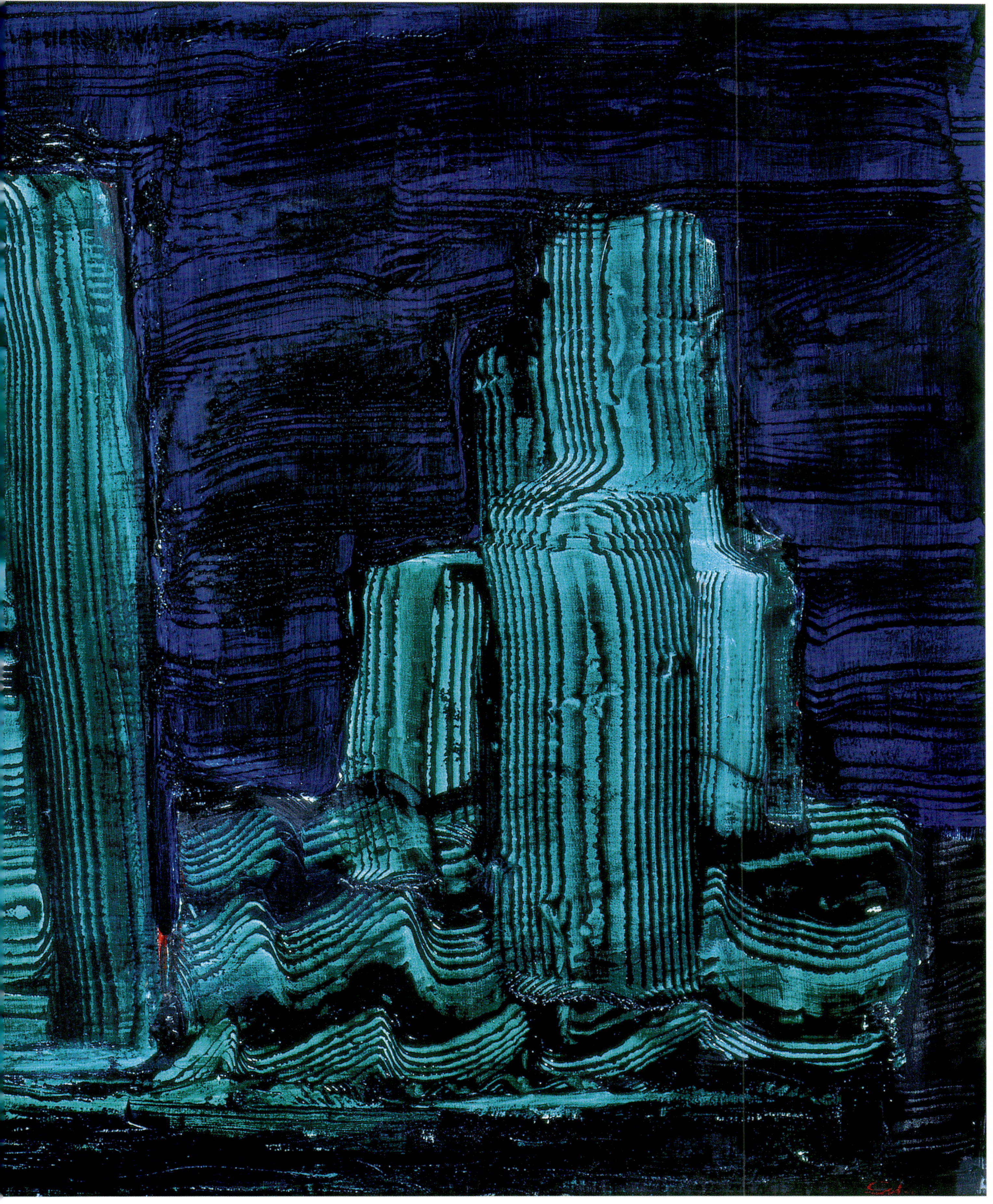

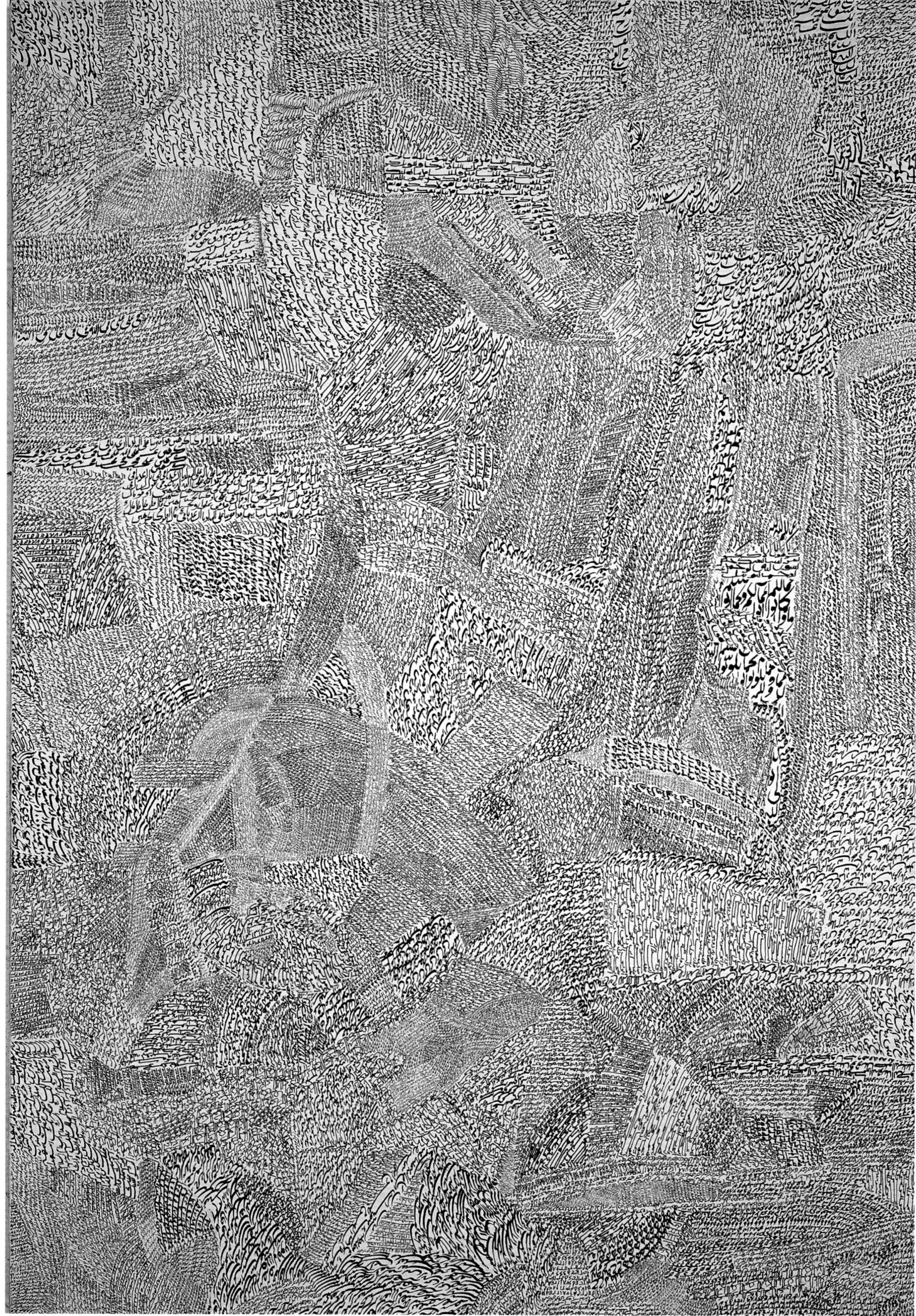

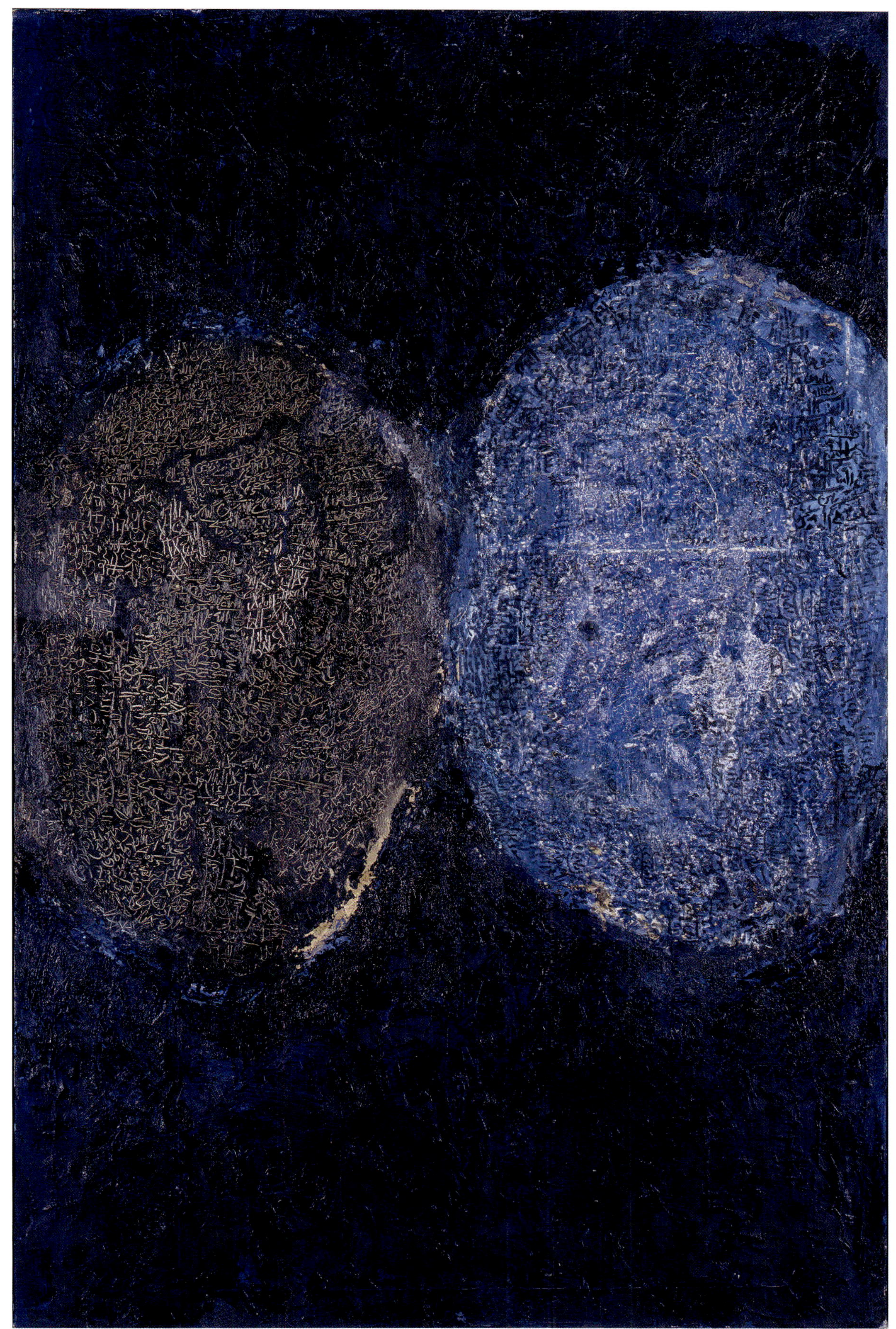

Opposite
Siah Armajani
Calligraphy, 1964
ink on canvas

Right
Siah Armajani
Prayer for the Sun, 1962
oil on canvas

Mohsen Vaziri-Moghaddam
Untitled, 1962
oil and sand on canvas

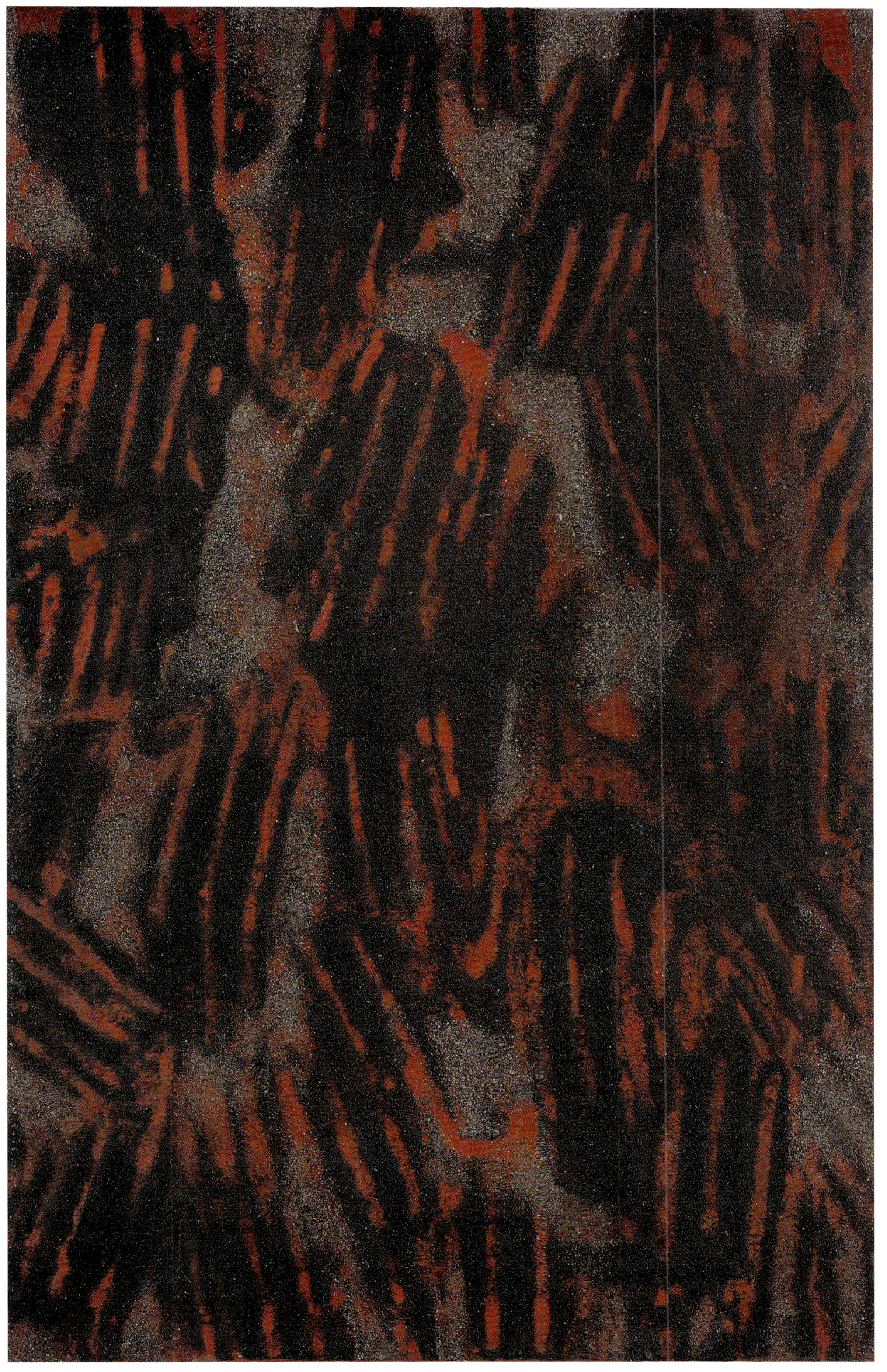

Sirak Melkonian
Untitled, 1972
oil on canvas

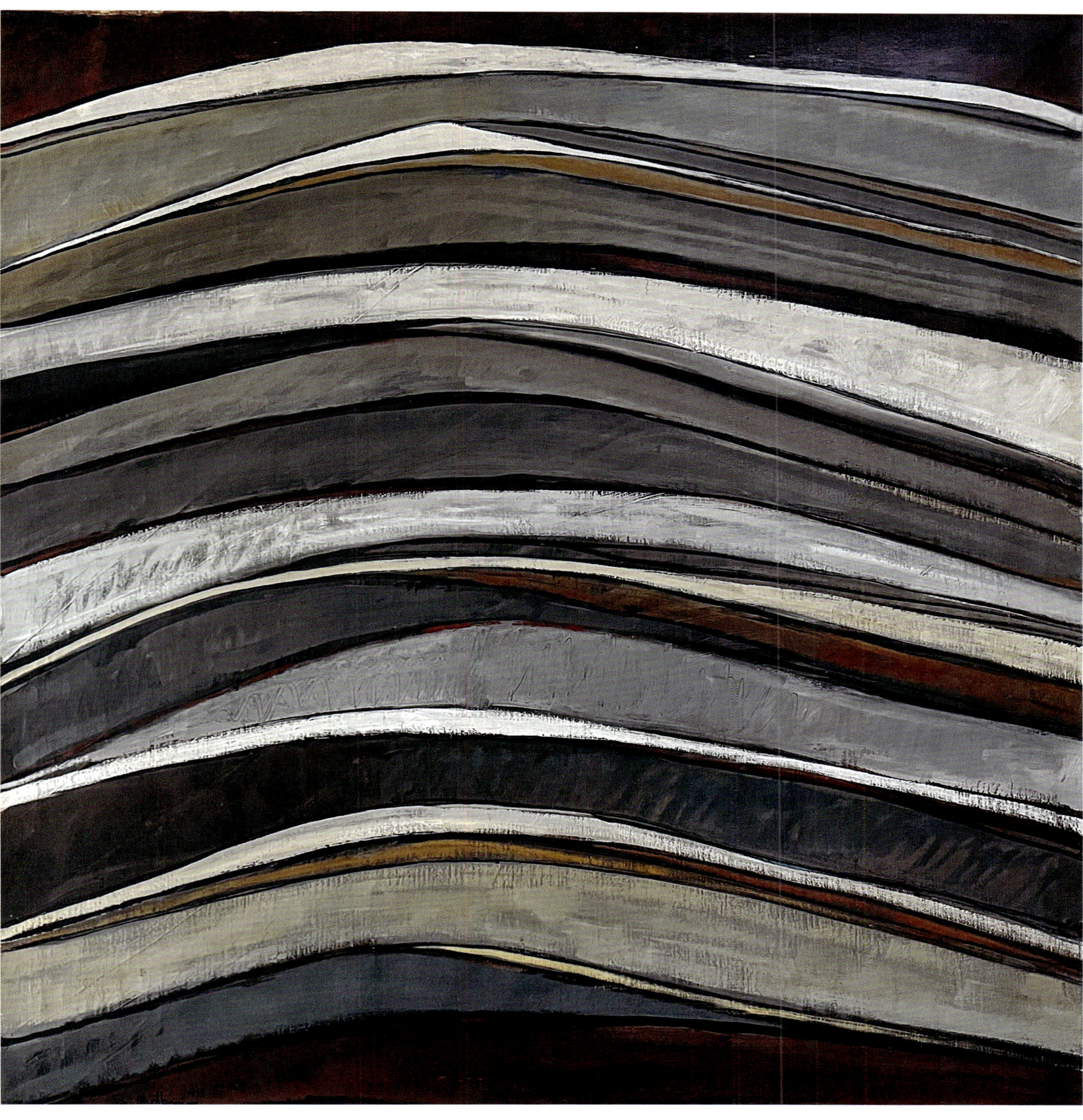

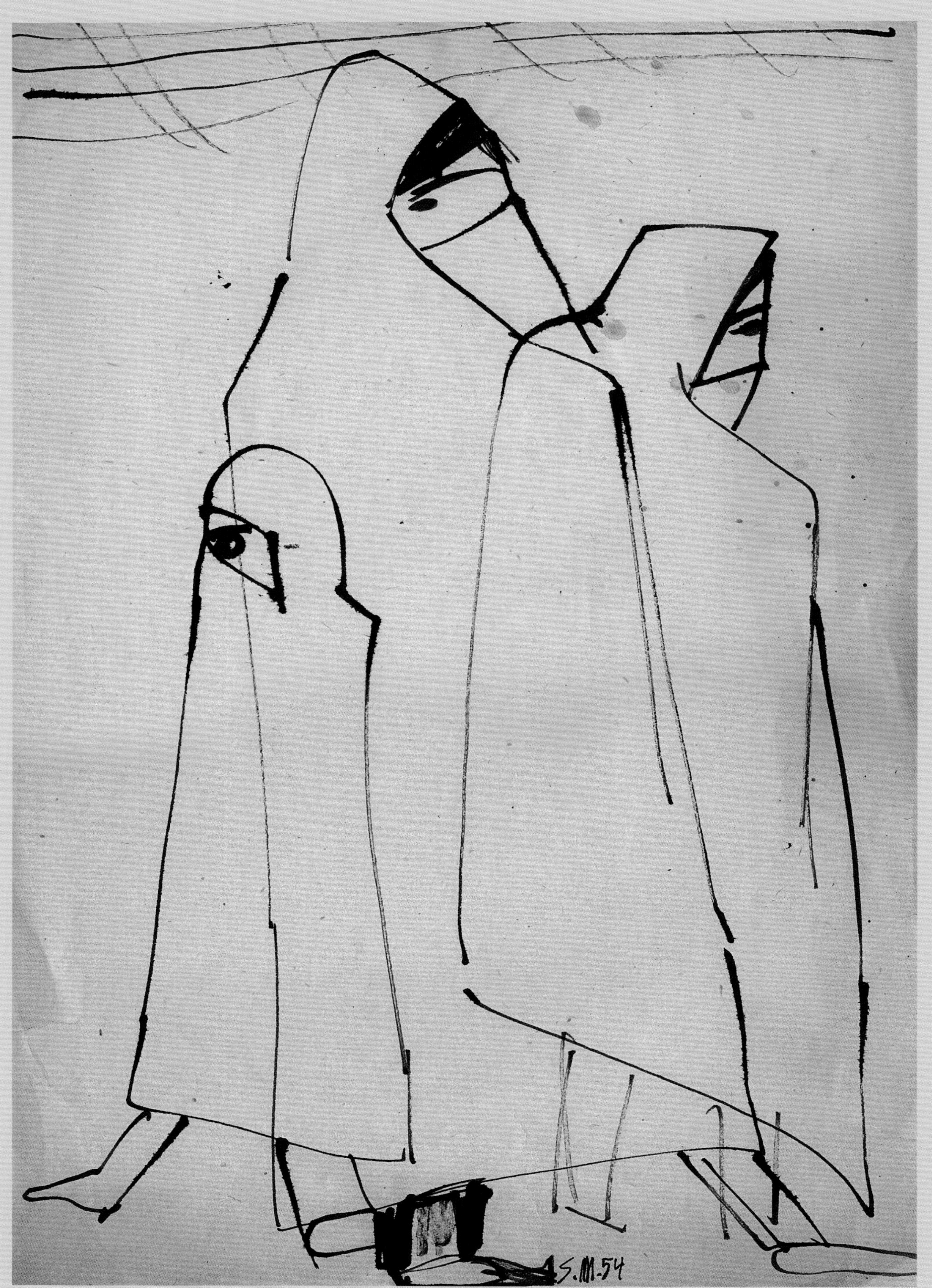
S.M.54

SIRAK MELKONIAN—A CONVERSATION THAT NEVER WAS

Davood Madadpoor

Vancouver – Berlin, 2024

I always carry hope; without it, we aren't alive. My hope isn't just for painting—it's hope upon hope, filling each breath and every moment. I hope my hand remains steady; I've never known the weight of despair, for even in the darkest moments, I find a flicker of light. My wife's illness strikes me like a wound that renews with every heartbeat, yet I refuse to give in to despair. If I have strength, I'll use it to help; in hope, I find life.

He invites us on a journey to the realm of imagination and reality, where these two intertwine with grace. For Sirak Melkonian, imagination is a bridge linking emotions to the realities of life, guiding us to witness unseen and unheard facets of existence. Here, the artist's role is challenging; he must construct a bridge between imagination and reality, both a voice for truth and a window into dreams.

In the aura of memories, Melkonian dances with his past, where childhood and its purity become a beacon of inspiration. Like a stream, memories flow into the canvas he brings to life, whispering echoes of the past with each piece; is this how the scent and innocence of childhood reflect in every line and colour of his work? Melkonian invites us into this realm of memories, perhaps offering us a glimpse of inspiration, too.

Imagine a sparrow chick cracking through its shell, breaking into life—a process repeating for ages untold. This chick embodies a timeless ritual, an ancient instinct that speaks of a lineage beyond time. When I create, I feel connected to that same ancient human impulse, an echo of lives that have come before. It's not calculated; it's beyond knowledge, beyond thought. We do things instinctively, often unaware, yet with a need to not harm. Artists like Tchaikovsky, Beethoven and Bach dive into this mystery, revealing pieces of their soul. Through their work, they leave a glimpse of their world while billions vanish unnoticed. The artist's role is to uncover these inner landscapes; so we know of Mozart, though countless others have faded. For years, I supported myself with graphic work and logo making, yet by evening, I was drawn back to my paintings. My work was never for money; art was my private sanctuary, untouched by commerce.

His art is a complex dance of interwoven cultures: Safavid heritage, Iranian and Armenian artistry and delicate threads from Western influence. How has this artist intertwined these strands to create a unique identity? Each stroke and line he crafts resonates with the voices of cultures interlaced from the depths of history. Melkonian seeks his distinct voice within these differences, striving toward unity.

I am deeply drawn to fossils, things aged beyond measure, steeped in timelessness. I yearn for my work to hold that same ancient essence. Imagine an authentic rug woven not for sale but for life, carrying the hands and heartbeat of its maker.

Sirak Melkonian
Untitled, 1954
ink on paper

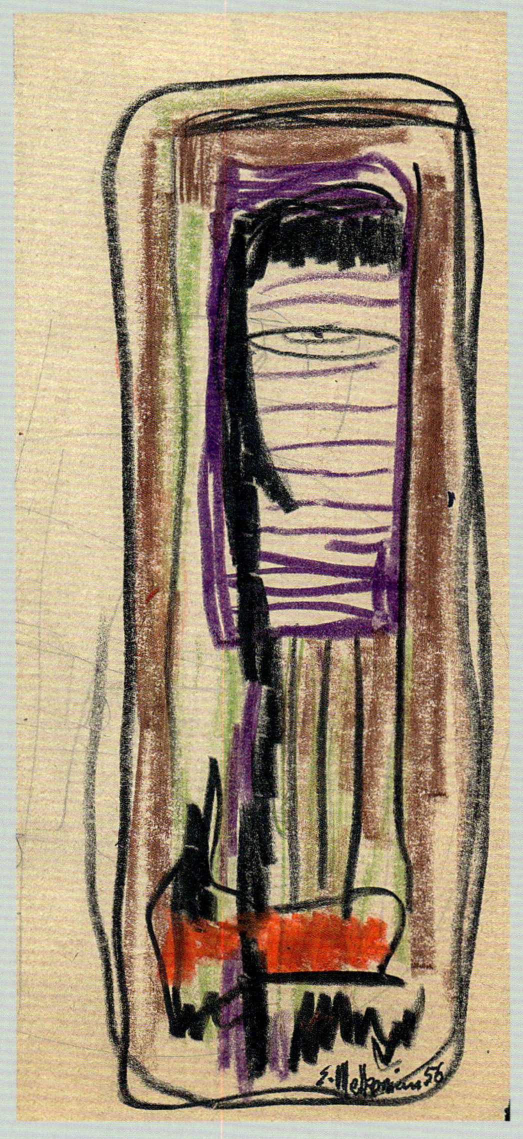

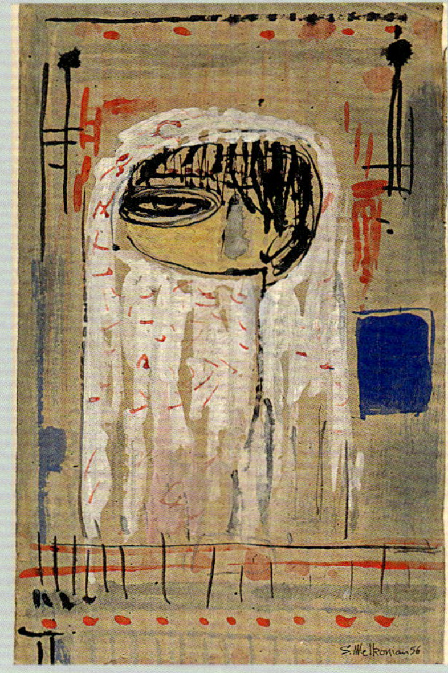

I revere such work, art born without pretense, where colours emerge naturally through movement and passion, creating something so pure that I bow to its authenticity. To me, these village rugs are the truest art.

He is mesmerized by the ancient remnants of time that echo across millennia. His art, too, seeks this timeless resonance. Like the cherished village rugs, woven not for sale but for life, his colours emerge organically, unforced, shaped by movement and love. For Melkonian, these works are sacred, unpretentious and born of pure intention. They are the most authentic form of art—a simple yet profound beauty woven into the fabric of everyday life.

For him, abstraction is the art of distillation, a removal of the ordinary to reveal the essence. His works are not entirely abstract—within them, one can still sense the echoes of life, fragments that speak of the world as it is and as it dreams to be. In these canvases, there is no room for melancholy, only distilled expressions of life; unlike the fleeting fashion trends that many follow, proper abstraction

Above, left
Sirak Melkonian
Untitled, 1956
pastel on cardboard

Above, right
Sirak Melkonian
Untitled, 1956
gouache on
posterboard

Opposite
Sirak Melkonian
Untitled, 1954
ink on tracing paper

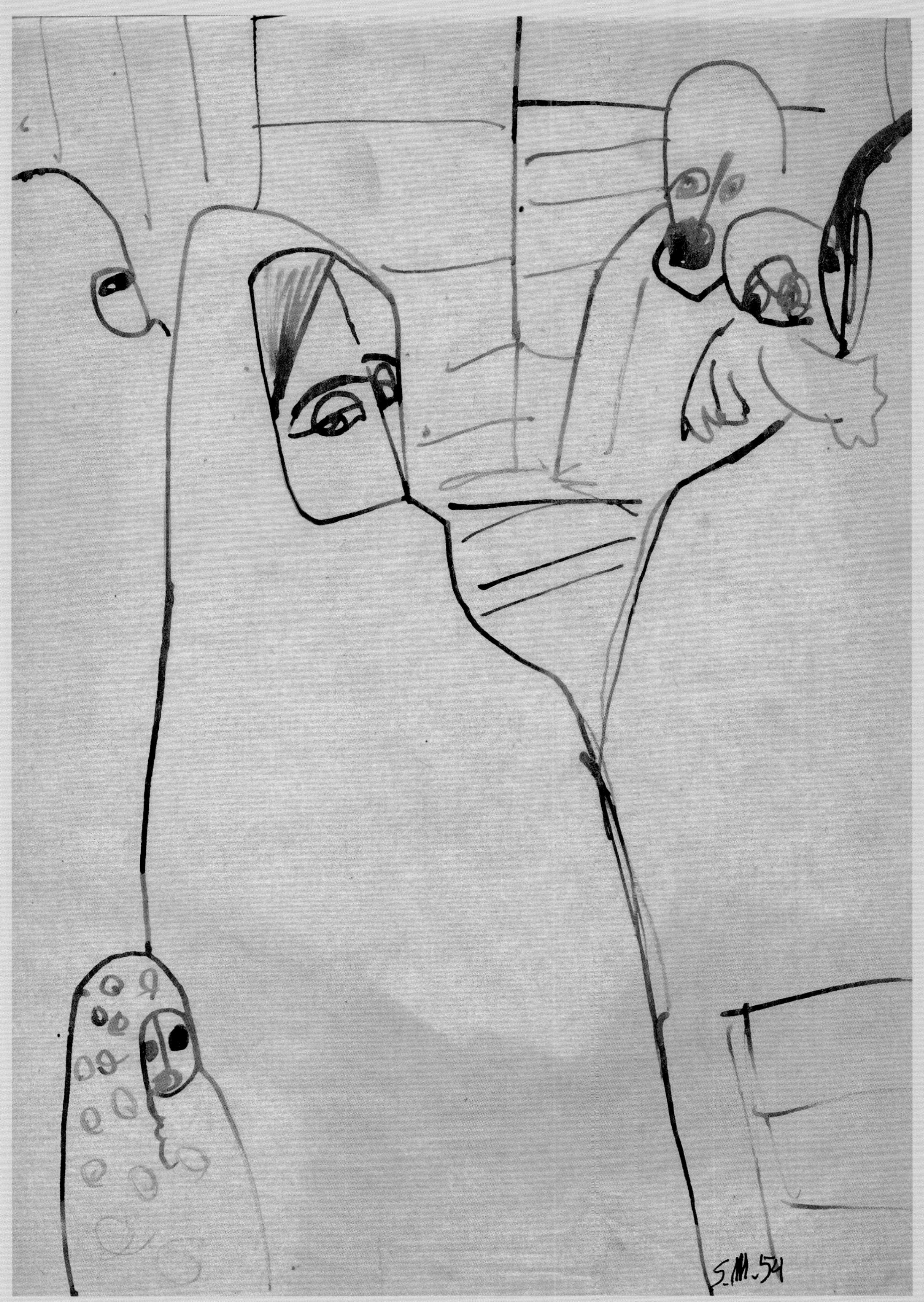
S.M. 54

demands depth, a surrender to its difficulty, like an unspoken challenge. He sees in Pablo Picasso's spaces a silent mastery—the abstraction not of the subject but of the silence left behind, empty spaces charged with the unspoken. Here lies true abstraction: a form untouched, a meaning distilled.

My work isn't purely abstract, you can still sense and see fragments of life. My paintings are not meant to evoke melancholy but rather to distill life into forms that breathe. Abstraction is no easy path; it's as relentless as it is revealing, not a playground but a demanding art. Picasso wasn't abstract, but he left spaces where the subject faded, opening up room for interpretation. In those moments, he brushed up against abstraction, leaving parts untouched, off-topic—yet filled with meaning.

I have painted countless faces, thousands, etched from moment to moment. Each face I call "life's scratches"—traces of joy, sorrow and endurance imprinted by time. Life leaves its trace upon every visage, just as lines cross our palms. Each face tells its tale, a quiet pain and stolen joy.

And that everyday life—the endless and ceaseless flow through the streets and marketplaces—is it simply routine? Not for him; he observes, he contemplates, and from these simple movements, he creates timeless moments. What seems insignificant to a passing gaze becomes a wellspring of inspiration for Melkonian. He captures this daily flow with abstract, nuanced expression; it is as if his paintings are the soft whispers of life's truths, the small joys and perhaps its quiet sorrows.

Sometimes, I sit, gathering my energy and contemplating colours and textures until I am ready to begin, my mind like a locomotive. I use the simplest materials—often paper napkins—creating small sketches wherever I go.

Melkonian is an artist who separates politics from his art. But can a gap exist between the everyday and art? He believes art can transcend politics, becoming a space for exploration and reflection. For him, art springs from the heart of nature, not from the hand of politics; it is art crafted to reveal a pure, human truth. Even for this artist, however, the line between life and art can sometimes be as delicate as a thread.

He also teaches us that art is not a mere imitation of nature; the artist must add something to it, embedding a part of themselves into the work. Thus, art is a blend of humanity and the world. Melkonian understands the ever-present risk of art being used as a tool for others. But with his artistic prowess, he draws clear boundaries, restoring art to its independence. To him, art is neither propaganda nor a mere tool; it is a personal experience.

He lives in the pulse of hope, breathing it like air. Without hope, he believes, life would lose its very essence. His hope is not bound to his brushstrokes alone but radiates through every corner of his being. It's a mantra, a lifeline: hope upon hope upon hope. Even as life brings hardship, he holds steady, unfaltering.

He lives in the moment, unburdened by thoughts of permanence or legacy. To him, life is movement—a continuous walk where each step matters, though

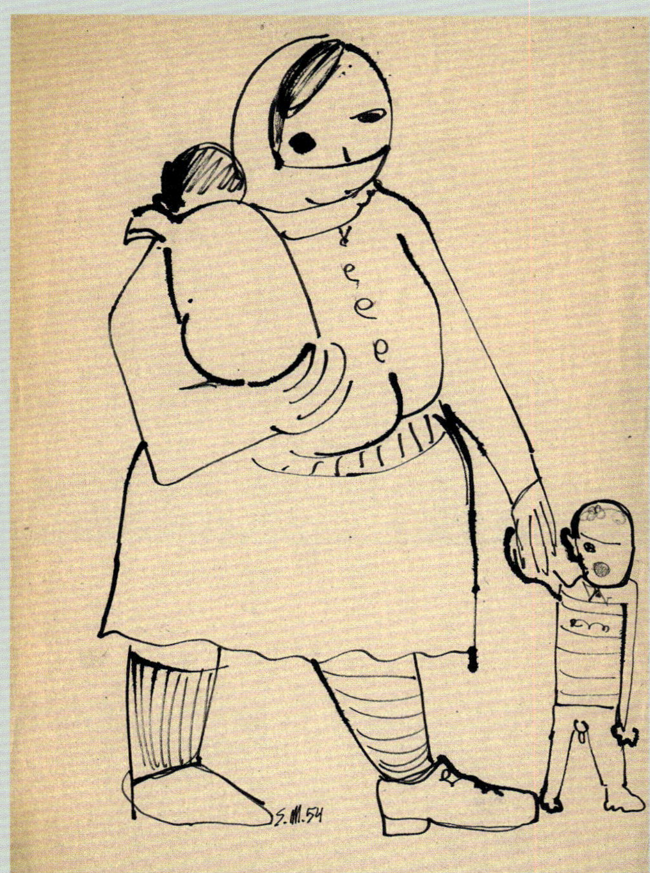

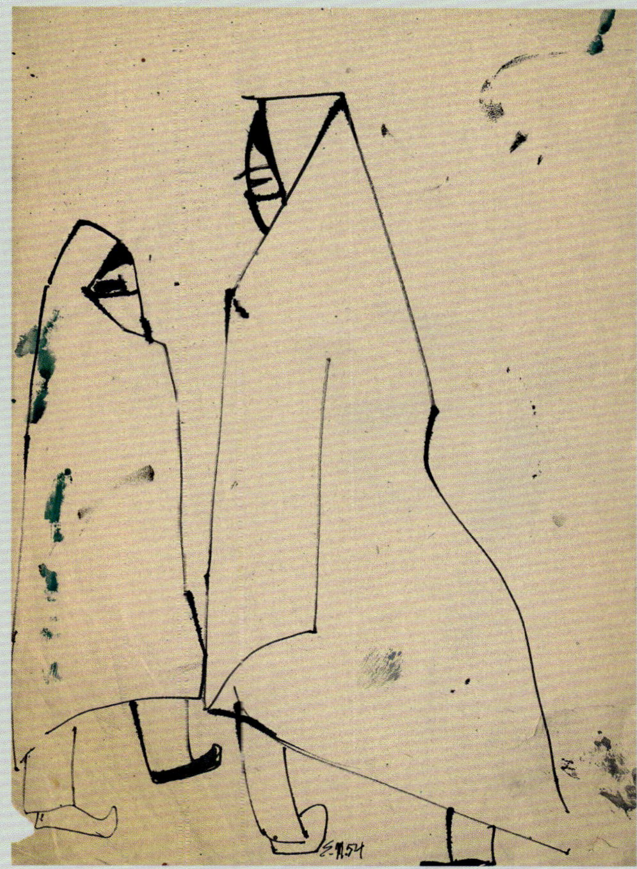

the destination remains unknown. He feels permanence is an illusion, irrelevant to the truth of existence. Just as a bird soars without concern for longevity, he, too, finds freedom in the present, unbound by time's weight. In his view, art is not for understanding but for feeling; it is an experience, an encounter. He sees himself not as the creator but as a part of the work, an energy embedded within the canvas. And as long as he lives, he will strive toward a destination he knows he will never reach.

There is art in everything—eating, walking, dressing. For me, as a visual artist, music stands supreme. It is intangible yet powerful, distilled into vibrations.

While Melkonian's life's work lies in visual art, he holds music in the highest esteem. Music, intangible and pure, resonates deeply, shaping his own art in subtle ways. In recent works, one can feel the influence of music—a silent rhythm that moves through his paintings, connecting them to something beyond the visible.

I listen to Beethoven's Symphony No. 7: IV. Allegro con brio*—each time alone, with the volume just right—and I feel how deeply he lived. How did he endure such depth, where joy mingles with pain? Beethoven absorbed his world, transforming it into a universal language that resonates even now. This, to me, is art—its vision expands, reaching out to infinity.*

Left
Sirak Melkonian
Untitled, 1954
ink on paper

Right
Sirak Melkonian
Untitled, 1954
ink on paper

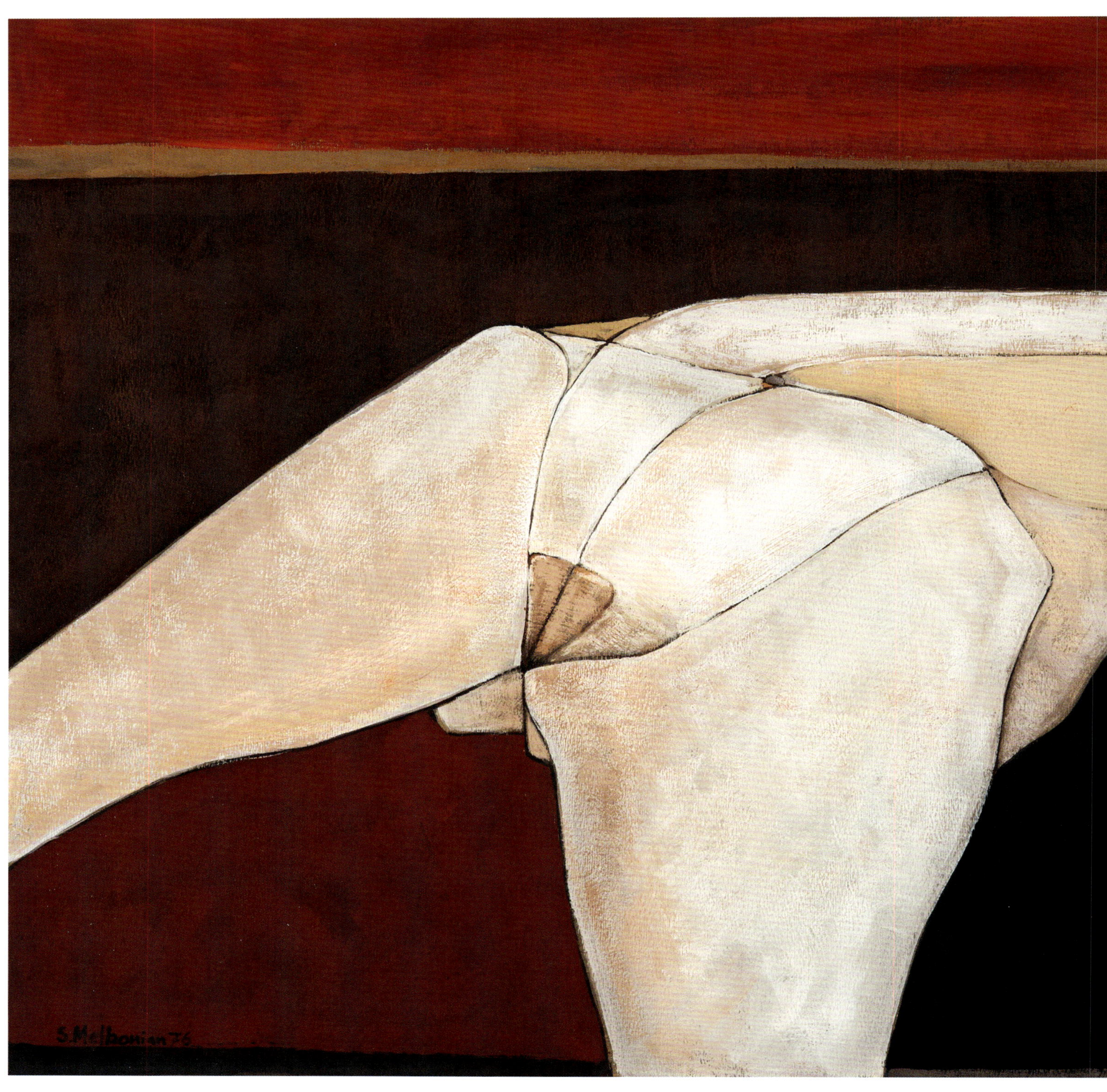
S.Melkonian 76

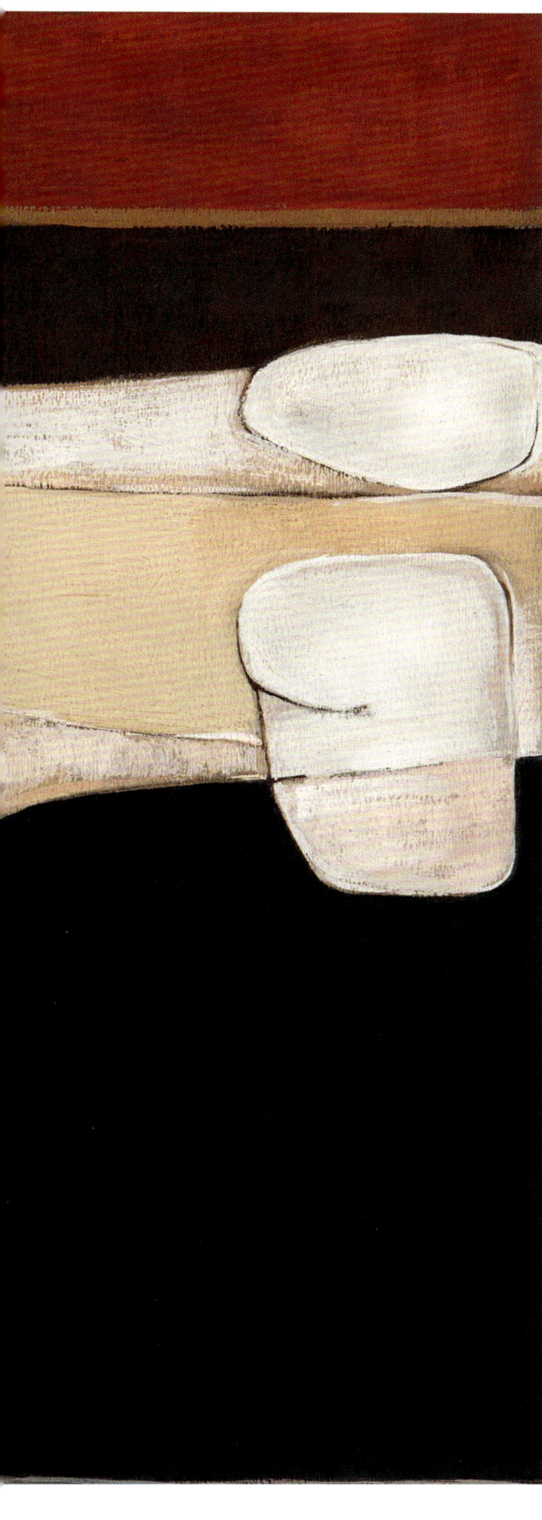

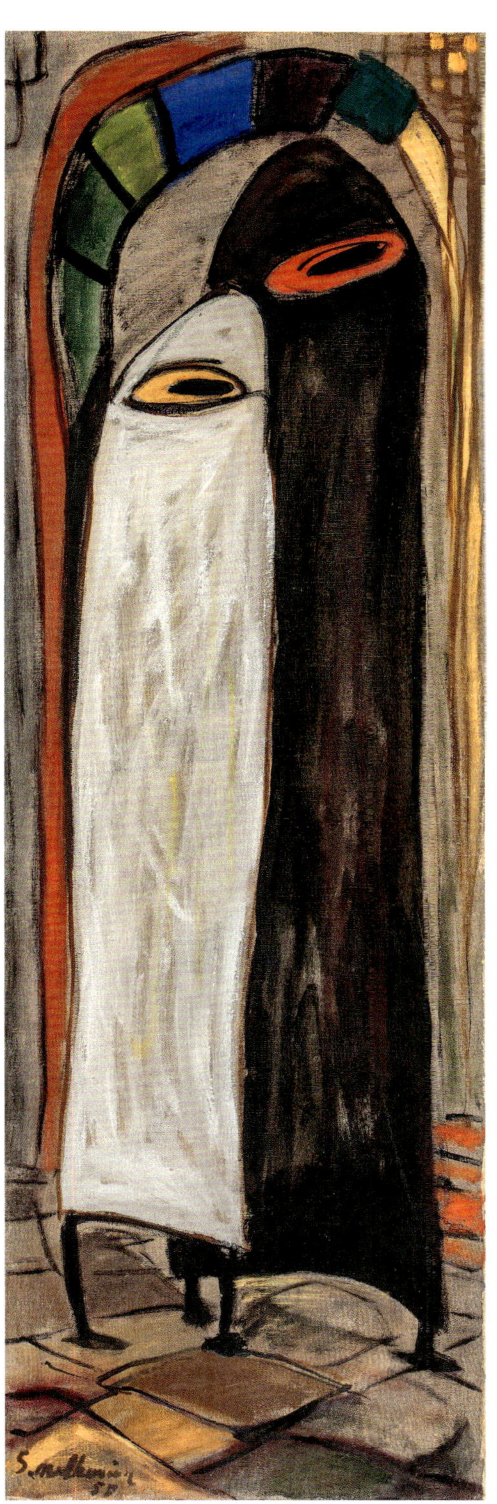

Left
Sirak Melkonian
Untitled, 1976
gouache on paper

Right
Sirak Melkonian
Veiled Women, 1958
oil on canvas

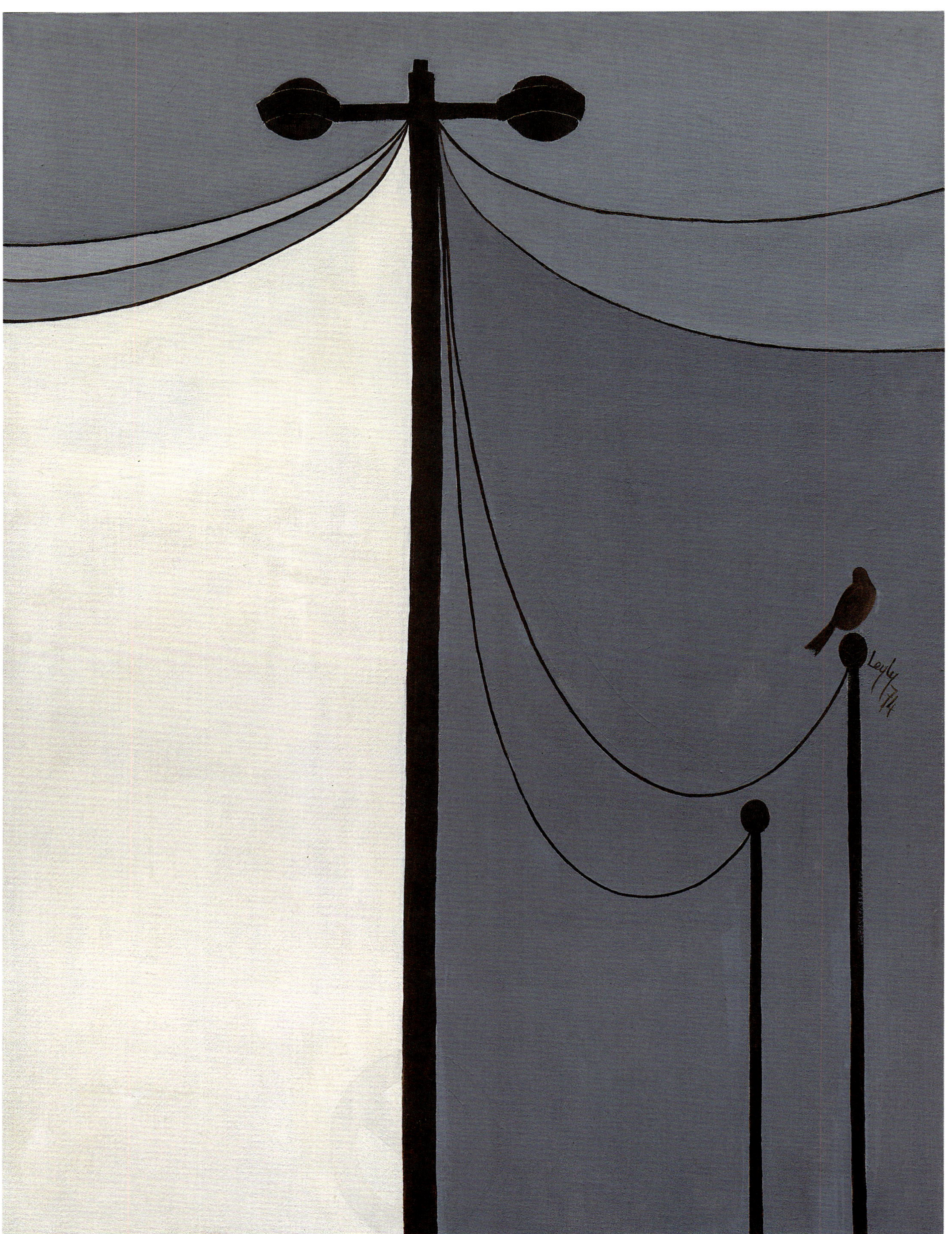

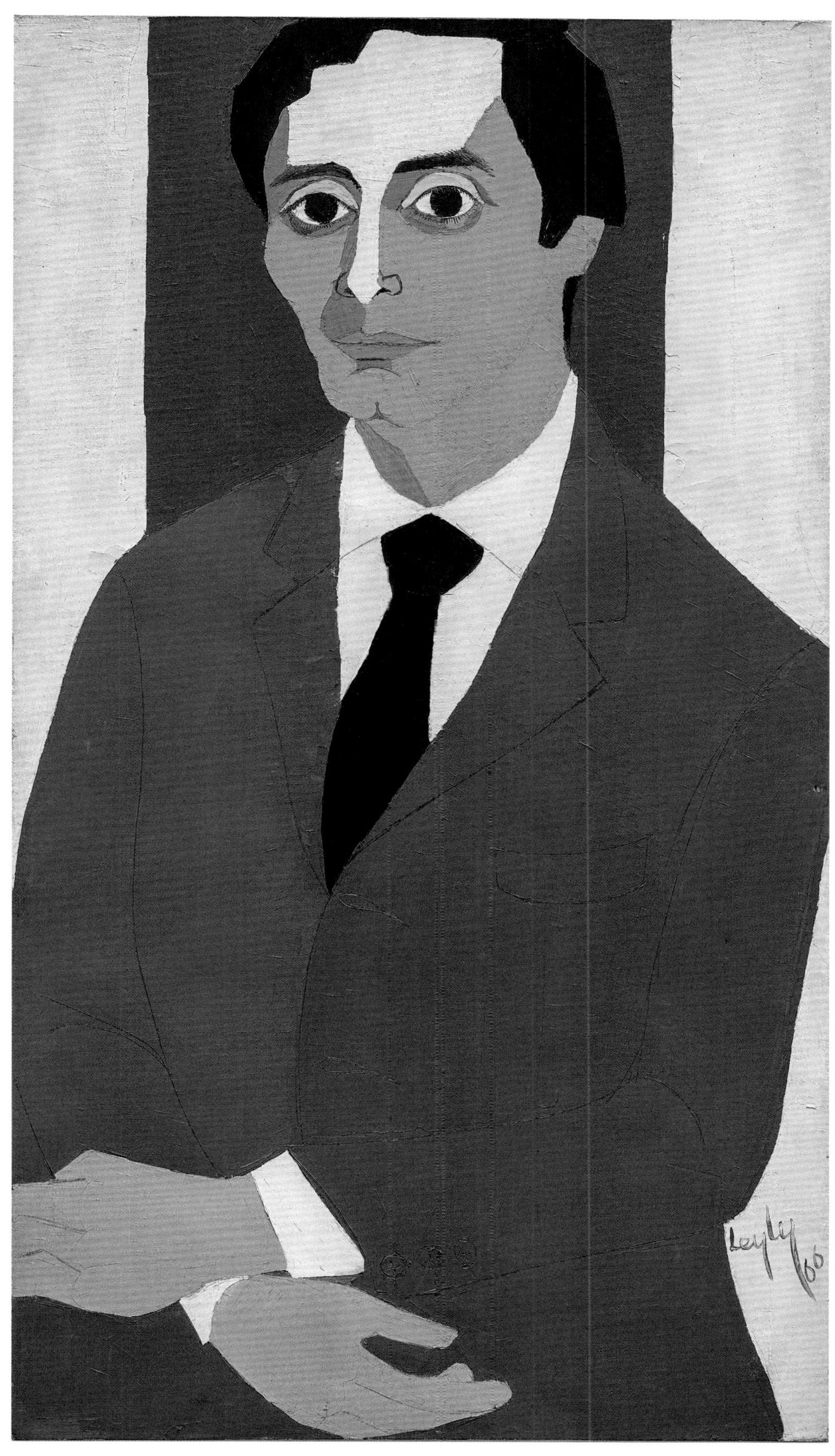

Opposite
Leyly Matine-Daftary
Untitled, 1974
oil on canvas

Right
Leyly Matine-Daftary
Majid, 1966
oil on canvas

Bahman Mohassess
a la mémoire du Forough Farrokhzad, 1966
mixed media on board

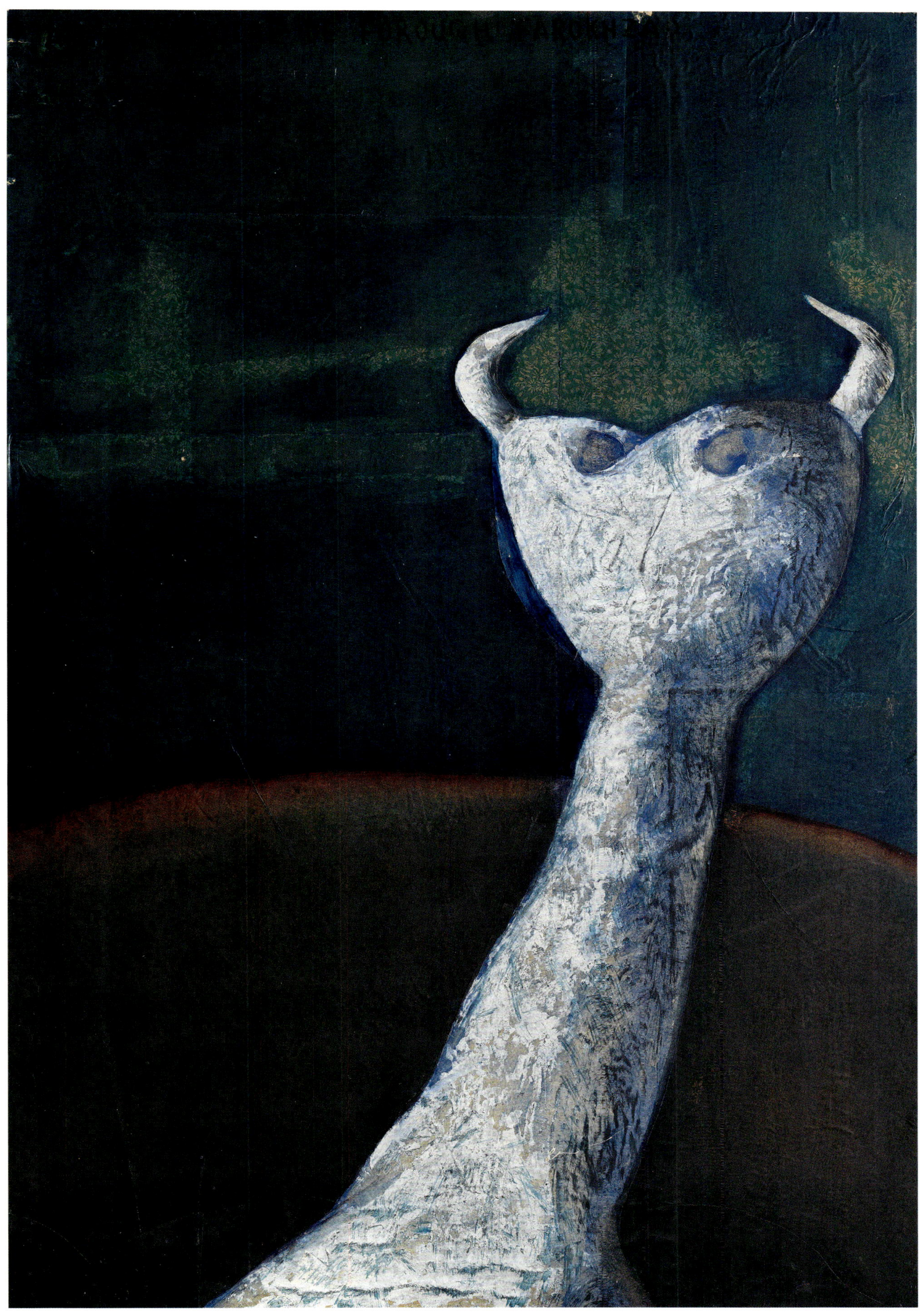

Bahman Mohassess
Bull, c. 1960s
bronze

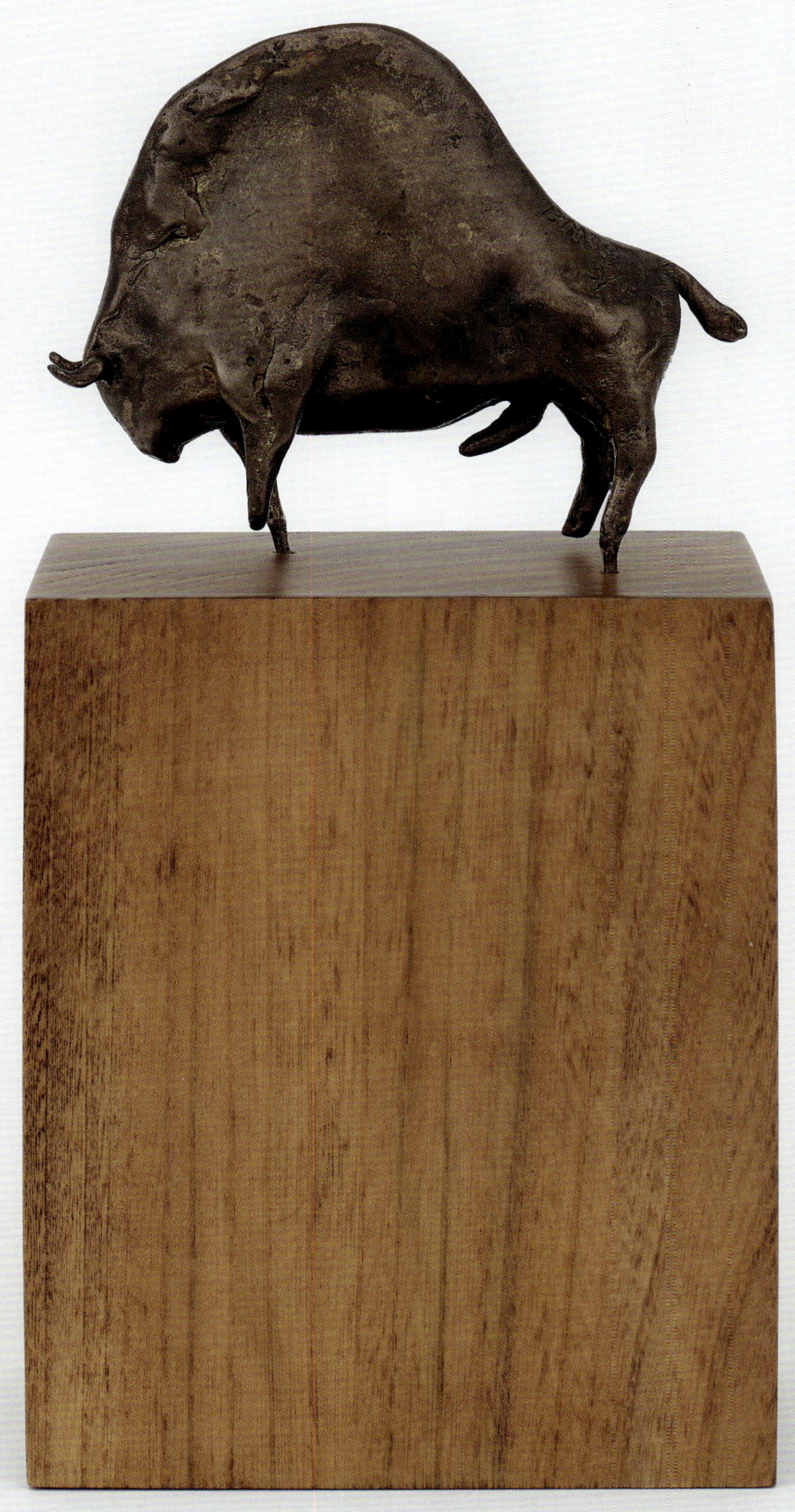

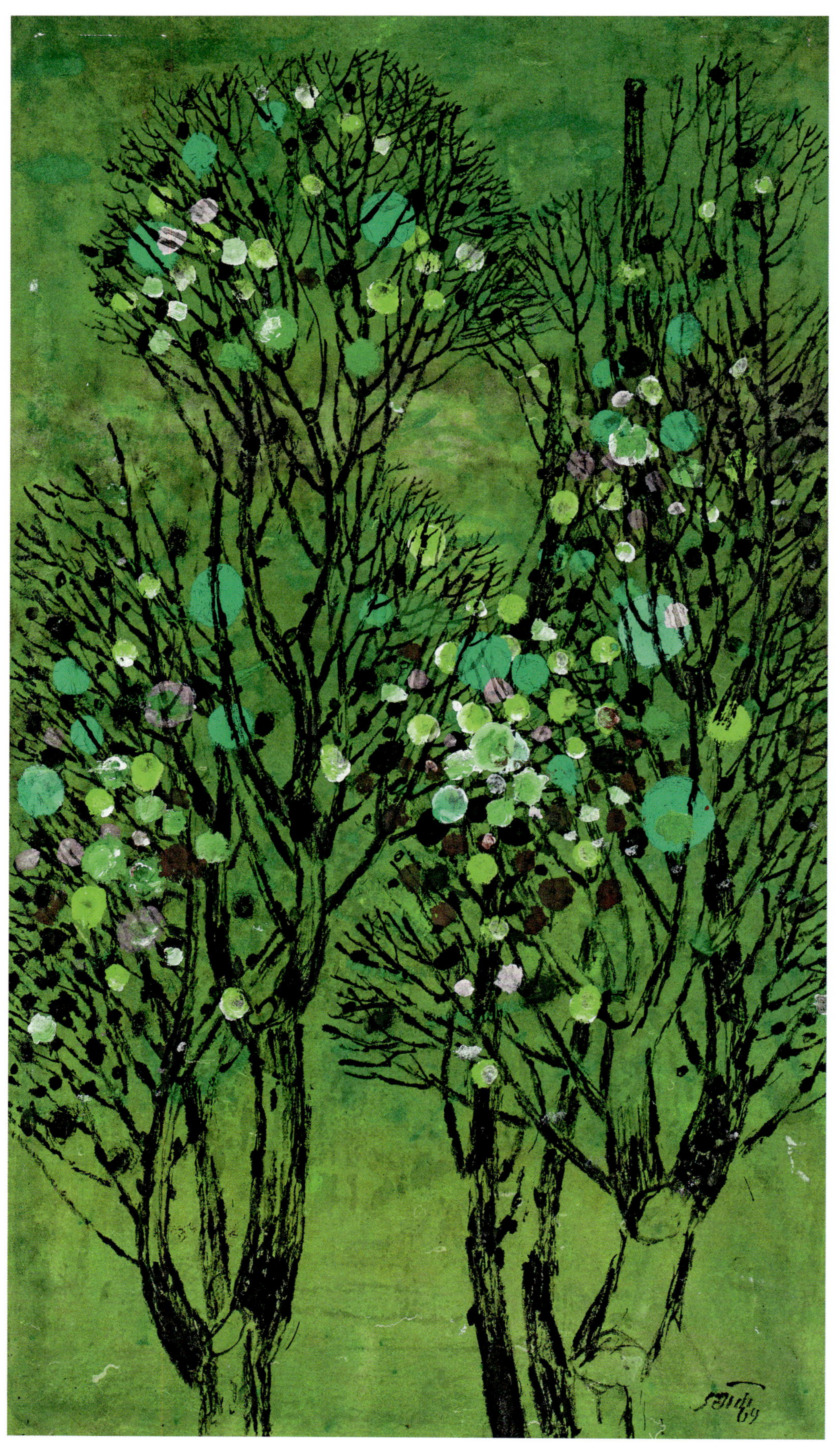

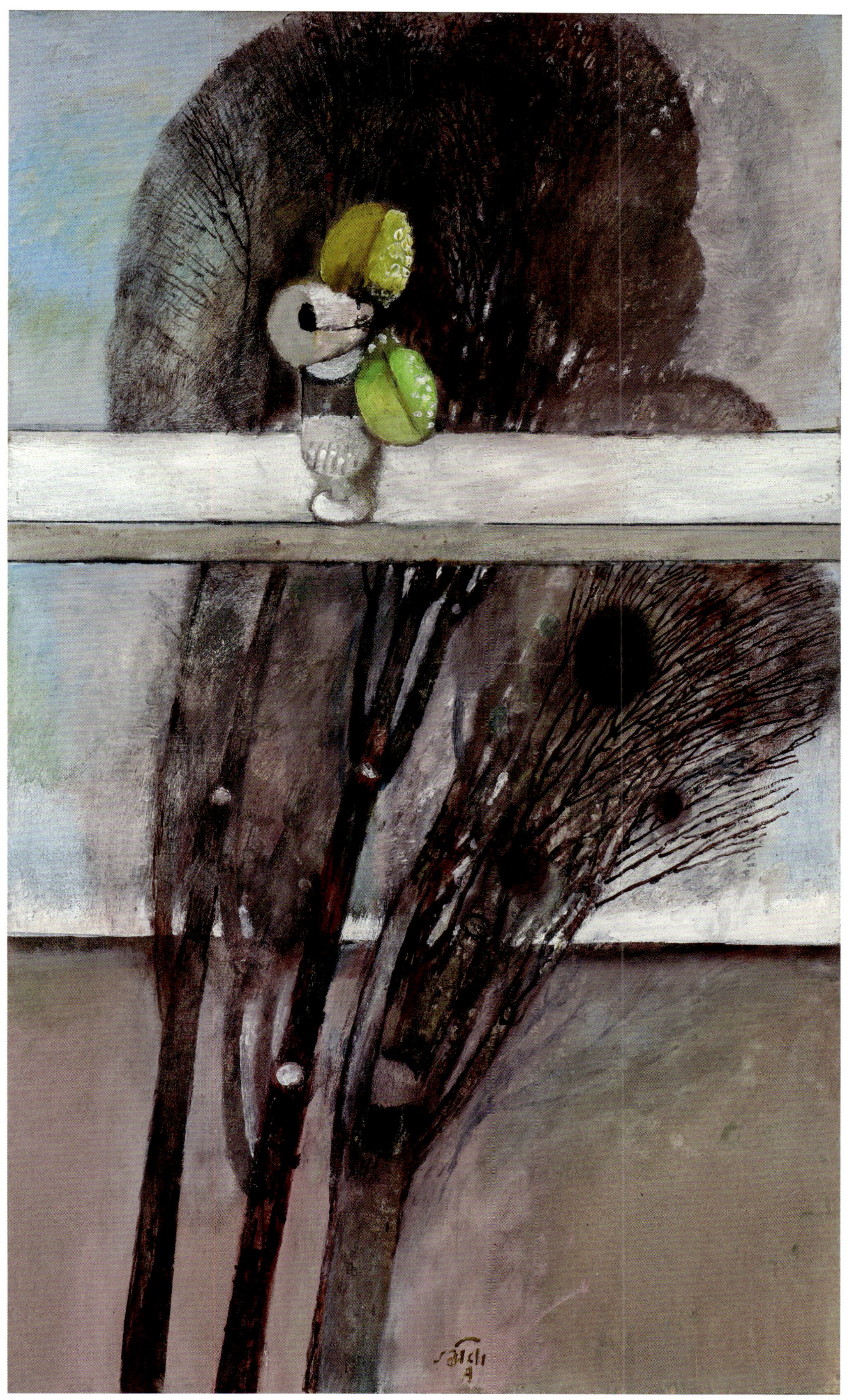

Opposite
Abolghassem Saidi
Untitled, 1969
oil on board

Right
Abolghassem Saidi
Untitled, c. 1970s
oil on canvas

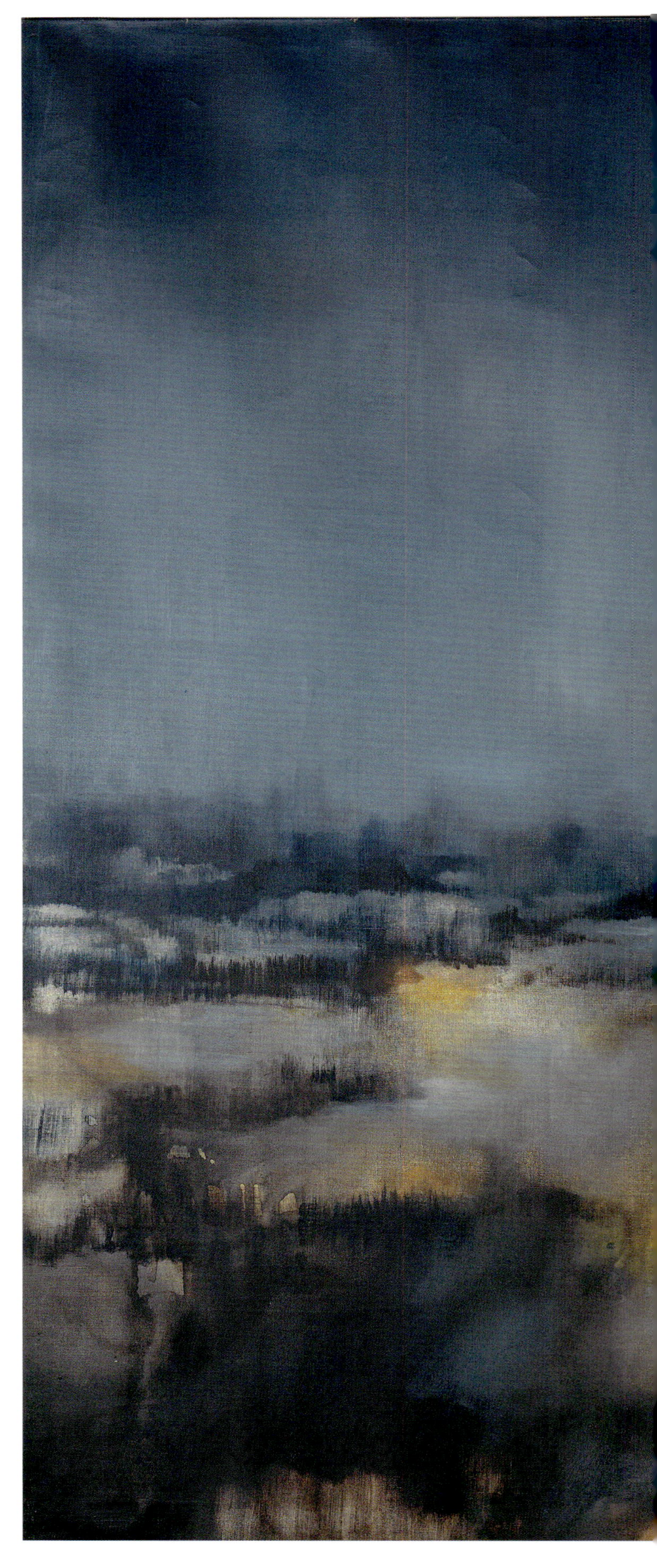

Iran Darroudi
Untitled, 1976
oil on canvas

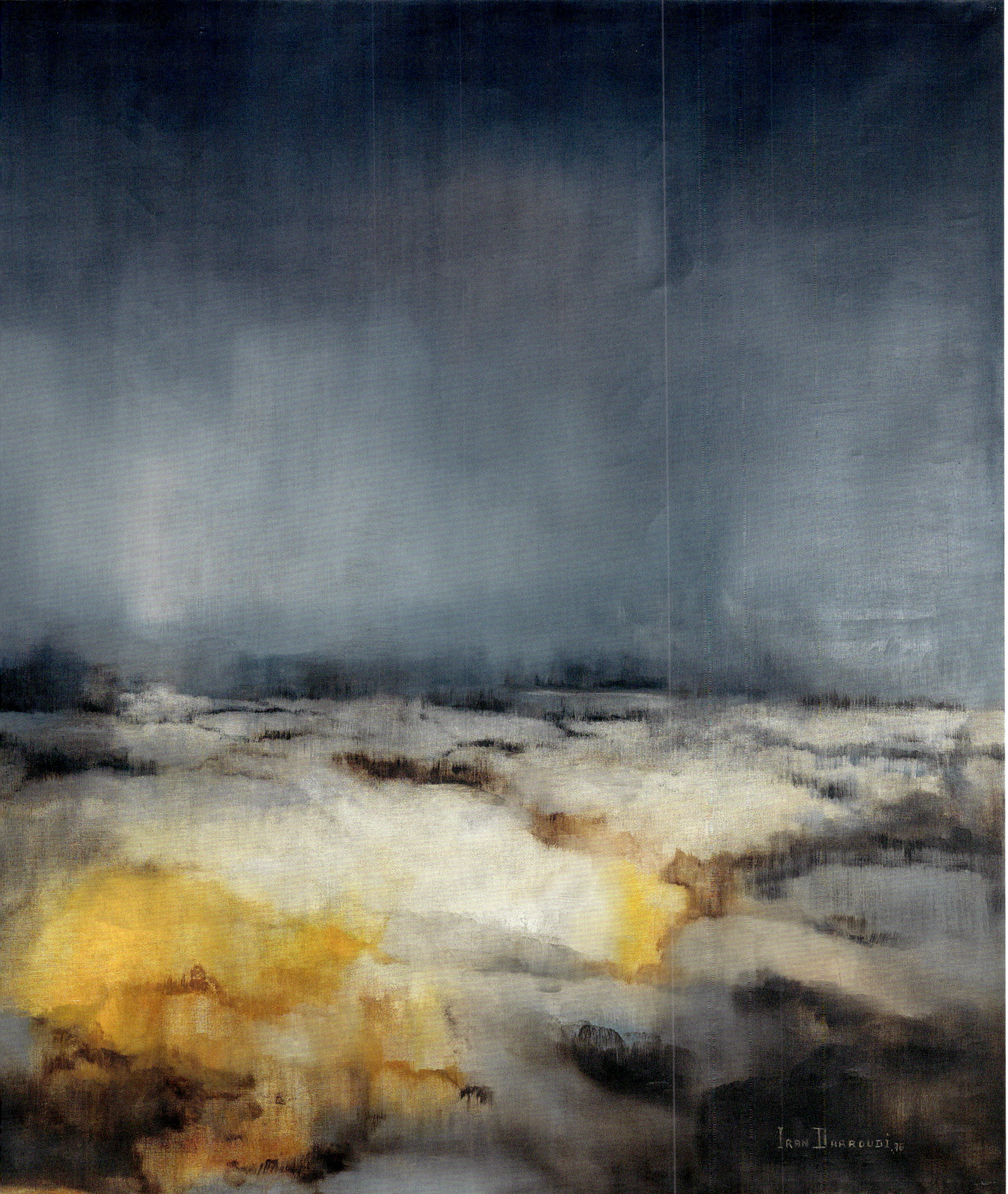
IRAN DARROUDI, 76

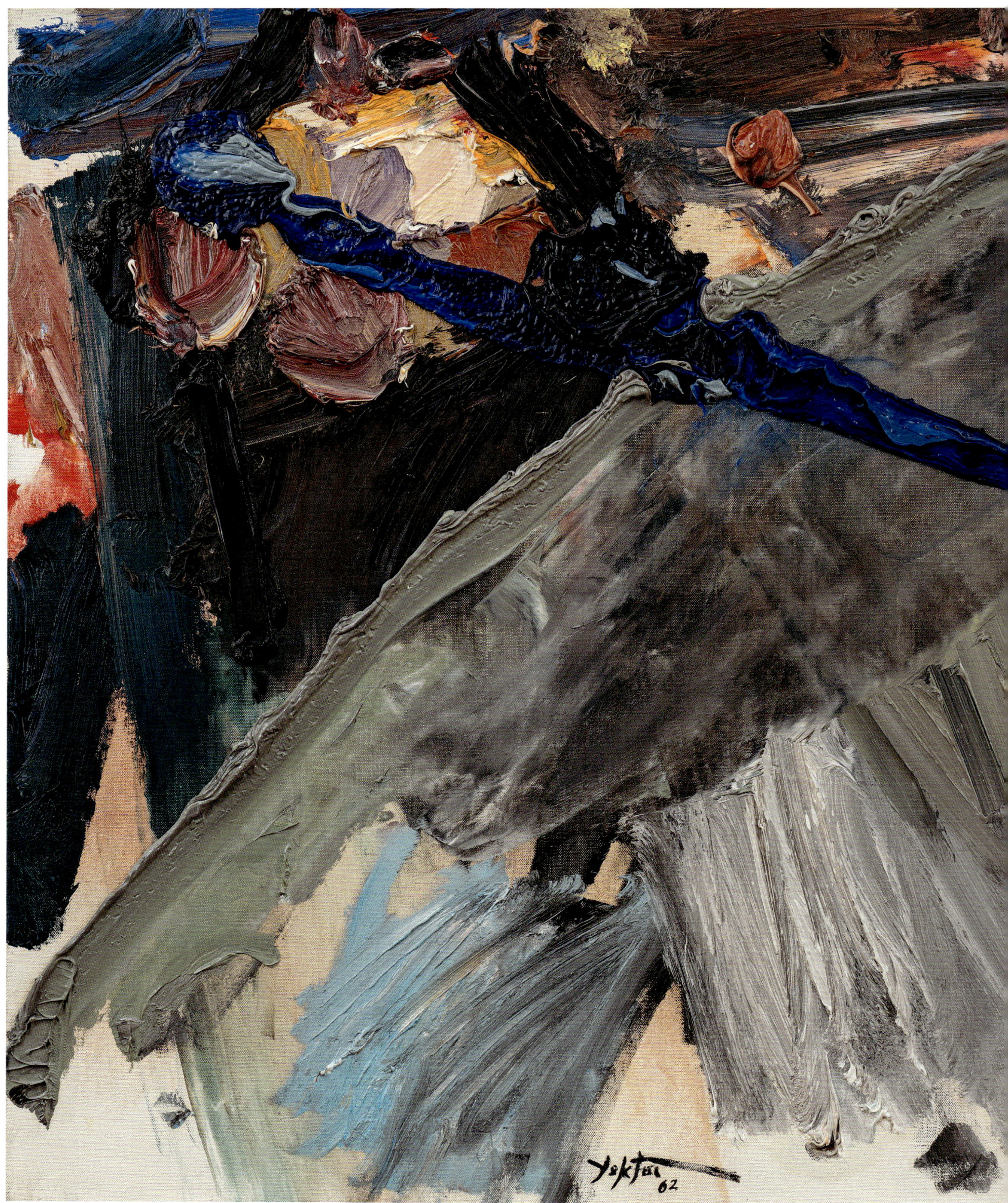

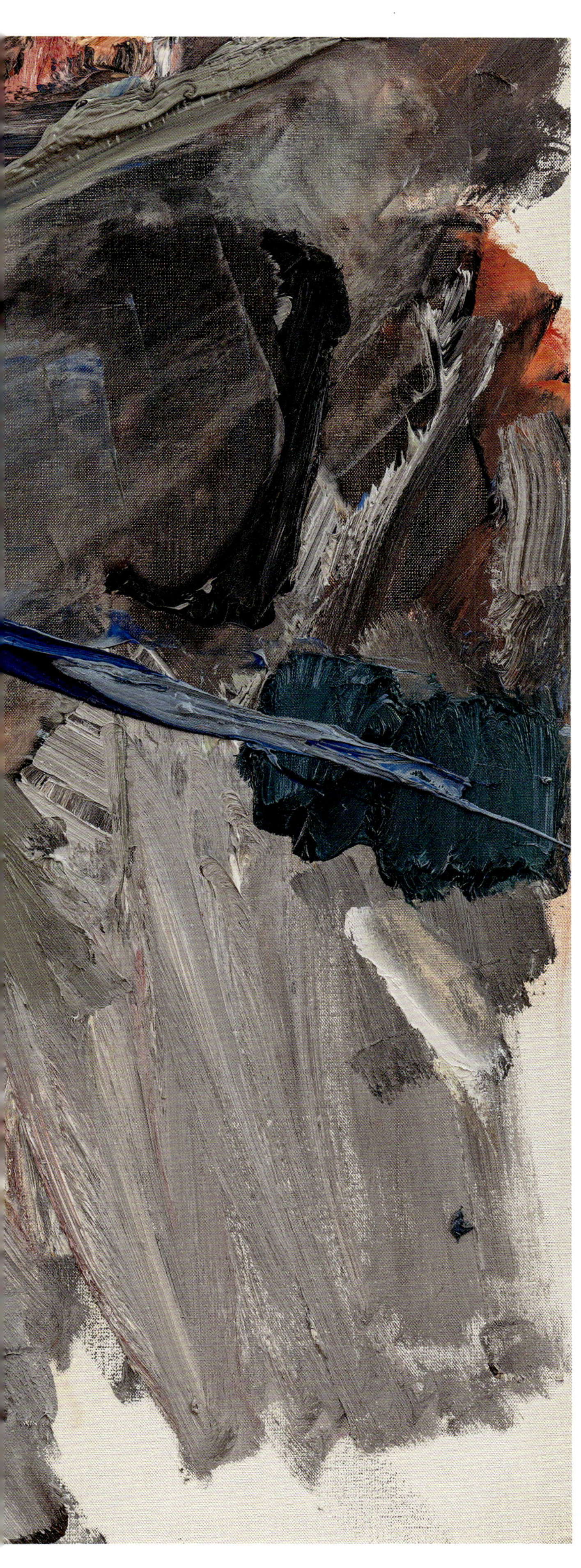

Manoucher Yektai
Untitled, 1962
oil on linen

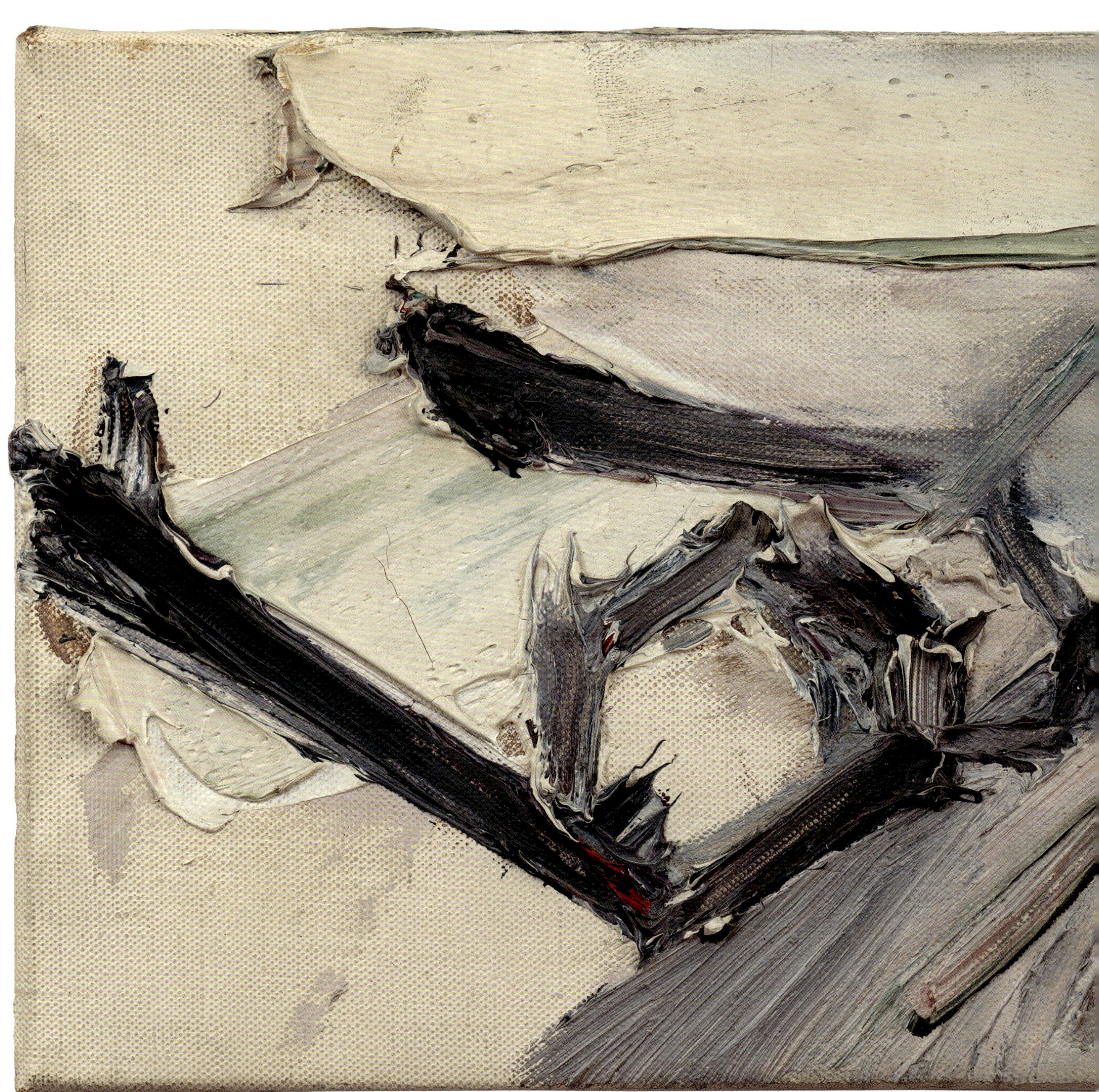

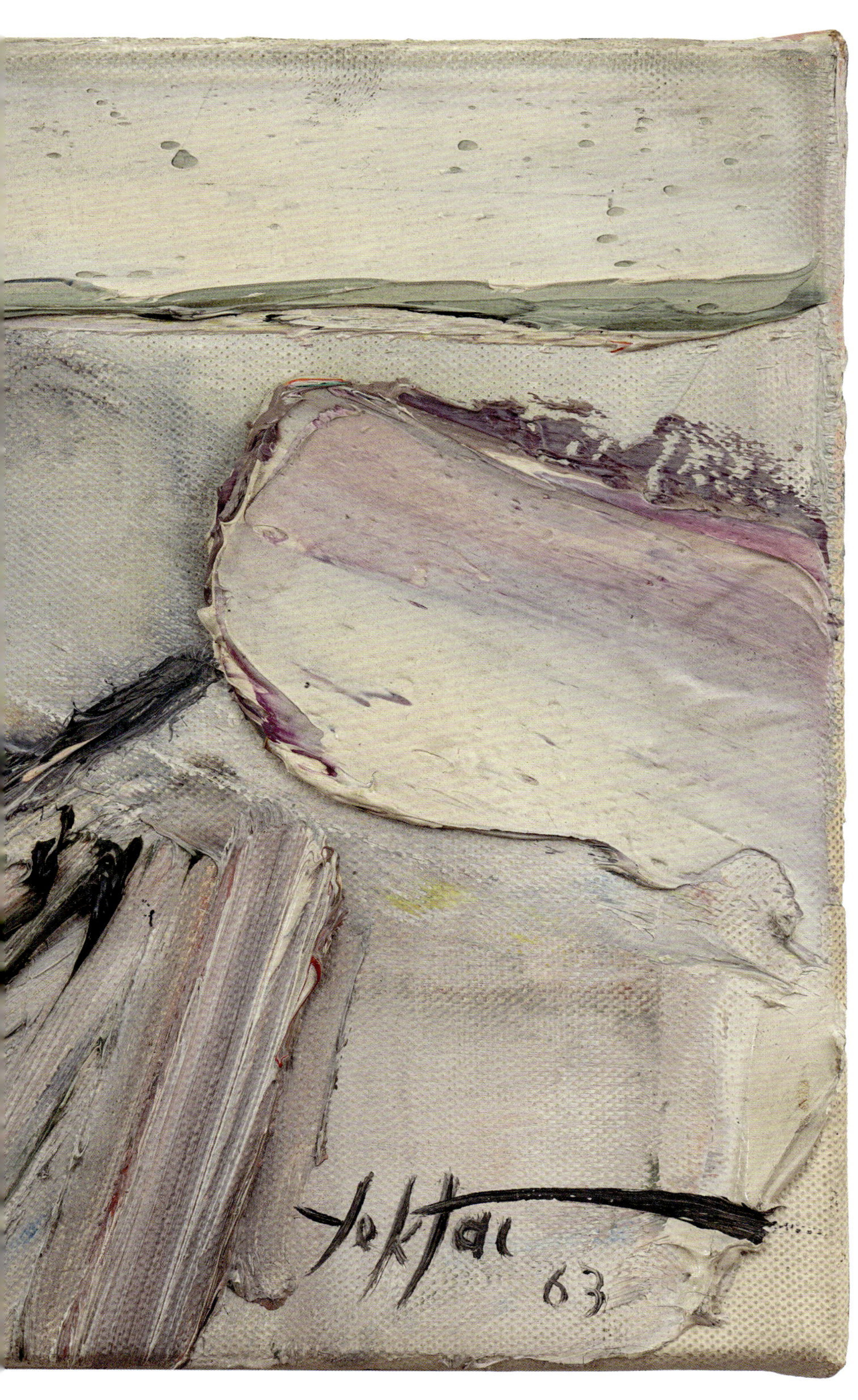

Manoucher Yektai
Untitled (eyeglasses on table), 1963
oil on linen

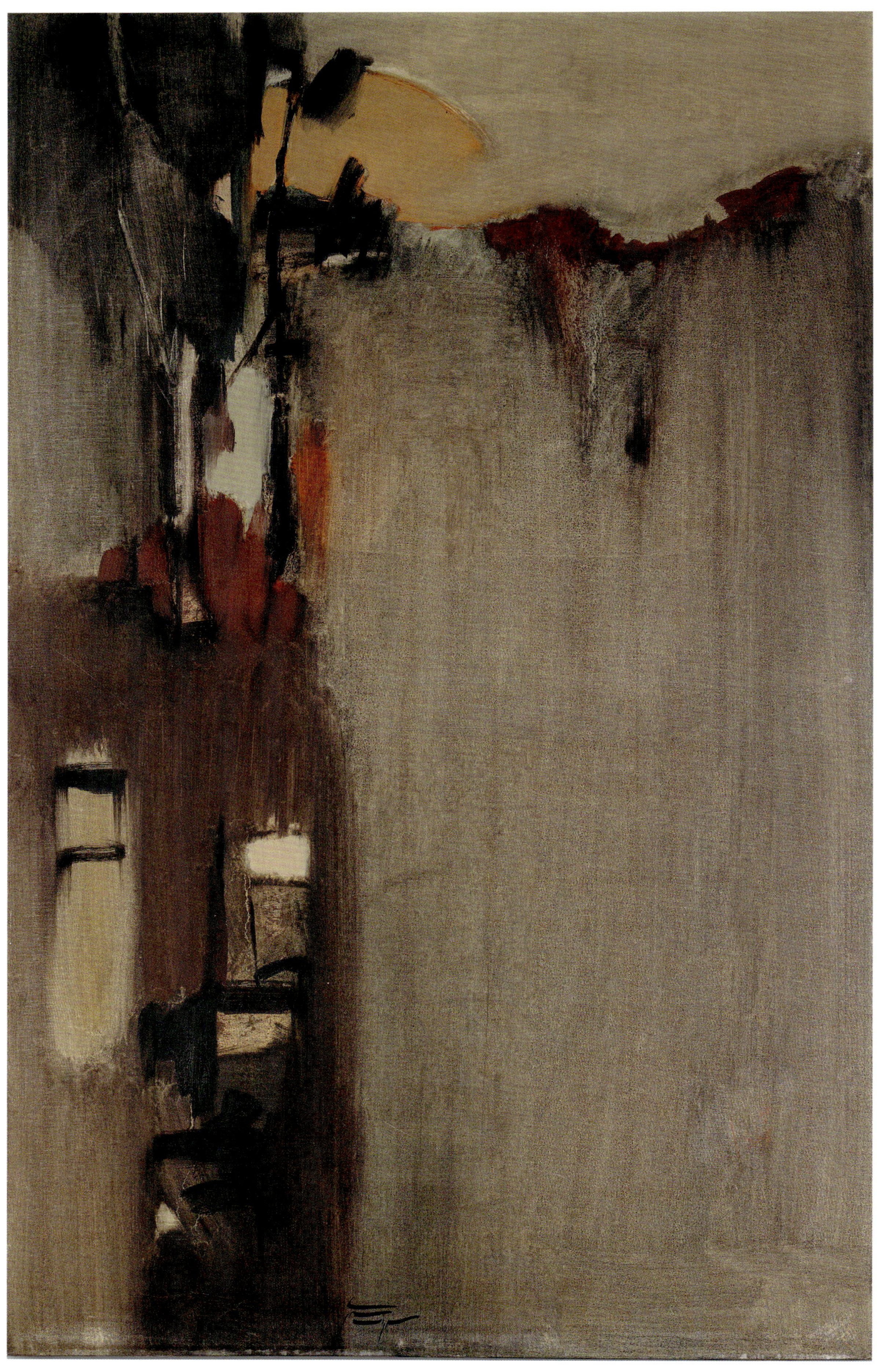

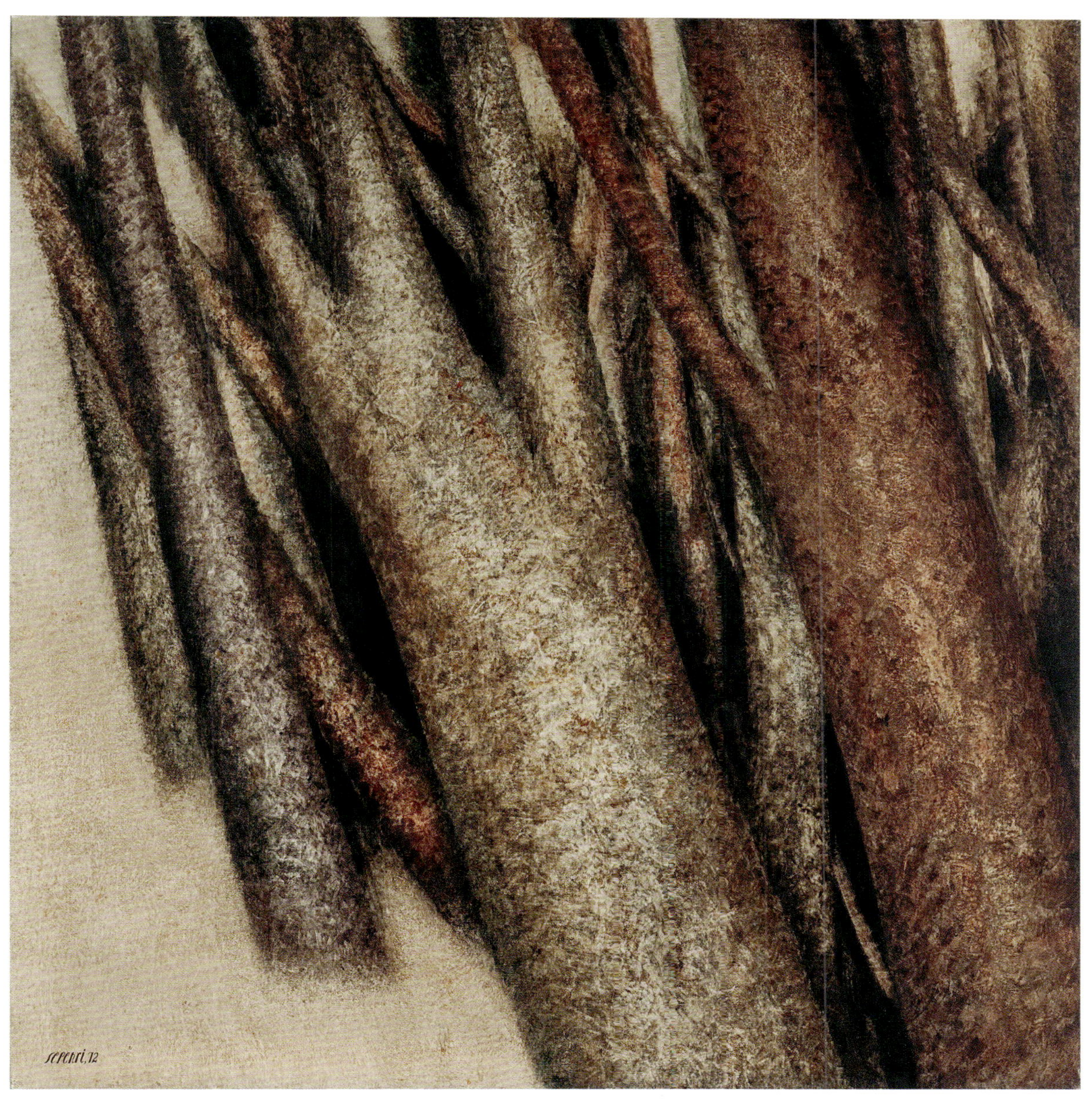

Above
Sohrab Sepehri
Untitled, 1972
oil on canvas

Opposite
Sohrab Sepehri
Untitled, 1972
oil on canvas

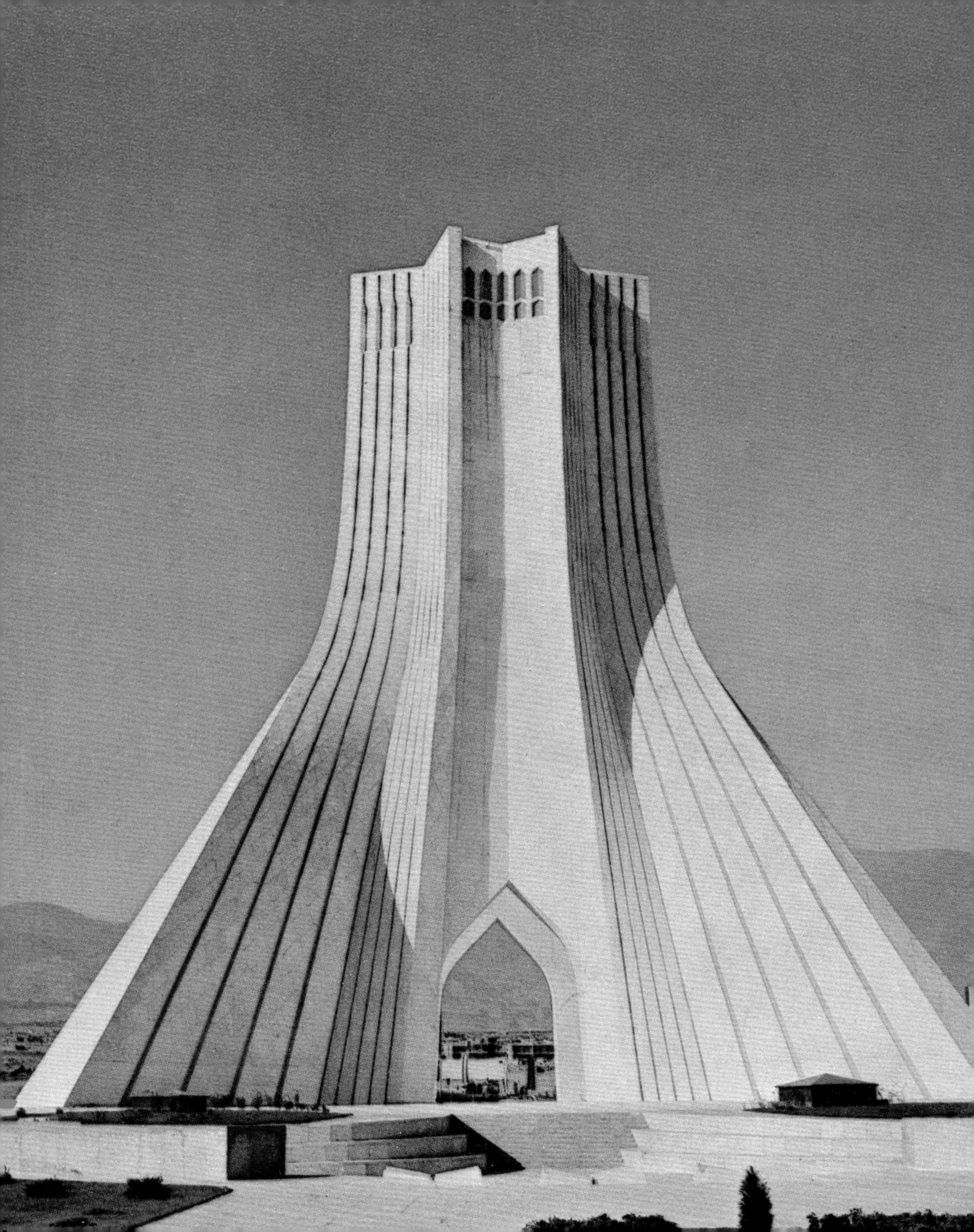

THE ARCHITECTURE, POETRY AND ART COMPLEX IN IRANIAN MODERNISM

Jeff Derksen

Like many nations that positioned themselves within the emerging world system as it took shape in the first half of the twentieth century, Iran initiated an innovative dynamic of architecture, culture and tradition to distinguish itself within this global modernizing process. However, an extraordinary set of historical forces took Iran, and its relationship to modernism, on a particular path, a path that negotiated the tensions between the nation, its history, its cultural traditions and its evolving political structures and struggles. Iran's encounters with Western modernization are globally shaped and yet historically distinct.

While Iran's move into modernism appears similar to projects around the world, the complexities of that nation's project are visible when viewed alongside similar gestures by Brazil, Venezuela and, later, Canada. For instance, Canada, entering late into this movement, expanded its university system in the early 1960s up until 1972, gathering international attention for Simon Fraser University in Burnaby, British Columbia, and the University of Lethbridge in Alberta—both designed by Arthur Erickson—and Ron Thom's Trent University in Peterborough, Ontario. Combined with the architectural and cultural success of Expo 67 in Montréal, Canada appeared as a fresh nation at "the apex of [its] postcolonial moment," even as it doubled down on its colonial structures.[1] Venezuela, flush with oil funds, built modernist schools and the beautiful University City of Caracas, alongside housing projects influenced by the International Congresses of Modern Architecture, with the country's modernist intensification taking shape under the hand of the dictator Marcos Pérez Jiménez.

Hossein Amanat
Shahyad Tower (now Azadi Tower), Tehran, 1971
Reproduced in *The Inauguration of Shahyad Tower*

Perhaps the most successful in terms of global recognition and influence was the wave of building and urbanism in Brazil between the late 1930s and the early 1960s. In this period, Brazil defined a form of modernist architecture for the Global South, drawing together the tenets of modernization—education, health,

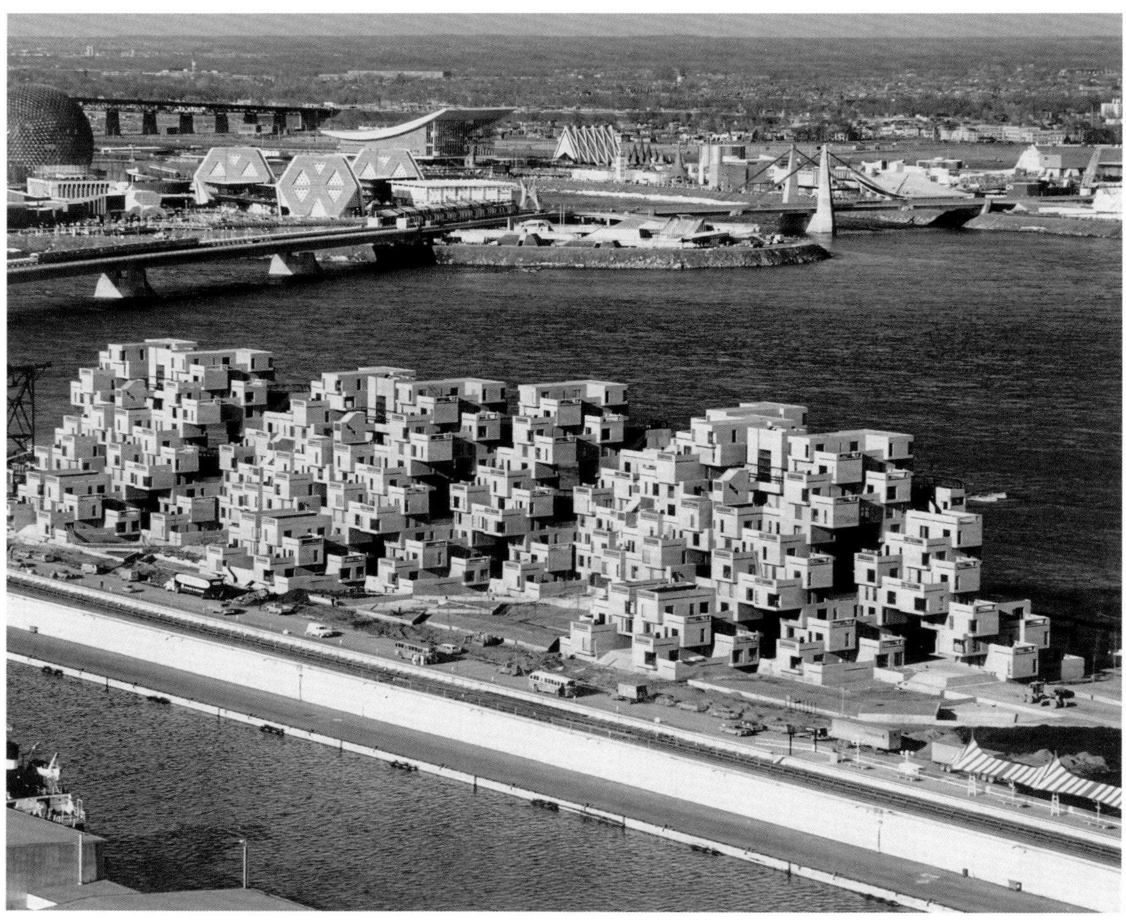

culture and governmentality—into a series of buildings realized by Brazilian architects in dialogue with the French master Le Corbusier. The building for the Ministry of Education and Health (1942) in Rio de Janeiro's Centro district drew immediate international recognition, which led to the *Brazil Builds* exhibition at the Museum of Modern Art, New York, in 1943. As the architectural historian Valerie Fraser puts it: "This is the paradigmatic way in which Latin American architects used European ideas as a basis for an alternative modernism, and those outside Latin America sat up and took notice."[2]

The local and national conditions that influenced and coloured modernization and the alternative modernism that emerged in Iran evolved over a long period. Modernization was initiated at the end of the nineteenth century in Iran, as a response to political and economic conditions: the modernist promises of political freedom, social equity and rule of law could be answers to the country's "so-called underdevelopment and despotic monarchy," as the sociologist Jamshid Behnam puts it.[3] However, as those ideals were not delivered, and following the Constitutional Revolution of 1905–06, the reforms of the 1920s and into the post–World War II period, critiques from Iranian intellectuals turned toward modernization. Informed by the 1960s global political movements and rejection of US influence, Iranian questioning of a Western form of modernism, as well as dissatisfaction with its top-down application, set the ground for what Behnam characterizes as an "era of return."[4] But, this period of the late 1960s and the

Above
Moshe Safdie
Habitat '67, Montréal, 1967

Opposite
Lúcio Costa
Ministry of Education and Health, Rio de Janeiro, 1953–54

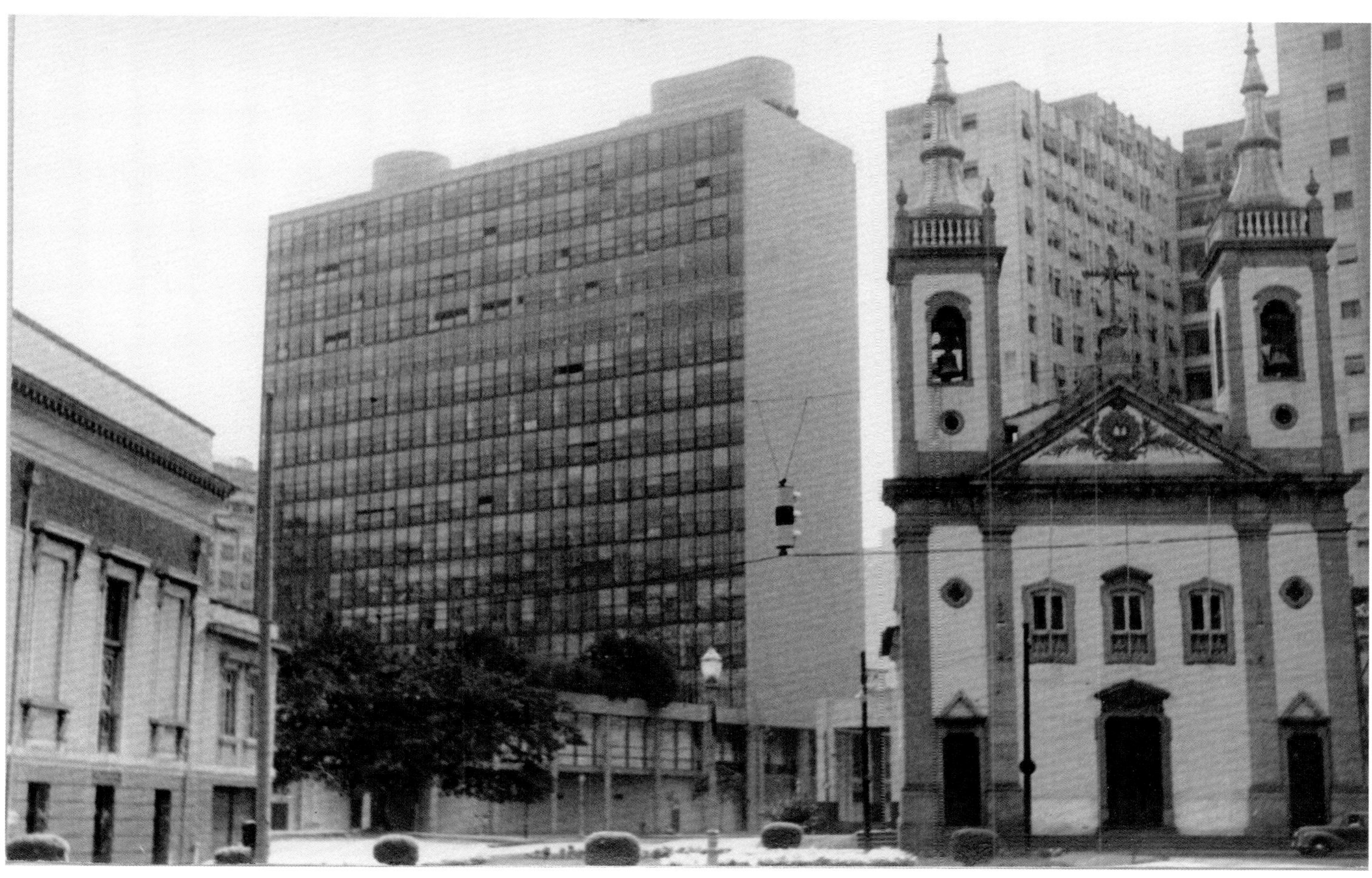

1970s was not uniform—it was not a period of retrenchment to tradition in the face of modernity but rather was a time deeply informed by a politics rejecting the world order sculpted by the West and challenging existing economic and cultural forms. Middle Eastern studies scholar Stephanie Cronin characterizes this time in Iran as one in which a "historical shift, from the hegemony of a more or less secular leftism to that of a political Islam, which worked itself out over decades elsewhere, was compressed into a moment."[5]

Modernism in Iran was immediately set in the tension between modernization's own destructive forces against an existing society and the robustly rooted knowledge of Iran's cultural history. This relationship between "modernity" and "tradition" shaped the dialogue of modernism in Iran as much as it shaped the actual design of cities, the aesthetics of architecture and the role of culture. However, the dominant idea of modernism as a break from, and a possible erasure of, tradition to construct a new society along Western lines of thought was moderated in Iran by the concept of "*tajaddod*," a term used by intellectuals and the Pahlavi state to shift modernity's definition toward "renewal" to more easily fit with ideas of continuity and reform. However, philosopher Ramin Jahanbegloo adds a layer of historical complexity when he argues that a central tension in Iran's relationship with modernity "appears to be less an irreconcilable clash between 'modernity' and 'tradition' than a series of ontological and anthropological encounters between them."[6] Jahanbegloo provocatively proposes that the reception of modernism in

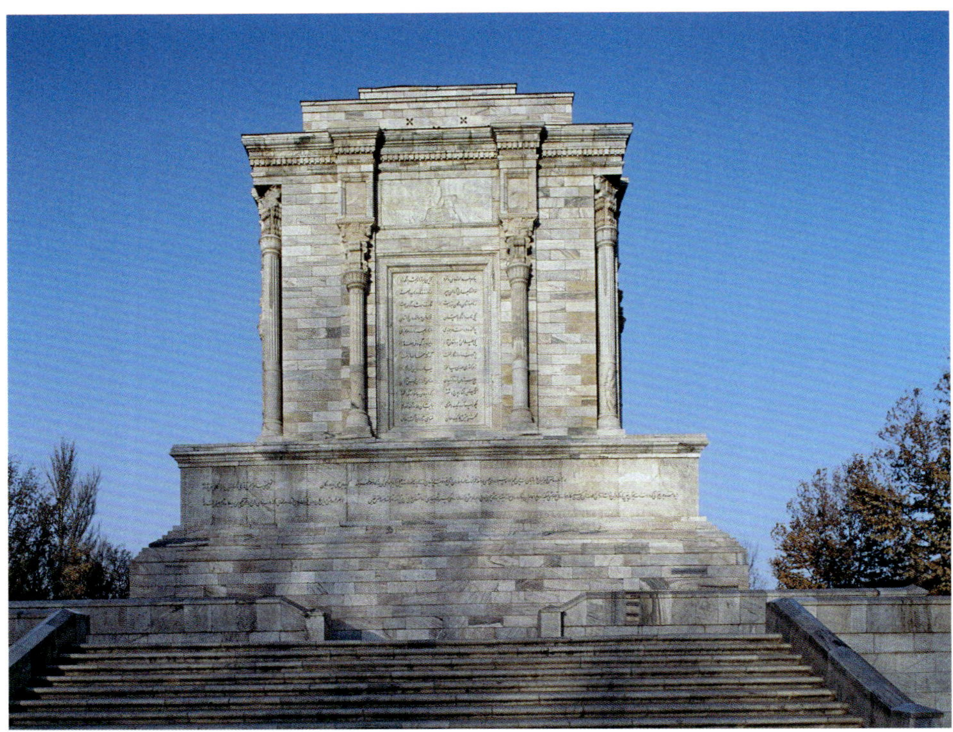

Iran set off a both a dialogue and a struggle due to a deeply ambiguous relationship to modernity that was not constructed by a simple tension between the (Western) new and tradition. "Rather," he proposes, "the uncertainty occurs because we know how to create a dialogue between our tradition and modernity."[7] This positive perspective locates the ability for such a dialogue within Iranian culture and avoids the binary pitting modernity against tradition.

Architecture scholar Esra Akcan calls this dialogue a "translation movement," a term she uses to describe "those historical moments when countries opened themselves to the foreign more consciously and effectively than before, and through translation enriched themselves, refusing to see the foreign simply as a threat."[8] This concept of translation can help break down the processes of Western modernization and modernity. Such a translation movement shows how modernism was reshaped by cultural knowledges and social practices in different regions and cities. Akcan flips the dynamic of modernism as a force overriding the culture, experience and practices of nations, drawing them into a predetermined form of change; in contrast, she acknowledges the effective engagement of countries through an exchange with or translation of modernism.

But it was in the 1920s and 1930s that modernist urban planning and architecture was dramatically pushed onto Tehran and the city was remade following European planning, with much of its original structure torn down. By deploying grand boulevards (or Haussmannization, as it is called, after the designer of Paris), imposed on top of the historical city with its more organic development, Tehran's layout was turned into a grid. As Cronin points out: "The modernist project implied destruction as much as construction."[9] Not only did this push the poorest of the city out of their quarters, it also dramatically altered the model of living,

Above
Houshang Seyhoun
Tomb of Ferdowsi, Tus, 1968

Opposite
Houshang Seyhoun
Mausoleum of Omar Khayyám, Neyshabur, 1963

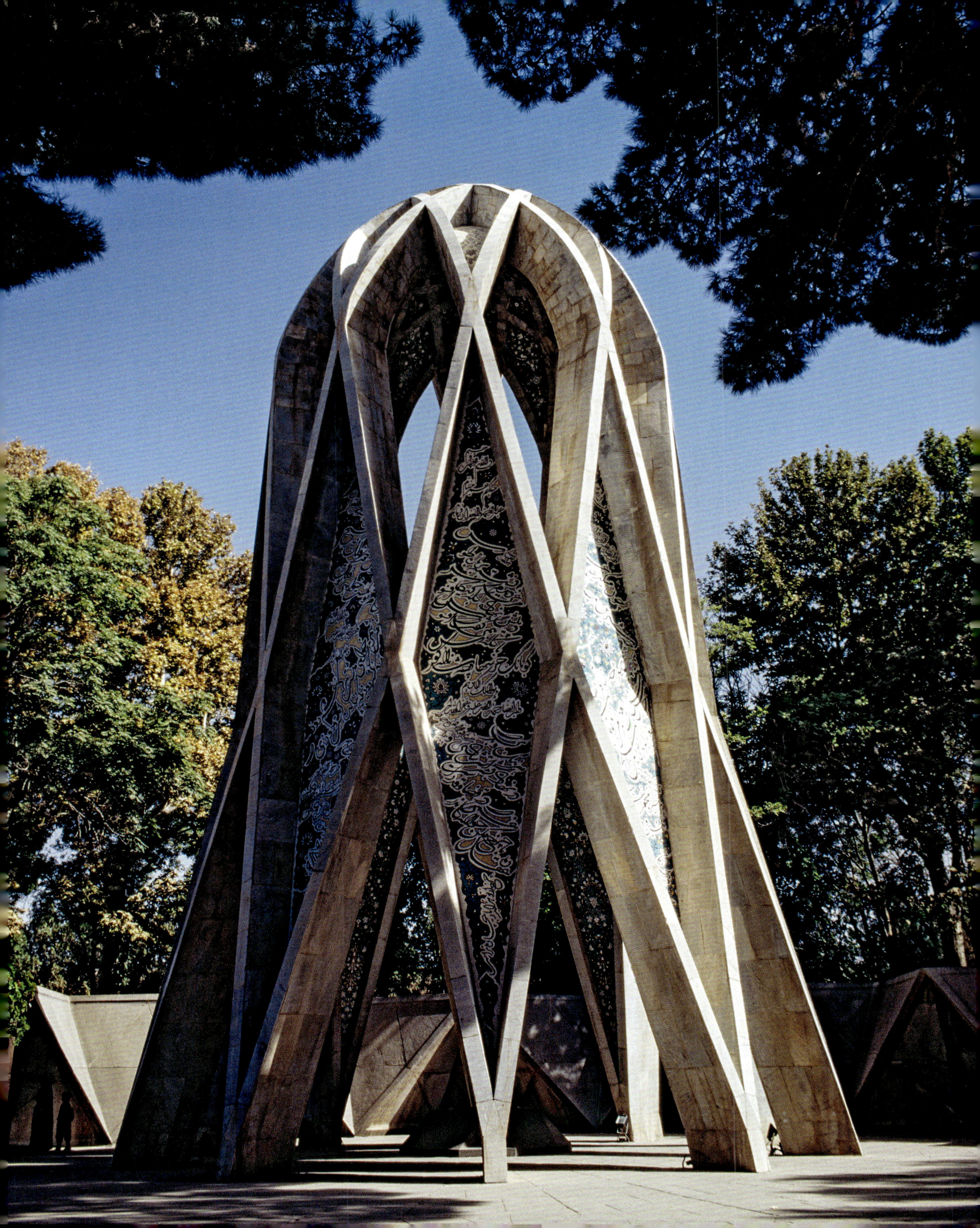

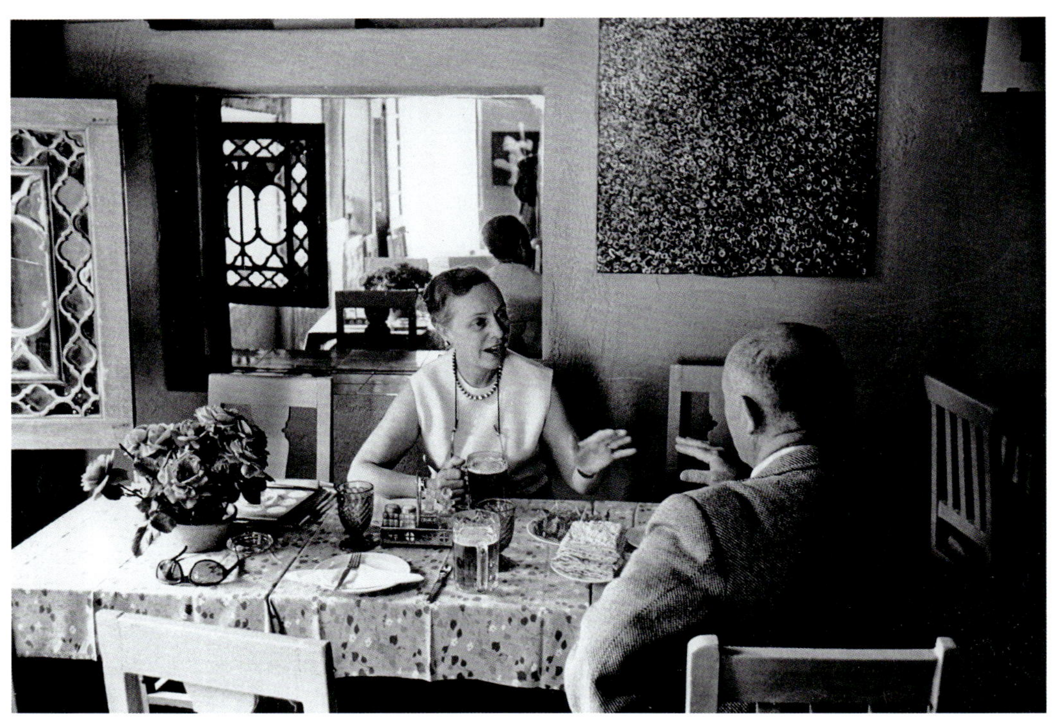

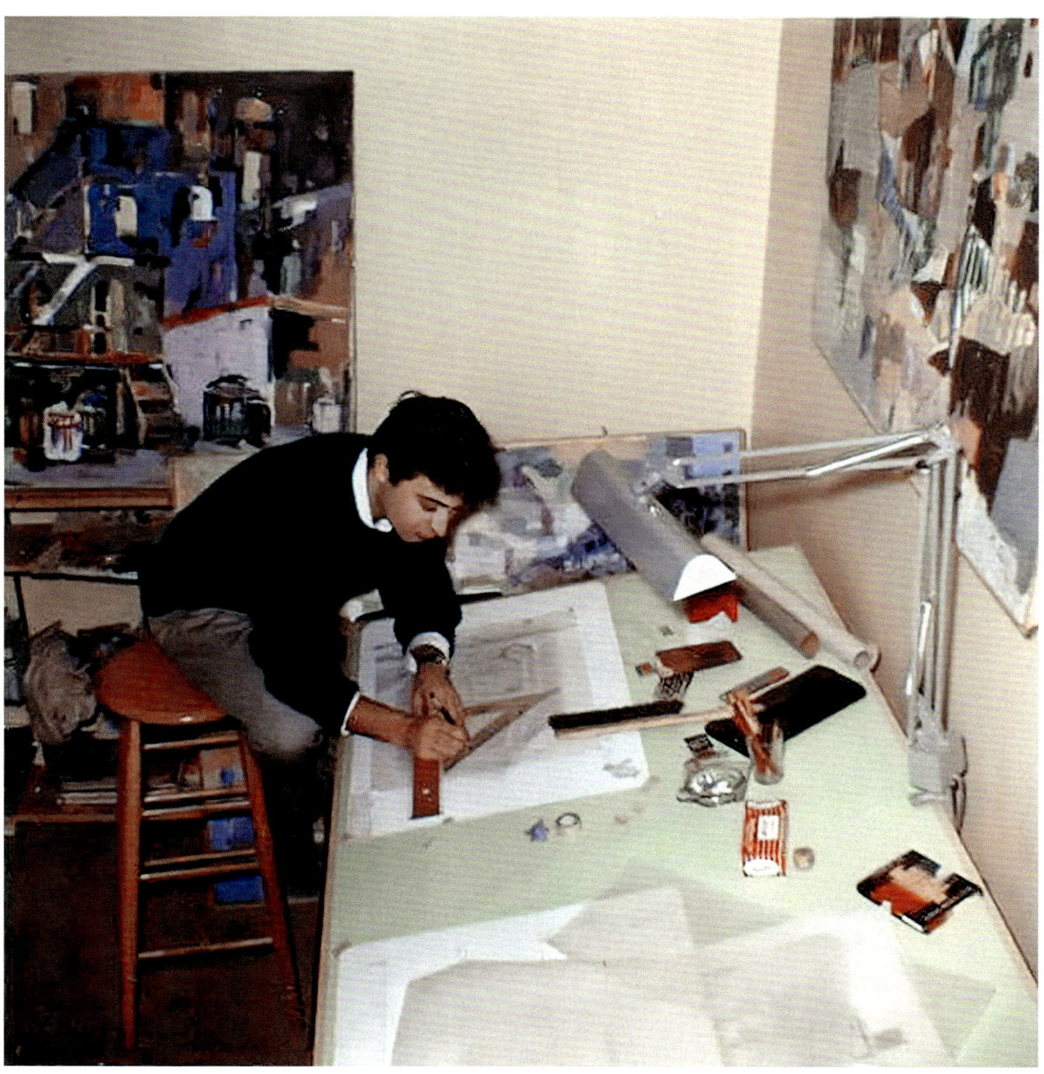

redefined domestic space and changed the spatiality of everyday and communal life toward a European vision. This urban development tore the urban fabric and broke a connection with past ways of life, modes of social organization and cultural practices that were now considered, through a European lens, archaic, unhealthy, dangerous and criminal. Yet, in architecture historian Talinn Grigor's perspective, this urban creative destruction had extended cultural effects: "The eradication of historical structures and urban pockets meant that a newly built environment could emerge free from the burden of history, geography, and colonialism. It also meant that a new historical continuity with the national past needed to be fabricated."[10]

This weaving, or fabricating, of a deeper past with a changing present is part of how nations have engaged with culture, in the broad sense, to create narratives to bring and hold the nation together, or to push a different identity. Canada did this with cultural programs, education, architecture and the Montréal Expo around the country's centenary, 1967. Similarly, the modernization process of the Iranian state reflects how history and culture are both constructed and lived, and contested and remade, at the national level. In Iran's case, the depth and variance of cultural traditions and the diverse external pressures, particularly in a moment of global political and cultural shifts, made these processes even more dynamic.

In this process, the relationship between tradition and modernism in Iran was shaped by the state through the formation of the Society for National Heritage (SNH) in 1922: from that point onward, the SNH solidified a continual and historical link between tradition and the present. The SNH, through its influence, guided the connection between architecture and heritage, privileging an architecture that embedded principles of Iranian cultural tradition. For the urbanist M. Reza Shirazi, this emphasis on the historical continuity of tradition did not "imprison" architecture in the past but instead allowed it to "anticipate new worlds and move toward never-ending authentic recreations."[11] Grigor, however, argues that the concept of tradition was based on an "exclusivist interpretation of its own tradition" based on Western knowledges.[12] Some of the earliest projects supported by the SNH were the remaking of the mausoleums for poets; at first European architects led these projects, but this choice eventually gave way to Iranian architects. The mausoleum for the epic Persian poet Abolqasem Ferdowsi was followed by a tomb and garden for the lyric poet Hafiz and a tomb for the poet, astronomer and philosopher Omar Khayyám. These mausoleums, gardens and tombs were important in strengthening a role for tradition within modernization, and they brought aspects of modern architecture and pre-Islamic and Sufi tradition together in a form of "public instruction." By drawing together poetry and architecture within the continuity of a national culture, tradition and modernity were joined; however, this articulation would be used in a very different manner by coming generations of architects and poets.

Top
Abby Weed Grey with American sculptor Jack Schnier at Rasht 29, Tehran, 1967

Bottom
Kamran Diba at Harvard University, Cambridge, US, 1960

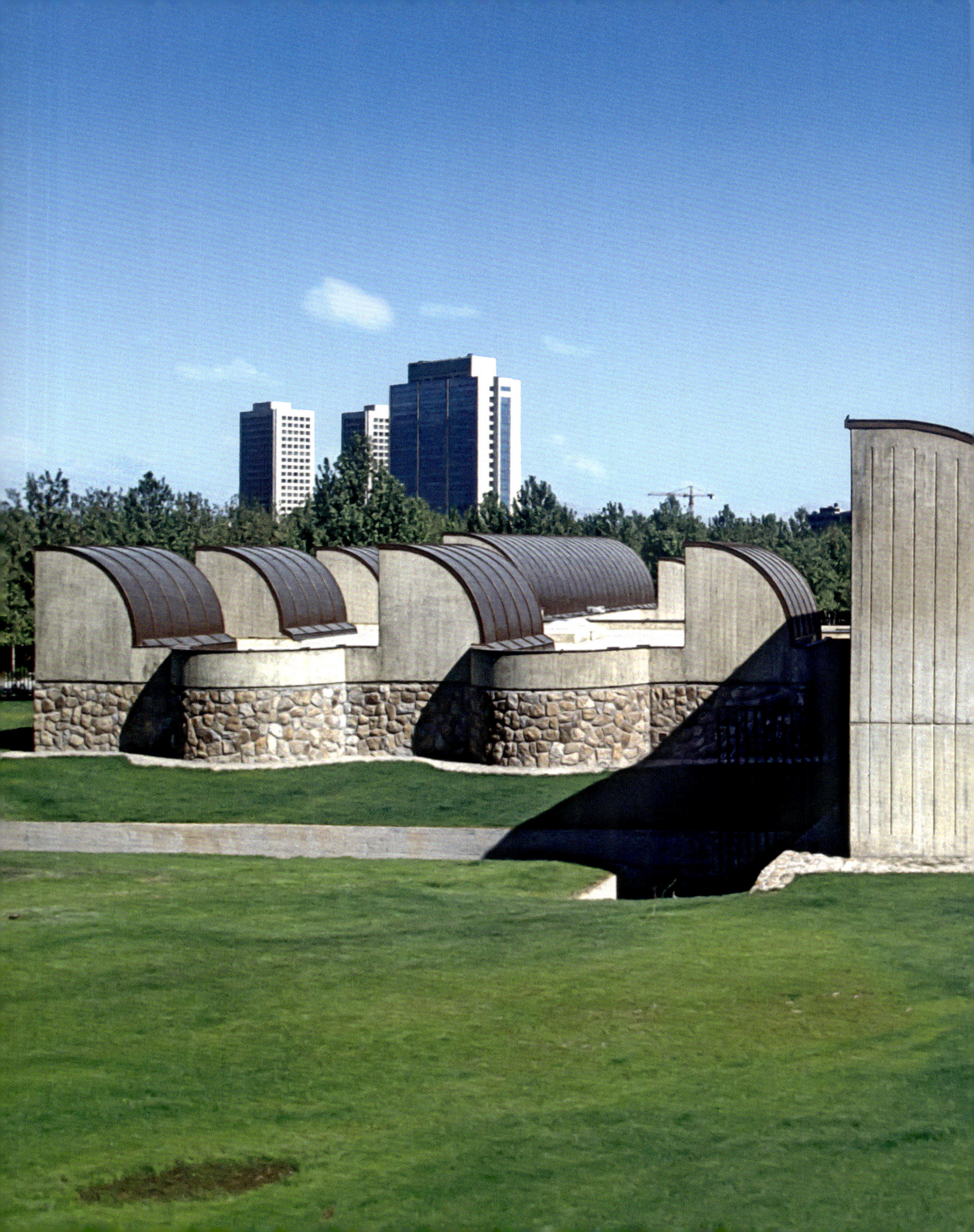

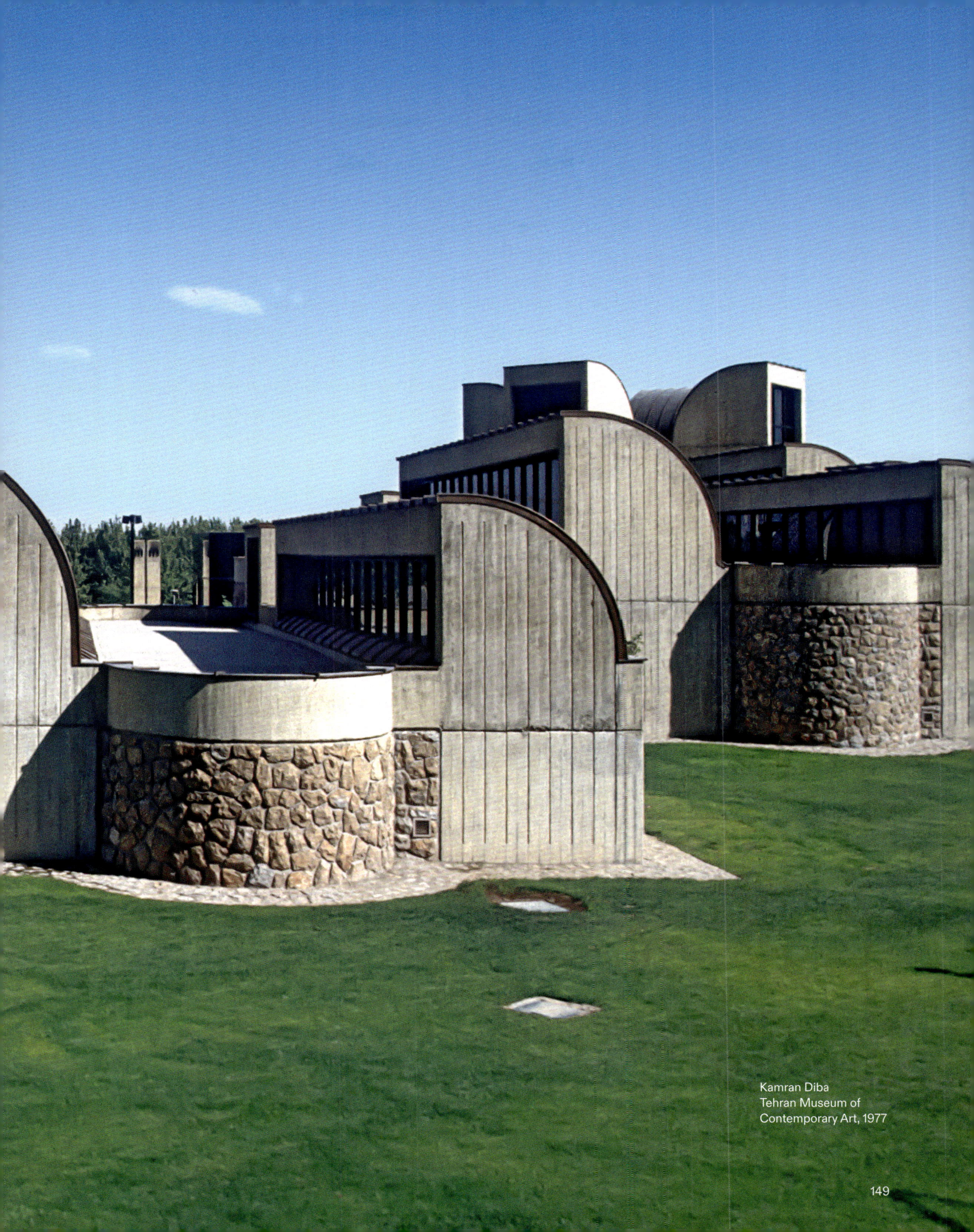

Kamran Diba
Tehran Museum of
Contemporary Art, 1977

This relationship of poetry and architecture in Iranian modernism later joined with art to sharpen as a form of criticism of the social and economic inequities brought by top-down modernism. This opposition blossomed in the liberatory light of the global 1960s, when culture and politics fused and the idea of new and freer societies—societies grounded in equity and creativity—fomented an explosion of new poetry, music and art. With large numbers of students studying abroad, young Iranians brought the politics and poetics of this global moment to their nation and their cities, and this would initiate a new critique of the form of modernism that had been directed by the state. It also opened culture through a reflective look at tradition within the context of Iranian culture of the 1960s. A deleterious effect of Iranian modernism before the 1960s was to create a split between high and low culture, and to criminalize thriving subcultural groups. As Cronin remarks, "The first half of the twentieth century saw the emergence and fostering of a profound and entirely novel gulf between high and low culture, the former elite and the modern, the latter traditional and the preserve of the poor and uneducated."[13] But a group of young artists, poets and architects, loosely designated as the Saqqakhaneh group, opened spaces such as the Rasht 29 Club in Tehran, where the rift between high and low culture could be overcome. This approach to culture sought to close this cultural divide of high and low and critiqued the conditions of the urban poor as well as the lack of social reforms and political and cultural openness that modernism had promised. In the realm of architecture, historian of architecture Niloofar Amini writes,

> Architects like [Kamran] Diba (b. 1937) and Nader Ardalan (b. 1939) knew that the public arts were important to create common concerns and public discussion. Since the majority of the Iranians did not receive an aesthetic education, and had no contact with the arts, they believed that their projects, rather than serve and entertain the cultural elite, should function as educational initiatives.[14]

Public instruction was levered toward creating a new society shaped through cultural practices, through the work of poets, artists and architects.[15]

The art and architecture critic Hal Foster has argued that a unique relationship between art and architecture, which he calls "the art-architecture complex," is central to the global cultural economy: "Sometimes a collaboration, sometimes a competition, this encounter [between architects and artists] is now a primary site of image-making and space shaping in our cultural economy."[16] The implications of this complex are not only the ways in which architecture and art work together or are juxtaposed but also how such ensembles have changed the nature of cities, and how architecture creates images of space and place. Foster locates this complex largely in North America and Europe, but he provides a fertile template to look at how architecture and art have come together in other times and other

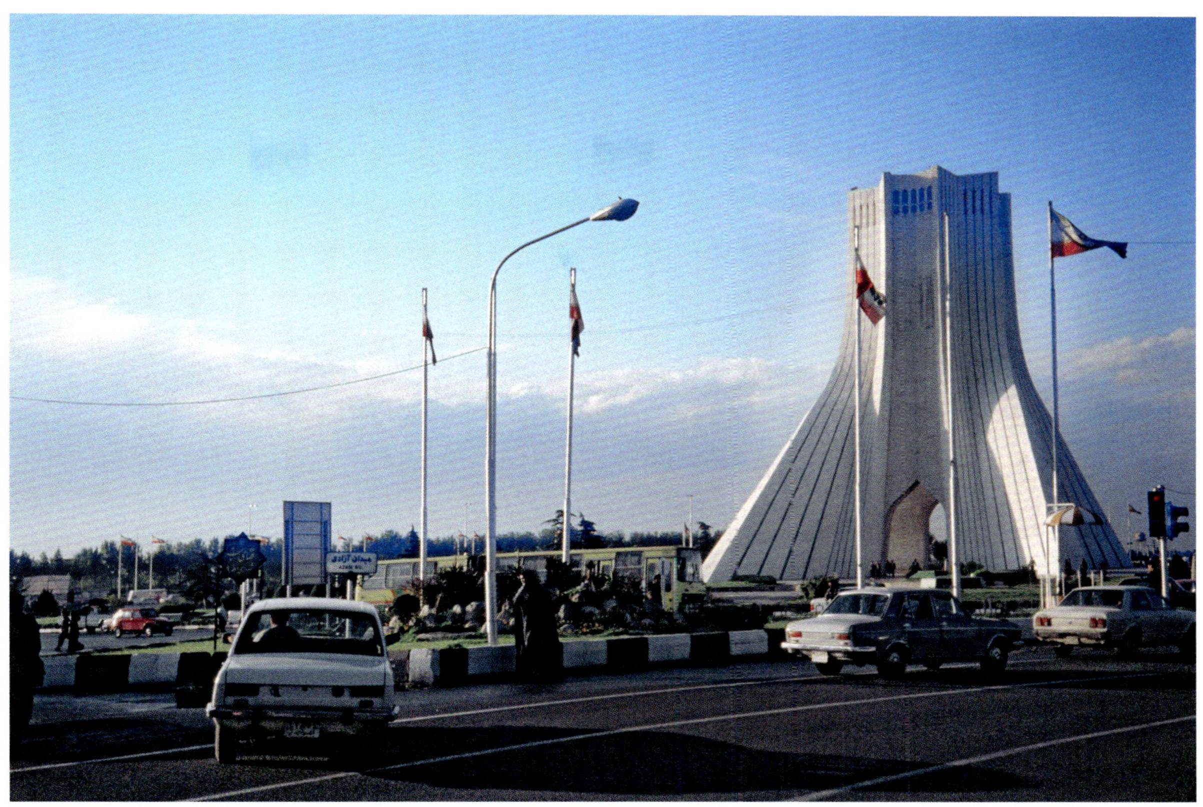

Hossein Amanat
Shahyad Tower (now known as Azadi Tower), Tehran, 1971

places. For Iran, this art-architecture complex is joined with poetry to form an art-poetry-architecture complex that carries the particularities of Iran's history and is shaped by the relationship of modernism to tradition. The nexus of architecture, art and poetry provided an energy through which, in a translation movement, ideas of modernism could be altered and reshaped—even turned upside down—to adapt to Iran's situation. Within this unique nexus, an architectural aesthetic sprung from the vibrant sense of tradition and, when understood through poetry and other arts and crafts, produced new forms of public space for modern citizens.

The role of poetry in Iranian architecture, through its cultural influence and its aesthetics, stands out within international modernism: poetry carries a cultural tradition in the present that can be translated into modernist ideas of architecture and space. Perhaps the best example of this collaboration between art, poetry and spatial knowledges is Tehran Museum of Contemporary Art (TMoCA, 1977), designed by Kamran Diba. Situated in a public park with a sculpture garden, TMoCA and its grounds created new forms of public space and used modernist sculptures to shift the scale and intent of public art away from monumentality. The materiality of the building itself is foregrounded by the use of concrete as an aesthetic material (Arthur Erickson was a key proponent of this), as well as the use of stones and copper to make the building's loop of seven gallery spaces textured but not ornamental. Likewise, elsewhere on the gallery grounds, a minimal, sculptural prayer room (Namaz Khaneh), with its inner room open to the sky and oriented toward Mecca, brought in a modernist aesthetic as an agent to produce a different type of public space, one grounded in tradition yet read through modernist materiality.

Hossein Amanat's Azadi Tower (originally Shahyad Tower), an optimistic structure built in Tehran's Azadi Square (Freedom Square), is another example where a poetics of tradition and modernism cohere in an elegant and meaningful architectural and social structure. Amanat, a recent graduate of architecture at the University of Tehran at the time, entered the design competition for a monument to celebrate 2,500 years of Iranian history. Shirazi writes that the tower is "a poem in which the solidity of geometry is softened by the delicacy and elegance of the arches, ornaments, and colours, generating a lyricism in which the inner geometrical logic never undermines the manifestation of the architectural vocabulary."[17] If we use the perspective of international poetic modernism to look at the tower, it is not a symbol as much as it is a compelling example of Iranian senses of balance and unity. The tower is an image and an "objective correlative" for cultural optimism, based on the weight of history. The poetic modernist sense of sincerity, as a direct treatment of material within its social context, also provides a frame to understand how the tower's design is informed by regional architecture, landscape and design as well as the choice of its building materials.

Esra Akcan makes a compelling case that Iranian architects reversed the flow of architectural and cultural knowledge from the so-called Third World to the First with their collective contribution, *The Habitat Bill of Rights*, to the UN Conference on Human Settlements, held in May and June 1976 on Vancouver's Jericho Beach. Not only was this an important and consequential UN conference, but Habitat I was a major public event within Vancouver, bringing the discussion of housing to a city that was a centre for environmental activism, yet a city that would come to evolve one of the most difficult housing situations in the world. *The Habitat Bill of Rights* was commissioned by the Iranian Ministry of Housing and Development and published by the Hamdami Foundation in Tehran, and it used Iranian architecture as a case study. This collaboration between the architects Nader Ardalan (Iranian), Georges Candilis (Greek), Moshe Safdie (Canadian) and Josep Lluís Sert (Catalan) grew out of the previous UN conference in Persepolis. The report presents a critique of the state of housing globally—filled with warnings that are prescient today—and international modernism's tendency to ignore the relationship to place, to misalign material to the local climate and to not consider the culture of the people who would live in its buildings. One right declares: "The layout of the new dwellings should incorporate...the cultural values and living patterns of prospective residents."[18] Pointedly, this right could address the top-down 1920–30s transformation of Tehran, which altered the living patterns, spatial practices and cultural values of those who would live in the city's new buildings. Akcan makes an intriguing point that not only did *The Habitat Bill of Rights* lay out what were understood to be universal rights regarding housing, it also made a clear argument for an affirmation of "indigenous architecture." The collectively written bill of rights is grounded in the dialogic relationship of tradition and the modern in Iran and proposes an architectural answer to the central tension that sees modernism as a break with tradition. Akcan's research figures Iranian architects as key players in a global dialogue of architecture that challenged the legacy of the International Style and the developmental impulses of modernization by turning the discussion of "critical regionalisms," and the role of national and local architectural and spatial histories and cultures, into a rights-based question. Along with architecture that deserves recognition as beautiful modernist design and innovative thought, the architectural debates in Iran also created a critical legacy of the translation of modernism and modernization, one that reshapes the narrative of modern architecture and the International Style.

ENDNOTES

1 Doug Saunders, "In 1967, Change in Canada Could No Longer Be Stopped," *Globe and Mail*, January 1, 2017, https://www.theglobeandmail.com/news/national/canada-150/in-1967-the-birth-of-moderncanada/article33466250/.

2 Valerie Fraser, *Building the New World: Studies in the Modern Architecture of Latin America, 1930–1960* (London: Verso, 2000), 146.

3 Jamshid Behnam, "Iranian Society, Modernity, and Globalization," in *Iran: Between Tradition and Modernity*, ed. Ramin Jahanbegloo (Lanham, MD: Lexington Books, 2004), 5.

4 Behnam, "Iranian Society, Modernity, and Globalization," 5.

5 Stephanie Cronin, *Social Histories of Iran: Modernism and Marginality in the Middle East* (Cambridge: Cambridge University Press, 2021), 24.

6 Ramin Jahanbegloo, ed., introduction to *Iran: Between Tradition and Modernity* (Lanham, MD: Lexington Books, 2004), x.

7 Jahanbegloo, introduction to *Iran*, xi.

8 Esra Akcan, *Abolish Human Bans: Intertwined Histories of Architecture* (Montréal: Canadian Centre for Architecture, 2022), 1.

9 Cronin, *Social Histories of Iran*, 113.

10 Talinn Grigor, "The King's White Walls: Modernism and Bourgeois Architecture," in *Culture and Cultural Politics Under Reza Shah: The Pahlavi State, New Bourgeoisie and the Creation of a Modern Society in Iran*, ed. Bianca Devos and Christoph Werner (London: Routledge, 2014), 97.

11 M. Reza Shirazi, *Contemporary Architecture and Urbanism in Iran* (Cham, Switzerland: Springer International Publishing, 2018), 78.

12 Grigor, "The King's White Walls," 166.

13 Cronin, *Social Histories of Iran*, 154.

14 Niloofar Amini, "The Aesthetic Resistance of Iranian Architects and Artists During the Late Pahlavi Era," *Studies in History and Theory of Architecture*, no. 8 (2020): 199.

15 This is characteristic of the 1960s political moment, when culture was pushed to the forefront rather than being seen as a mere adjunct to social change.

16 Hal Foster, preface to *The Art-Architecture Complex* (New York: Verso Books, 2013), i.

17 Shirazi, *Contemporary Architecture and Urbanism in Iran*, 65.

18 *The Habitat Bill of Rights*, quoted in Akcan, *Abolish Human Bans*, 48.

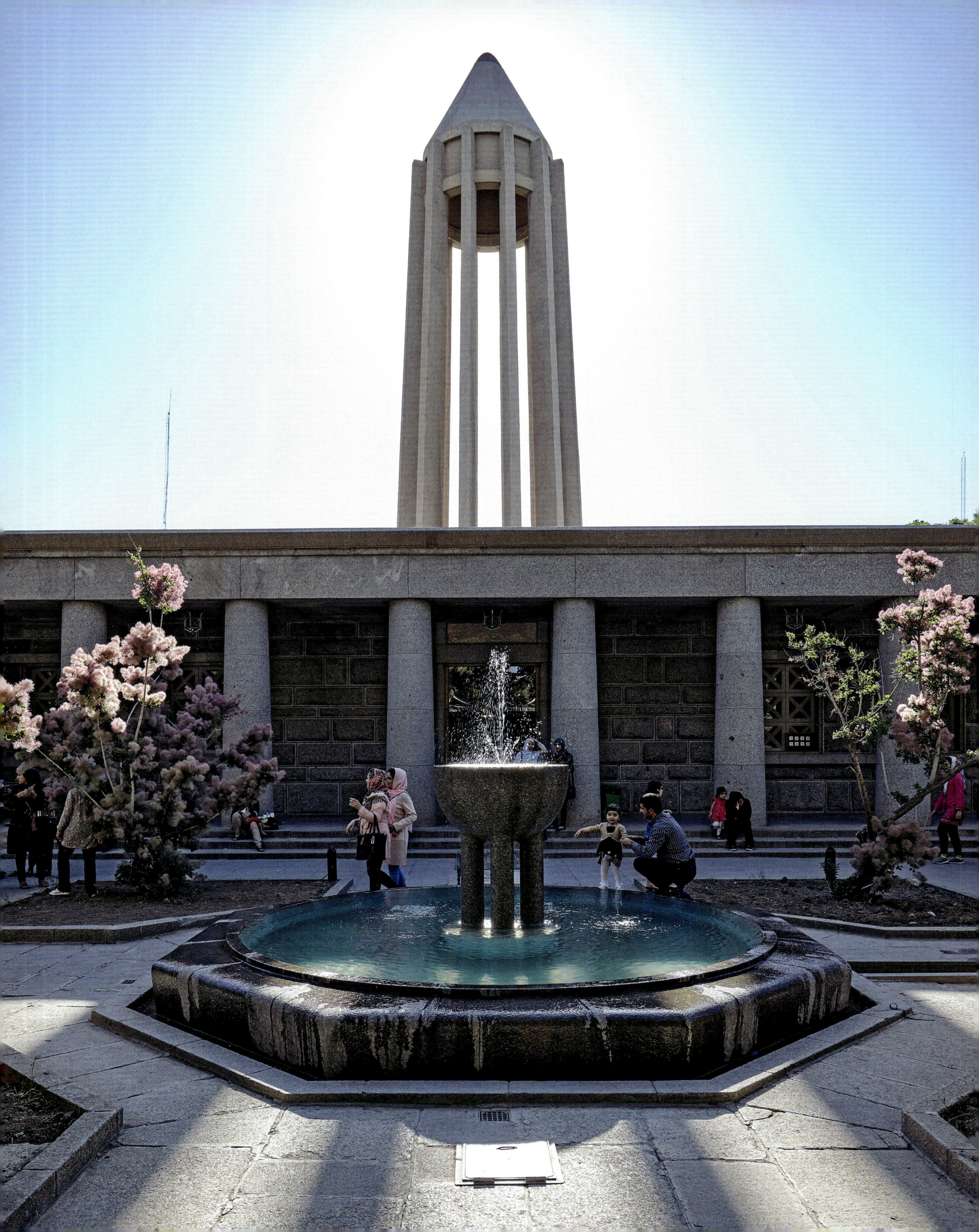

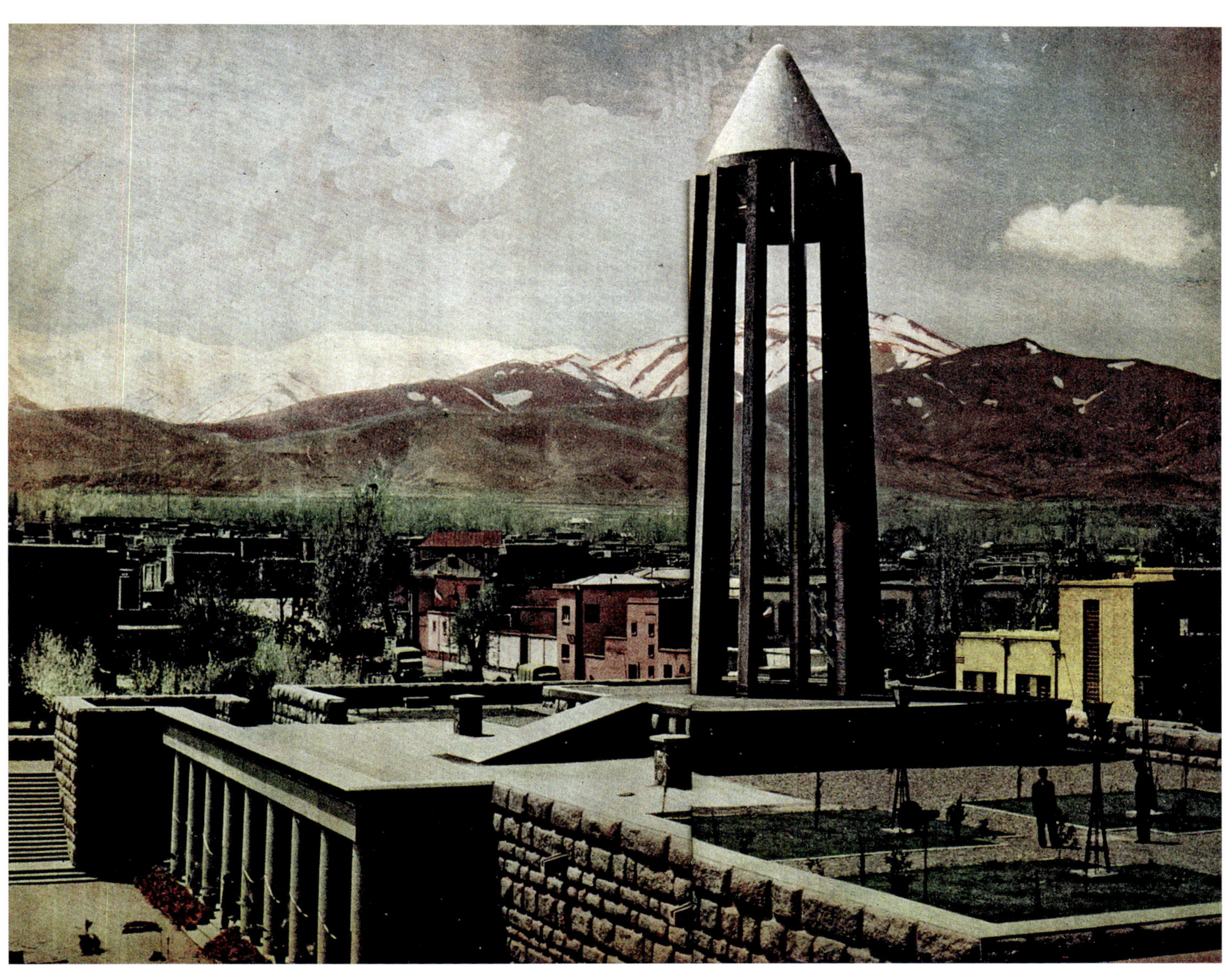

Houshang Seyhoun
Mausoleum of Avicenna,
Hamadan, Iran, 1954

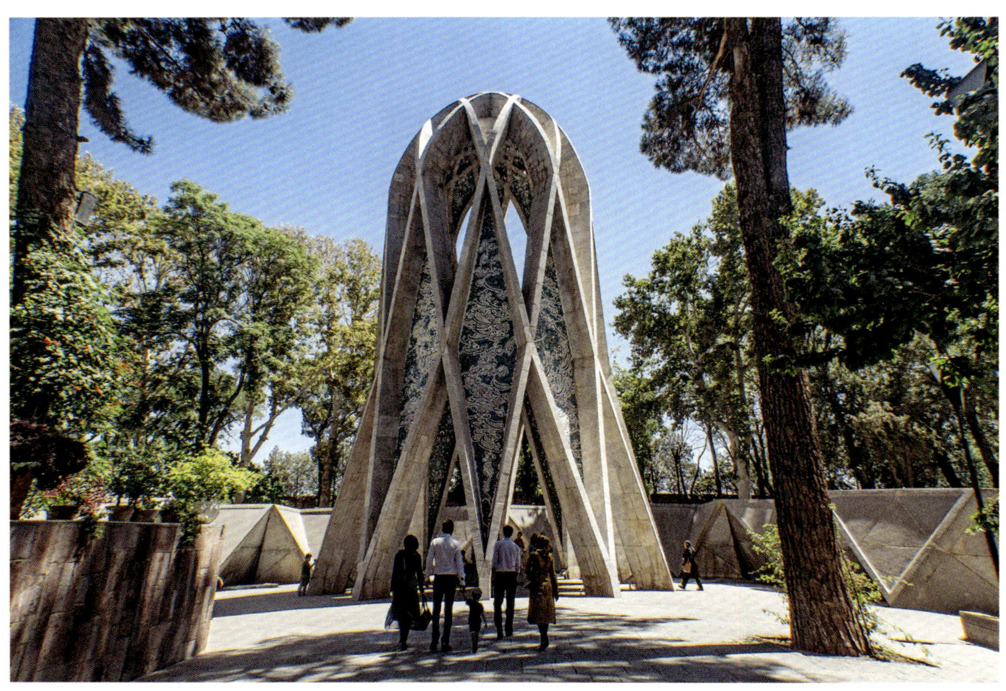

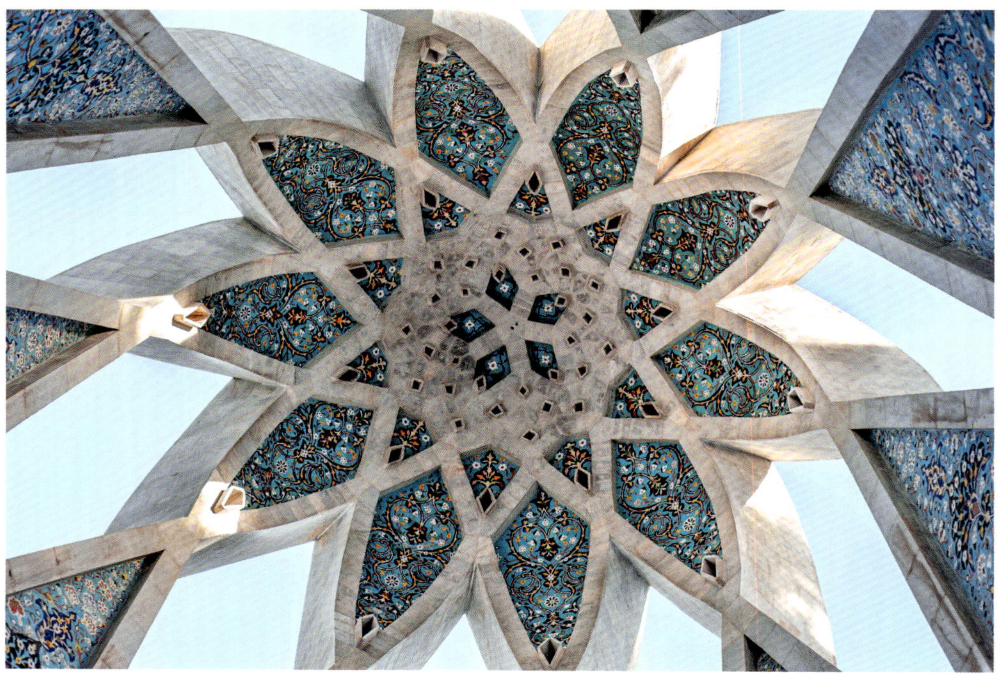

Houshang Seyhoun
Mausoleum of Omar
Khayyám, Nishapur,
Iran, 1963

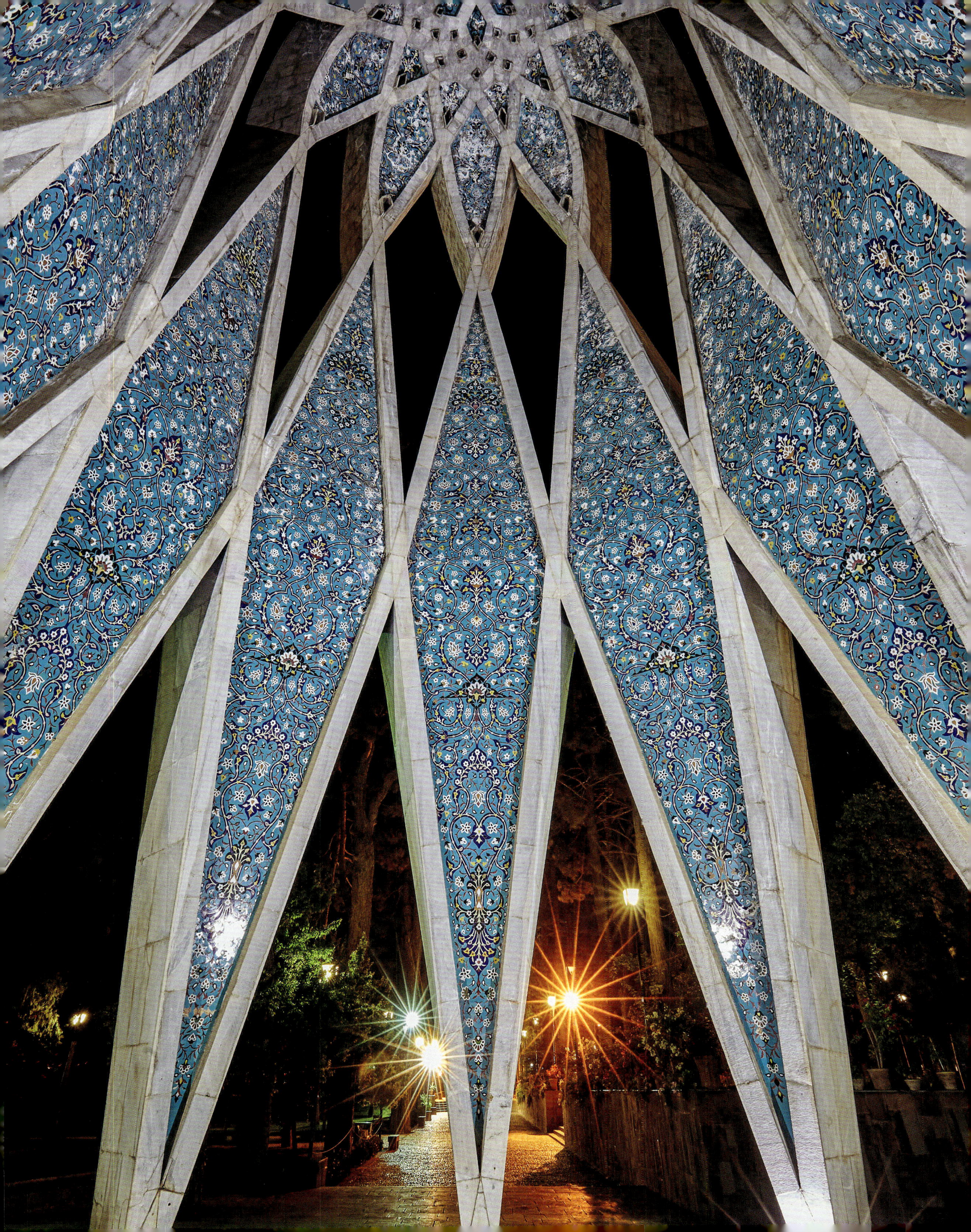

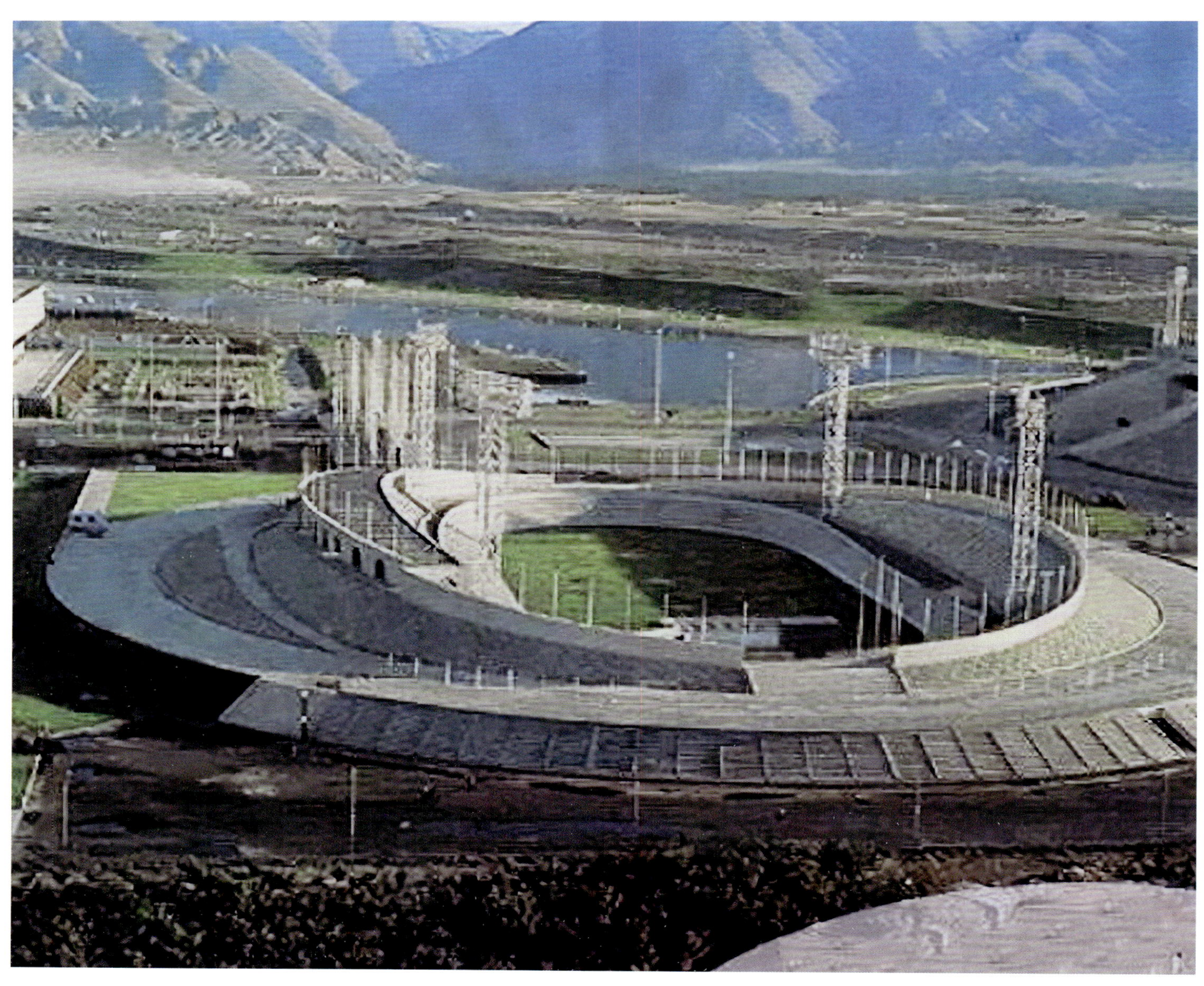

Abdol-Aziz Farmanfarmaian
Aryamehr Stadium (now Azadi Stadium), Tehran, 1971

SHAHYAD HAS MANY MORE STORIES TO TELL: HOSSEIN AMANAT IN CONVERSATION WITH DAVOOD MADADPOOR

Vancouver – Berlin, 2024

DAVOOD MADADPOOR The Shahyad Tower stands as a striking fusion of pre-Islamic and Islamic architecture, bridging Iran's ancient history and modern aspirations. Over time, it has transformed from a monument initially meant to commemorate 2,500 years of monarchy into a powerful symbol of the 1979 Revolution, the 2009 Iranian Green Movement, the Woman, Life, Freedom protests of 2022 and many more events in the collective memory of Iranian society. This duality—embodying the nation's pre-revolutionary identity and its post-revolutionary transformation—mirrors the ever-evolving nature of Iranian culture. In a country where the socio-political landscape shifts rapidly and dramatically, Shahyad has become an enduring icon. It stands alone yet resonates deeply with the history and spirit of the people.

As we talk, I am reflecting on the timelessness of the Shahyad Tower's design. It seems that you, too, Hossein, were aiming to create something that transcends time when you conceived it. Correct me if I'm wrong, but it feels like you built something for a society whose history is eternal—a history that doesn't fade with time. You created a monument for culture and community that could serve both as a marker for the 2,500-year celebration and as a lasting symbol for future revolutions and new eras.

HOSSEIN AMANAT Yes, do you know why? Because the Shahyad Tower is deeply rooted in the culture of Iran. It draws its essence from there. It's very Iranian. Once, a student who was writing his thesis on Shahyad at a university here asked me to attend his defence. His professors questioned what value he saw in the building that specifically belonged to Iran. He explained that Shahyad couldn't be placed in Cairo, because Cairo is Islamic, or in one of the Gulf countries, because it wouldn't fit. It is only for Iran.

In many ways, Shahyad is like a poem by Hafiz or Saadi Shirazi. Just as their verses are deeply embedded in Iranian culture, Shahyad is born from the same roots. Forough Farrokhzad, Sohrab Sepehri and H.E. Sayeh—all are modern poets who continue the legacy of Rumi, Saadi and Hafiz, but with a different lens. They understood that poetic essence, the one that touches the human spirit. If you apply this same understanding to architecture, you can create something like Shahyad.

That's why, if you look at the Shahyad project, you'll see that every corner is inspired by the architectural principles of ancient Iran—like the arch and the geometry you find in the old domes. These are true masterpieces of Iranian architecture. Today, even with computers, it's challenging to replicate the complexity of those designs, but we try. But back then, they achieved the same complexity with bricks. Imagine that. This is the richness of Iran's architectural heritage—it offers so much for an architect to learn, even today, and it still has more to offer.

Hossein Amanat in front of the Shahyad Tower (now Azadi Tower), Tehran, c. 1970s

DM Please walk me through!

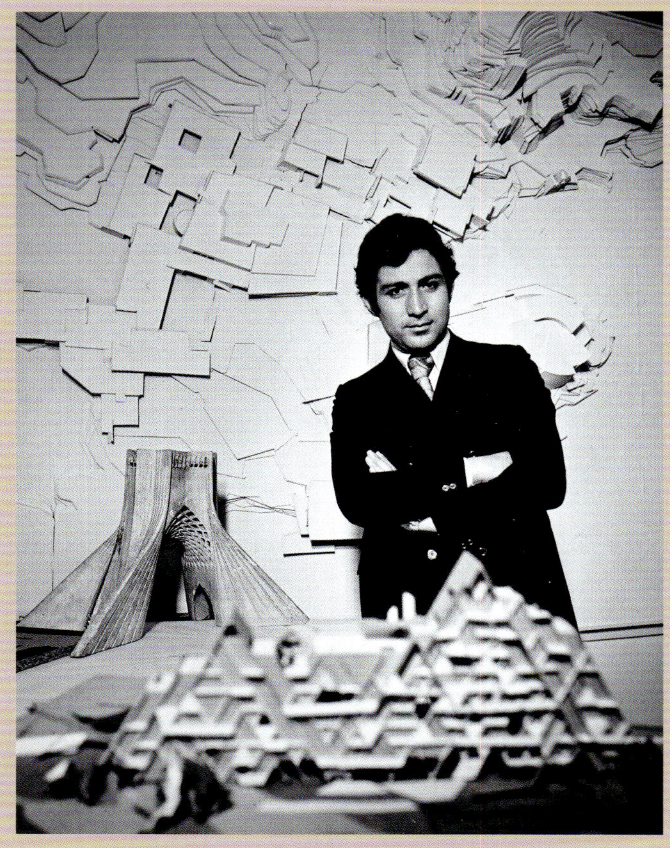

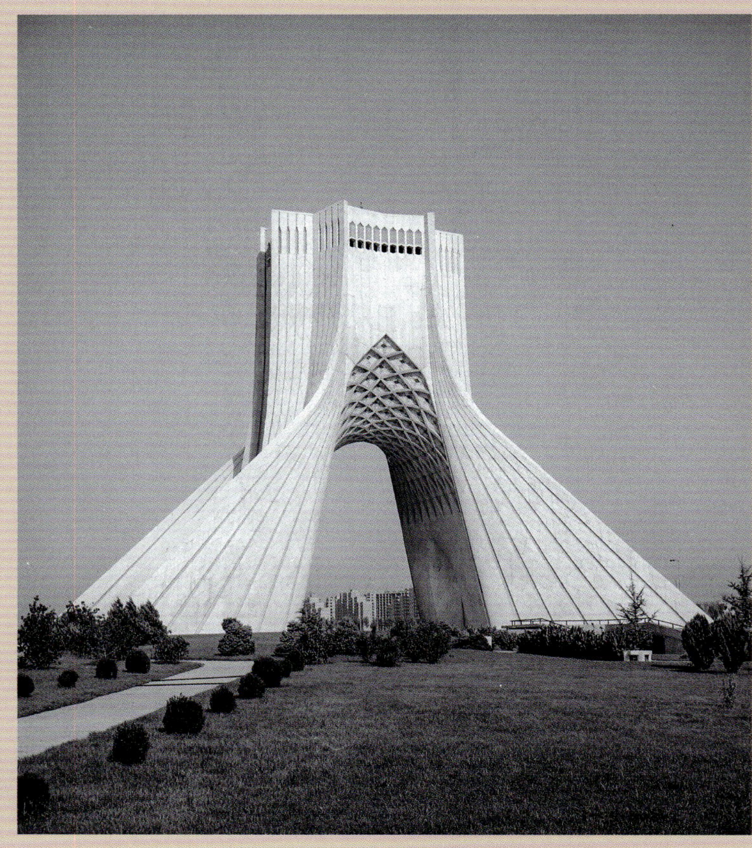

A Tapestry of Context
Back then, we believed—because it felt undeniably true—that everything of value came from the West. We all thought the future was happening in the West, and, naturally, I wanted to go abroad for my studies. But my father had a different idea. He insisted that I begin my education at home, and then when the time was right, I could go wherever I wanted.

So, I stayed.

I remember having a subscription to *L'Architecture d'Aujourd'hui* from France. We'd eagerly buy, see and read the books that arrived. But there was something special in our faculty library—a book by the art historian Arthur Upham Pope. *A Survey of Persian Art* was unlike anything else. Pope carefully documented Iranian architecture, drawing from the works that survived in Iran and the surrounding regions, which we call the Persianate. These places might have different names now, but they were once part of Persia or deeply influenced by its culture. At the faculty, our focus was on Western methodologies, particularly their advanced technology. But alongside that, my fascination with ancient Iranian architecture grew. I read Pope's book many times over—not every single word, no—but I was drawn to the parts that sparked my curiosity. The way those buildings looked, their design, their form—it all formed my imagination.

I proposed something bold for my diploma project—a tourist village by the Persian Gulf. And with that idea in mind, I decided to go south. This was when

Above, left
Hossein Amanat in front of a model of the Shahyad Tower (now Azadi Tower), 1972

Above, right
Shahyad Tower (now Azadi Tower), Tehran, n.d.

famine had gripped the southern regions, and there were no roads for the Red Crescent Society to deliver food to the remote villages. Those places were cut off from the world. My father, a trader involved in imports and customs, knew a man named Mr. Jahanmir, an officer at customs... My father introduced us. We travelled together to these isolated villages. We followed paths that had been carved out by smugglers because, otherwise, there was no way to reach these areas. What I saw there was unforgettable—breathtaking natural formations of stone, and places like Bandar Lengeh, which it felt like the world had forgotten. It had once been a thriving port known for producing pearls, but now it was like a surreal ghost town—empty but still holding traces of life.

As I worked on my diploma, I kept returning to a question that had been growing in my mind: What is it about certain spaces that draw me in so deeply that it makes me want to stop and just stay there, as if I'm hearing beautiful music? What makes these spaces so captivating? It was a question that gnawed at me as an architect. Why did some places make me want to linger, while others I passed through without a second thought? I began to believe that space—its volume, the light, the materials, the way it guides you from one place to another—profoundly impacts people. Together, these elements create a whole range of emotions within a space. In the end, my project was awarded top grades, and I became the top student. But, honestly, that wasn't what mattered to me. What truly mattered was that I had started down a path filled with questions—questions I knew I had to keep exploring.

An Announcement

A few months after I graduated, I saw an advertisement in the *Ettela'at* newspaper. I told my father that night: "There's an architecture competition." He asked: "Do you want to participate?" I said: "No." He asked: "Why not?" I replied: "Well, I have no connection to the system. I don't think I'll have any chance." But he said: "Look! You've already created such a large project for your diploma..." There were no printers at the time. We made the board, put Canson paper on it, and, as the French say, we "*dessin*-ed" on it and then rendered it. All the terminology was French because our faculty used that language. It's changed now, but the influence of the French education system still exists in Iranian architecture. Anyway, my father said: "Draw this one too; it won't be a problem for you. Just do it!" So, with two months left before the deadline, I started working on it. They wanted a building to commemorate 2,500 years of monarchy—a celebration of history. The design had to be forty-five metres tall, and no more, because it was near the airport.

I've always lived in a world of doubt, constantly questioning whether my work is good enough. It's part of the creative process for people like me. Not everyone is as obsessive. But for me, it's never easy to land on a concept, and it takes time. I spent the first month or two just piling up paper, layer after layer. I drew countless versions of the idea, but nothing felt right. Just a few days before the deadline, I thought, "You've wasted enough time. It's time to finalize it." A few friends helped me pull everything together. I still remember that night in my basement.

On the deadline day, I brought my design to the Council of Celebrations—the organization overseeing the project. They didn't even seem to remember there

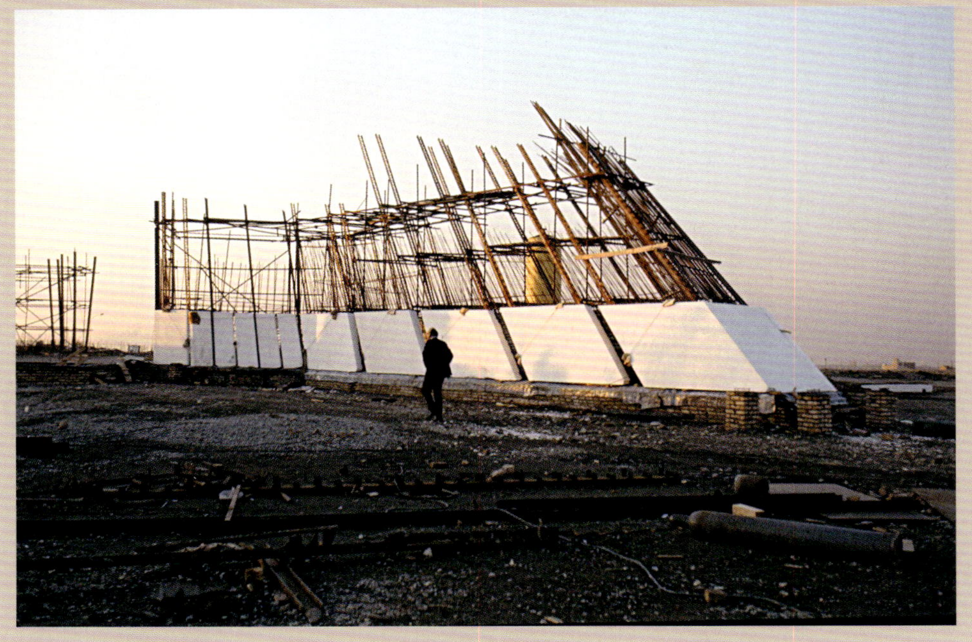

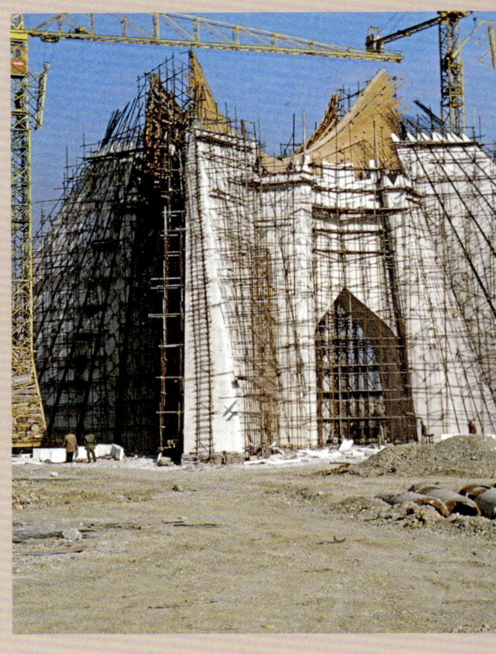

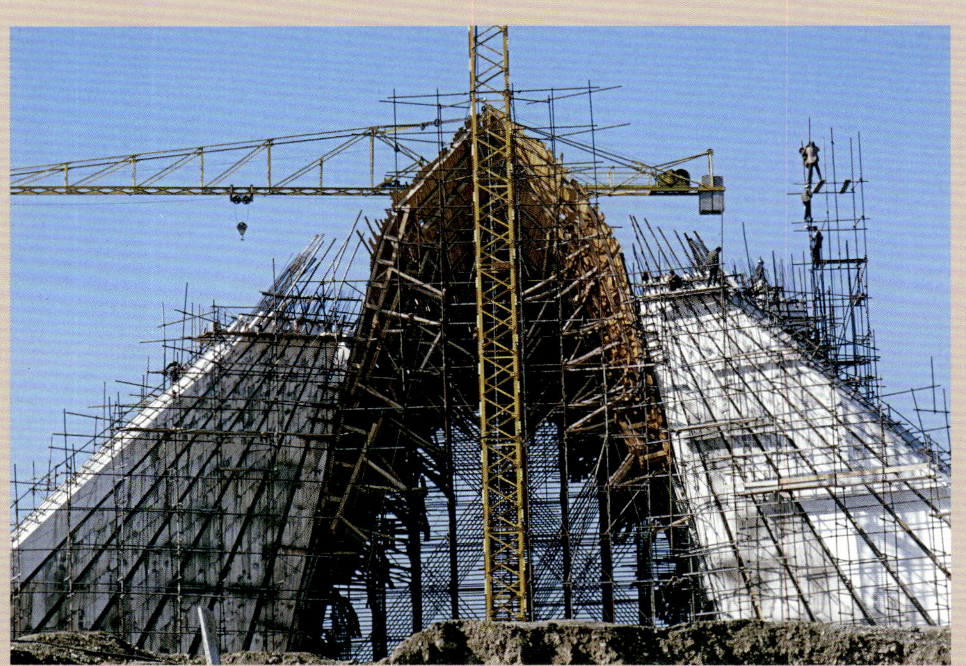

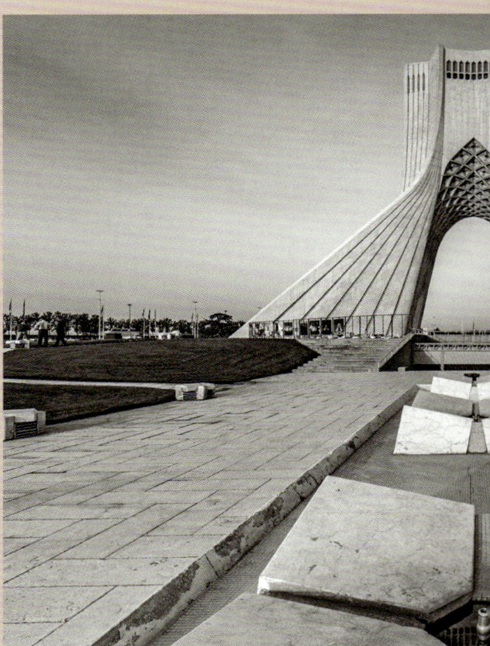

Shahyad Tower (now Azadi Tower) under construction, Tehran, c. 1970s

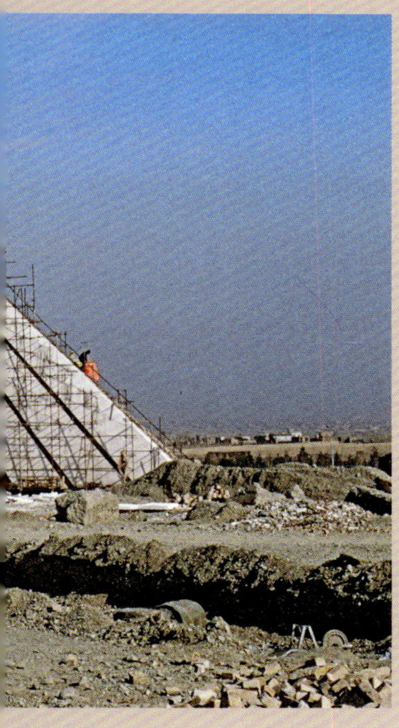

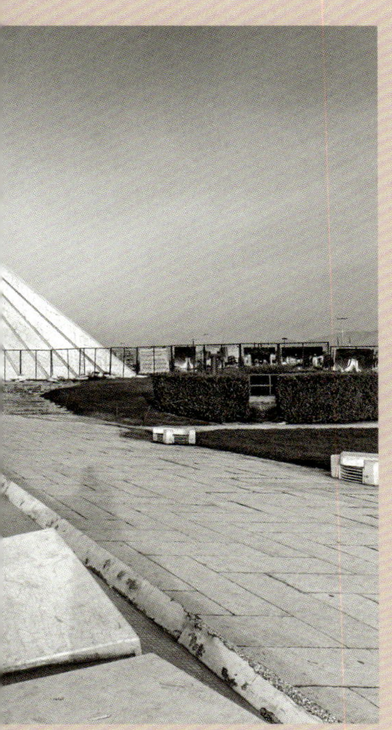

was a competition! I handed in my design at noon sharp. They looked at me and said, "Just put it in that corner." They weren't waiting for submissions, and I left without much hope. I didn't even ask for a receipt. I didn't dare. After weeks of waiting, I finally heard back. The jury said none of the designs were exactly what they wanted, but mine was the closest.

I kept waiting for them to contact me or at least call me. But there was no news. And I was very anxious because I was supposed to continue my studies at universities in America. I had been accepted, and everything was ready, but I didn't go. The reason they didn't contact me soon after, as I later learned, was that they suddenly decided to hold a coronation celebration before the 2,500th anniversary. All their attention shifted to that. I heard nothing until the celebration ended; they called me and said they wanted to sign a contract. When I signed the contract, two council members were present. As I signed, I told them: "Look, this isn't just an ordinary building for me. This project encompasses all my thoughts and love of Persian culture. It's essential to me." They nodded, but I don't know if they understood what it meant to me.

The question that has always stayed with me is: Why do those places I visit move me more than anything else? And because of that question, I found my way forward. I wondered if I could apply the principles that strongly moved me in my own work. Luckily, this project came along, and they asked me to design something that reflected the history and culture of Iran. They called it "Shahyad," but that didn't matter to me. I wanted to express the culture of Persia that I had always loved and admired. Since childhood, I have visited Persepolis and the mosques of Isfahan, and the beauty of that architecture has never left me. You know? That's what I wanted to capture.

Beneath the Scaffolding

They didn't realize what Shahyad would become at the time. They thought: This guy is building something here, or this is just an addition to the celebrations. No one could have imagined its grandeur and significance. When it first opened, people were excited. They lit it up at night, and it was there for all to see. But what is the true depth of its meaning? That came much later.

During that design time, I was in a dark place. I was submerged in doubt and depression, wondering if this project would ever lead to anything. I even had gloomy thoughts because I couldn't see the light at the end of the tunnel. That was my state fifty years ago, working on Shahyad. And now, when I look back, I understand. I realize that feeling of despair was part of the process. I've learned that I just need to wait until things come together. But back then, I didn't know that. I was just a student, uncertain of the future.

Now, fifty years have passed. The building's values have become clear to the people of Iran. They love it—not because it's tied to a specific place but because it resonates with Persian culture. It isn't just about a mosque or a single era; it speaks of ancient Persia, the Sasanian era and the time before and after Islam, all in a very abstract form. It's a modern reflection of the ancient culture of this country, a connection that transcends time. When the truth of something comes through in a building, that truth becomes eternal. The essence of Persian architecture has made Shahyad eternal. It doesn't grow old.

I will never forget the day I stood under that arch. A group of workers came to me and said, "Mr. Architect! The scaffolding has been taken down." Until that moment, the building had been wrapped in scaffolding. "It's down now," they said. "You can come see." I went up from the basement, climbing the stairs, and when we turned toward the arch, I saw it. I'm frozen. I've got goosebumps. I had imagined every detail of that tower a thousand times, but standing there, seeing it in reality for the first time, was something else entirely. It was the same feeling I had the first time I went to Persepolis. The awe, the weight of history and the artisans—it all hit me at once.

I remember that day so clearly.

Silent Tales
The stone used in this building is truly remarkable. Its thickness is twenty-five centimetres—unique. That's why, after all this time, even after all the abuse and mistreatment, it still stands strong. It comes from an era we're talking about—when craftsmanship was at its peak. The turquoise-coloured tiles are just as remarkable. Looking closely, you'll see an abstract quality in their forms. They reference traditional Iranian motifs but in a modern, subtle way.

Where did this stone come from? A man came to me, Ghafar Davarpanah. He said, "Ghanbar Rahimi has stone—let's see if it's what you need." For an architect, the first concern is the stone's colour, appearance and the strength of its veins. Ghafar told me, "Let's go to the mine together." So, we drove his BMW to see it. Ghafar was an interesting character—he was both a skilled stonemason and very well educated and cultured. We arrived at the mine, which belonged to Ghanbar Rahimi, a man who had taken advantage of the economic opportunities in Iran at the time. The security of that period allowed someone like him to discover and extract from a mine.

When I asked Ghanbar how much stone he could supply, he said, "Just get the permits, and I'll deliver as much as you need." I didn't know what kind of permission was required at the time, so I asked. Once we got that sorted, Ghanbar brought the stone to the Shahyad site, and we set up the workshop right there.

Nowadays, if you wanted to build something like the Shahyad Tower in Dubai, you'd need to bring stone carvers from Italy. Why? Because all those stones, each with its unique shape, required the skills of true artisans. In Iran, we had our sculptural tradition. The Iranian craftsmen understood how to carve those stones and bring the design to life. This was a testament to the artisan culture in Iran. It's all embodied in Shahyad. Every part of Shahyad reflects the advancements of Iran during that period. I told you about the stone, but the same can be said for the concrete work and the overall construction. Shahyad has many stories to tell.

At the time, I was reading the poetry of Sayeh. His poetry references the past, but what makes it beautiful is how he builds something new on top of that history. Sayeh's talent makes something timeless, just like the great poet Hafiz. His works resonate because he draws on lasting traditions while creating something unprecedented. We shouldn't just look at architecture alone. Look at Sayeh's poetry—how much of the past is in it, yet it's undeniably something new. That's why it endures. And that's what I aimed to do with Shahyad: to create something that feels both timeless and modern and draws on Iran's rich history but speaks to the present and future.

* * *

When you walk through the Isfahan bazaar, there's an underlying rhythm created by the arches. You don't even realize it—you're just walking. Sometimes, a shaft of light cuts through from above, illuminating a spot below, *ding!*—but all around you, life is buzzing. Then you arrive at the entrance of a *caravanserai*, a new stage in this journey. You pass through a narrow vestibule that suddenly opens into a small courtyard. The rhythmic melody you've unconsciously created in your mind carries on, reflected in the arches around the courtyard.

When you leave and step back into the bazaar, the rhythm continues, driven by that geometric order of the space. It's structured, but also free—it tilts here, straightens there, guiding you to where two bazaars intersect under a grand dome. From there, you walk further, passing through another entrance until, finally, you reach Shah Square in Isfahan. And it's like a spatial explosion—just like the powerful notes of Beethoven's symphony. "Ba ba ba bam!!!" It hits you—first in your head, then in your heart.

Shah Square has its own rhythm of notes, too. Surrounding you are arches that create a sense of order, and within that order are the larger, more pronounced notes. There's Ali Qapu Palace. There's the Shah Mosque. Then you see Sheikh Lotfollah Mosque. Each of these monuments is like another instrument added to the composition.

When you step inside Sheikh Lotfallah, there's a corridor that winds and turns, leaving you uncertain of where you're headed. And then, suddenly, you turn the corner, and there it is—the dome, like an explosion of beauty. That moment is breathtaking.

This is what great architecture does—it creates a symphony. Every step you take, every turn you make, builds that melody in your mind. And for me, good architecture is the kind that recreates this experience, this harmony, guiding you through space like a well-orchestrated piece of music.

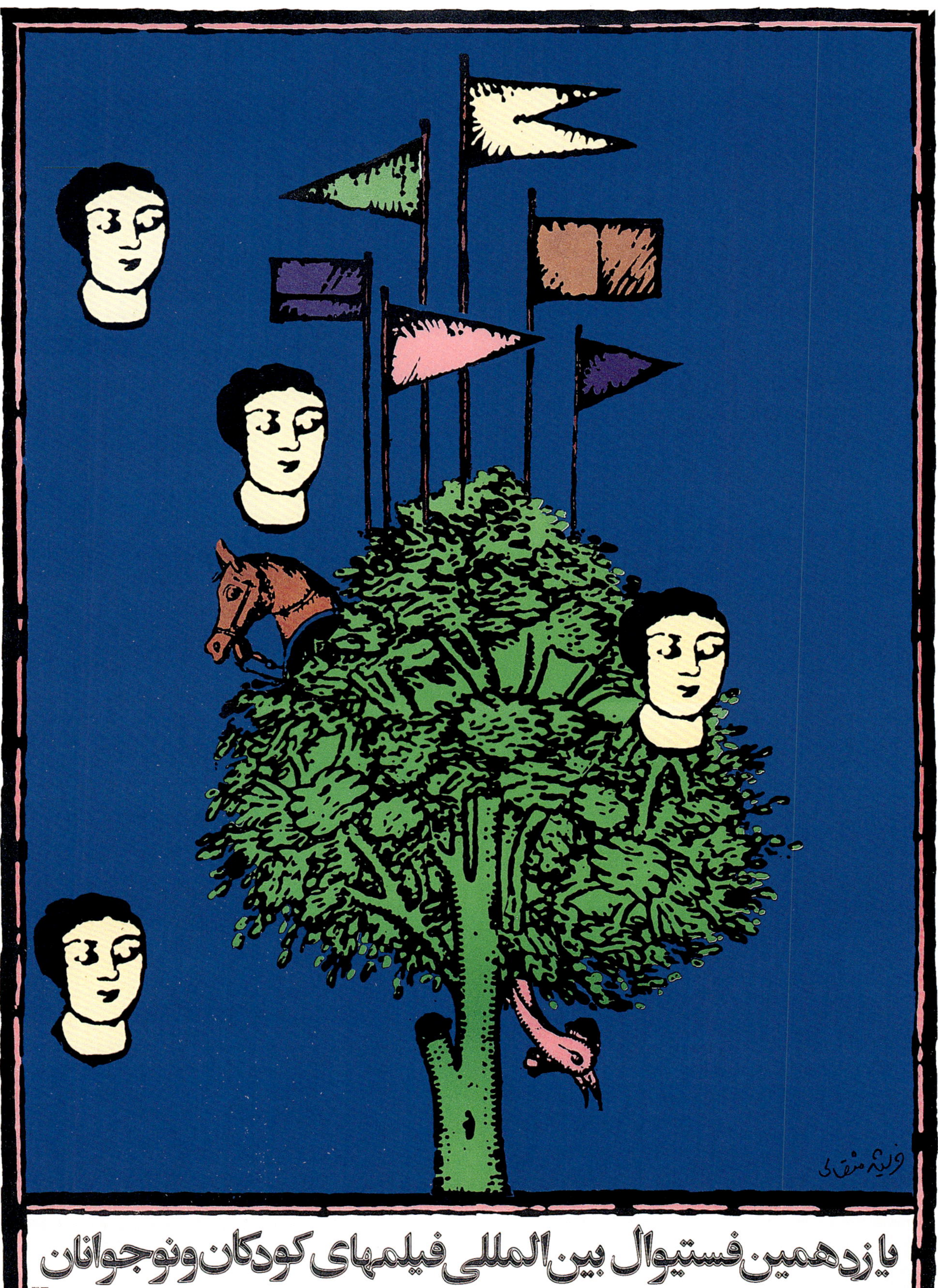
یازدهمین فستیوال بین المللی فیلمهای کودکان ونوجوانان
11TH TEHRAN INTERNATIONAL FESTIVAL OF FILMS FOR CHILDREN AND YOUNG ADULTS
31 Oct_7 Nov, 1976
۹ تا ۱۶ آبان ۲۵۳۵

VISUAL MODERNIZATION IN IRAN

Ali Bakhtiari

Finding the roots of visual modernism in Iran is complex, but several fundamental factors contributed to this transformation. Two objective factors were the introduction of the printing industry, which led to the development of graphic design, and the introduction of photography. But one of the most essential factors of this transformation was the mandatory issuance of birth certificates, which meant that every Iranian became an illustrated character.

In the 1940s, after the occupation of Iran during World War II, visual products did not have much of a market, but a change in Iranians' lifestyle, including new visual standards, can be traced in the surviving studio and amateur photographs from that era. Family photos, featuring contemporary attire, Pahlavi hats, women with trendy hairstyles, men sporting moustaches and the prominent presence of children, depicted the meaning of the modern family in a visual form.

The introduction of the printing industry meant that many visual manifestations were no longer limited to elite, one-of-a-kind pieces. Painting and calligraphy became accessible to the public, and images were no longer restricted to royal albums and books. More importantly, typography gave a new form to writing and script. Although magazines and newspapers had begun to expand during the Qajar era (1794–1925), the structural modernization of Iran's visual culture should be examined from the post–World War II era onward.

Farshid Mesghali
Poster for 11th Tehran International Festival of Films for Children and Young Adults, 1976

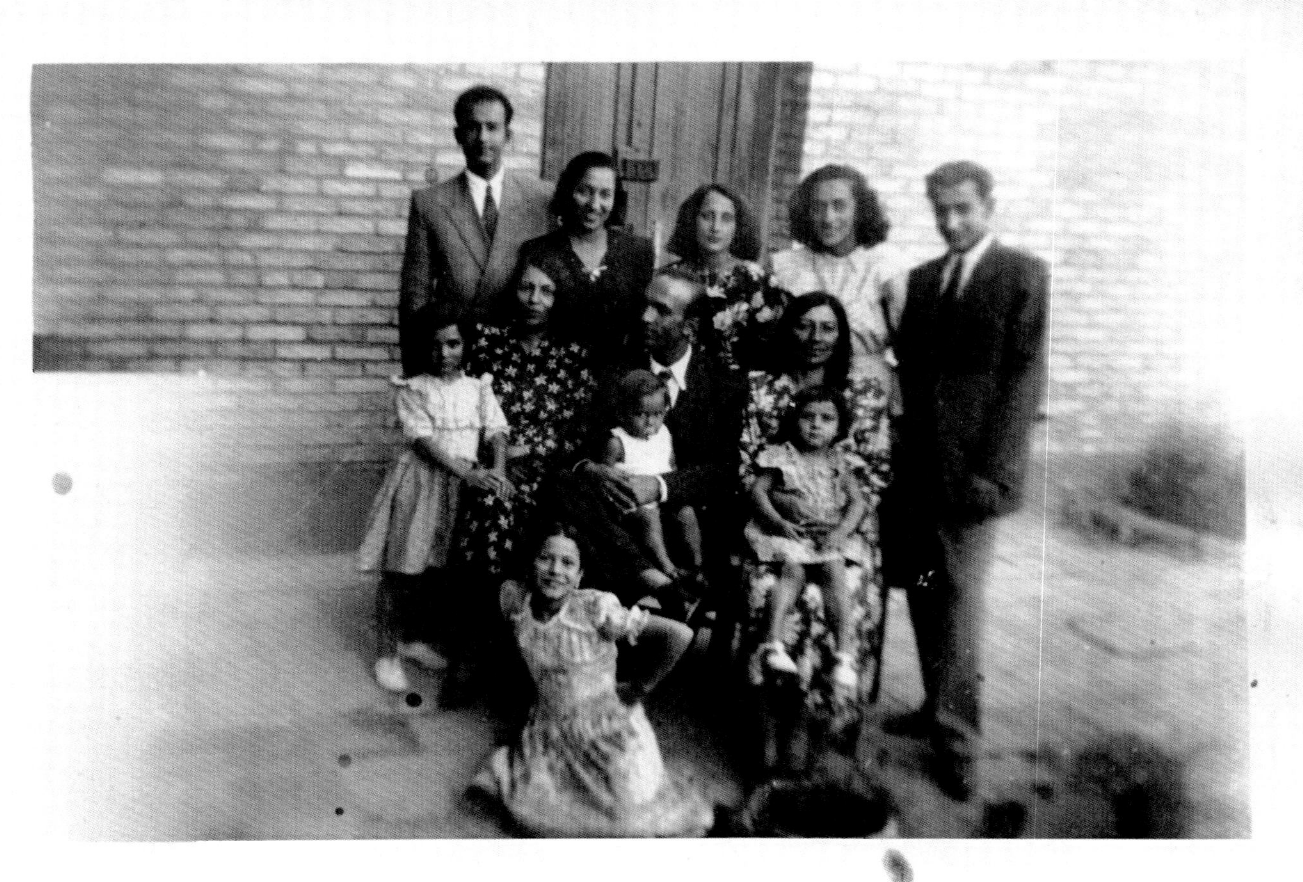

Above
Iranian family, Tehran, 1948

Opposite
Iranian family, Tehran, 1948

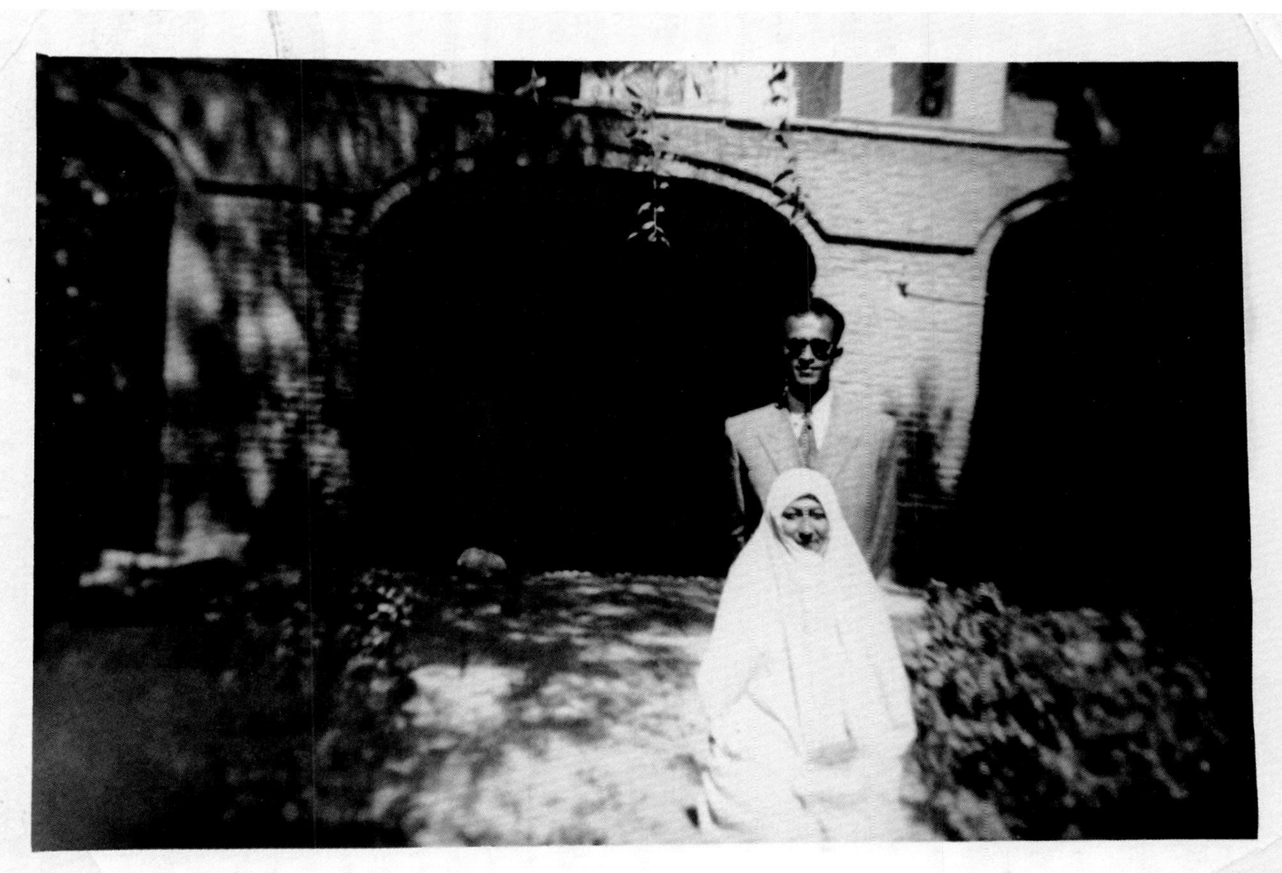

A significant part of the sociopolitical structure of the first half of the twentieth century was built on the historical revival of ancient Iranian culture. We can see this trend in everything from the publication of *Ancient Iran* by former prime minister Hassan Pirnia in 1927, to the celebration of revered poet Abolqasem Ferdowsi's one thousandth birthday in 1934 and opening of the National Museum of Iran in 1937, to the display of Iranian artifacts at the Cernuschi Museum in Paris in 1948, to the emphasis on Iranian arts and traditions at the Shiraz Arts Festival and Tous Festival through the 1960s and 1970s.

The first visual representations of this spirit emerged in the mid-1950s in the works of Mohsen Vaziri-Moghaddam, Marcos Grigorian and Houshang Pezeshknia, and then more strongly in the 1960s in the practices of the Saqqakhaneh movement. Each of the Saqqakhaneh artists focused on a part of Iran's visual history, attempting to recreate and redefine it using motifs, patterns and an understanding of Western art. However, in the 1960s and 1970s, there were also non-Saqqakhaneh efforts that focused on history that was less ancient, particularly Qajar art. This trend manifested in exhibitions of *eidi-sazi* (woodblock prints) and the illustrations of the religious epic *Hamleh Heidari* at Ghandriz Hall in Tehran; the work of Ali Asghar Masoumi in a dialogue with Qajar painting; the paintings of Ghasem Hajizadeh based on Qajar photographs; and the sketches of Ardeshir Mohassess, especially his *Stormy Weather* and *Kafernameh* series, which directly reference the narrative and epic illustrations of lithographic books.

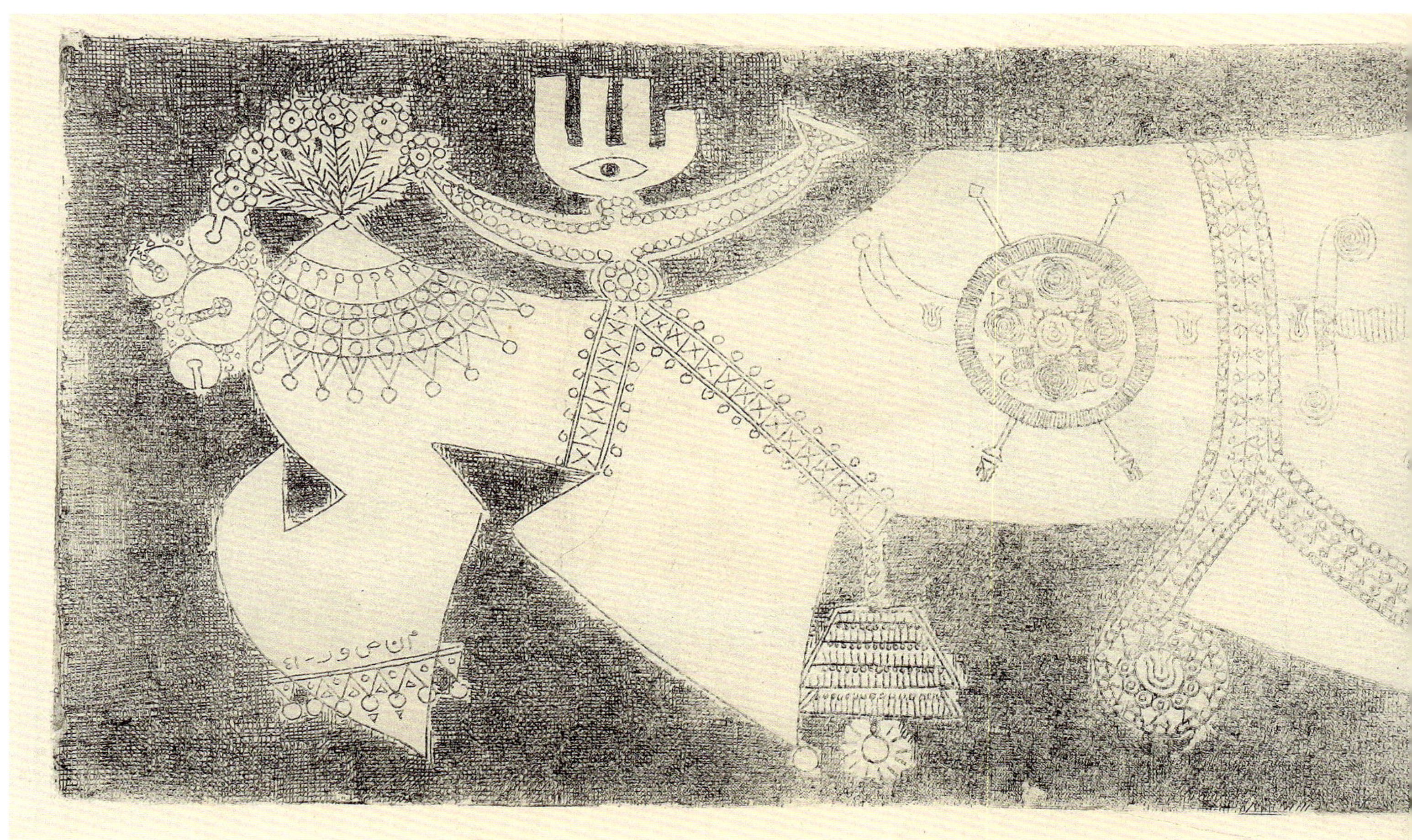

The establishment of the Faculty of Fine Arts at the University of Tehran, the School of Fine Arts for Boys and Girls,[1] and later the university's Faculty of Decorative Arts[2] was among the most important factors in the expansion and transformation of Iran's visual-artistic culture. The University of Tehran was founded in June 1934, through the efforts of the acting minister of education, Ali-Asghar Hekmat. In October 1940, the Faculty of Fine Arts was opened as an art school at the suggestion of Ismail Merat, the minister of culture, who invited architect Mohsen Foroughi and archaeologist and architect André Godard to run it. Then, in 1945, the design and construction of the faculty's workshops were overseen by Godard. By 1967, the central building, amphitheatre, sculpture hall, exhibition hall, library and buildings for visual arts and music were completed.

The curricula for the architecture, painting and sculpture programs, despite various disagreements, were based on those of the École des Beaux-Arts in Paris. The graphic designer Morteza Momayez writes: "The impact of the establishment of the Faculty of Fine Arts was such that it has even influenced the educational direction of other art schools in the country, drawing them toward its methods and casting a direct and indirect shadow over their activities."[3]

The activities at the Faculty of Fine Arts up to the 1979 Revolution can be divided into three phases: the first, from the faculty's founding until the end

Above
Mansour Ghandriz
Untitled, 1962
etching on paper

Opposite, top
Parviz Tanavoli
Lovers, 1962
metal relief on paper

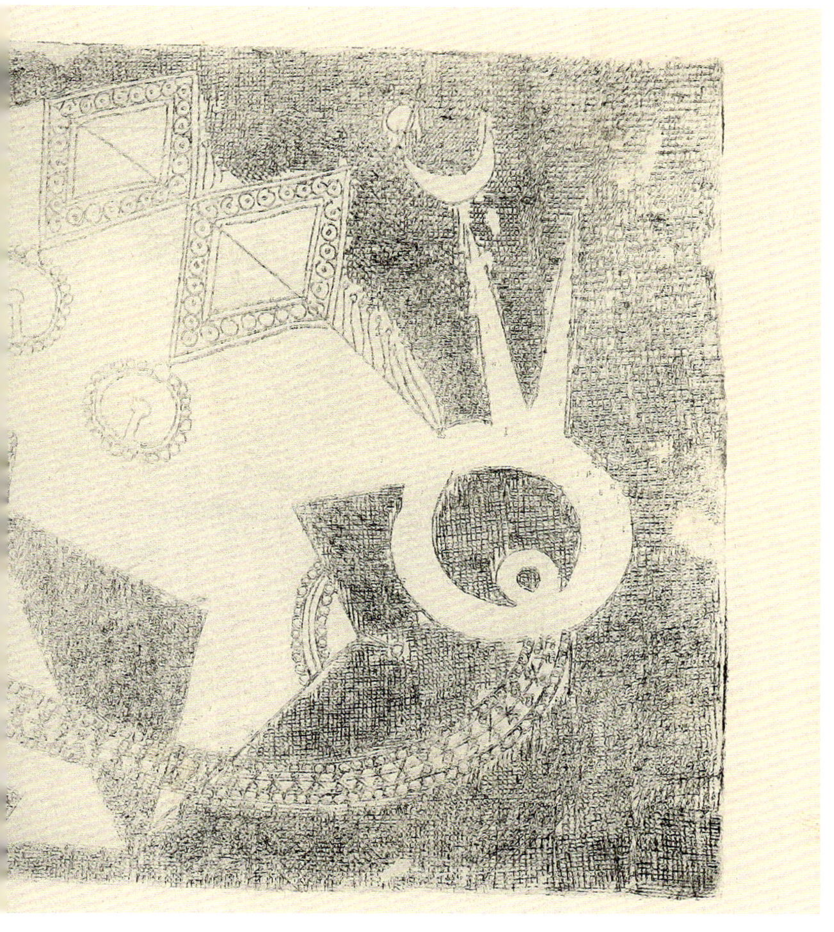

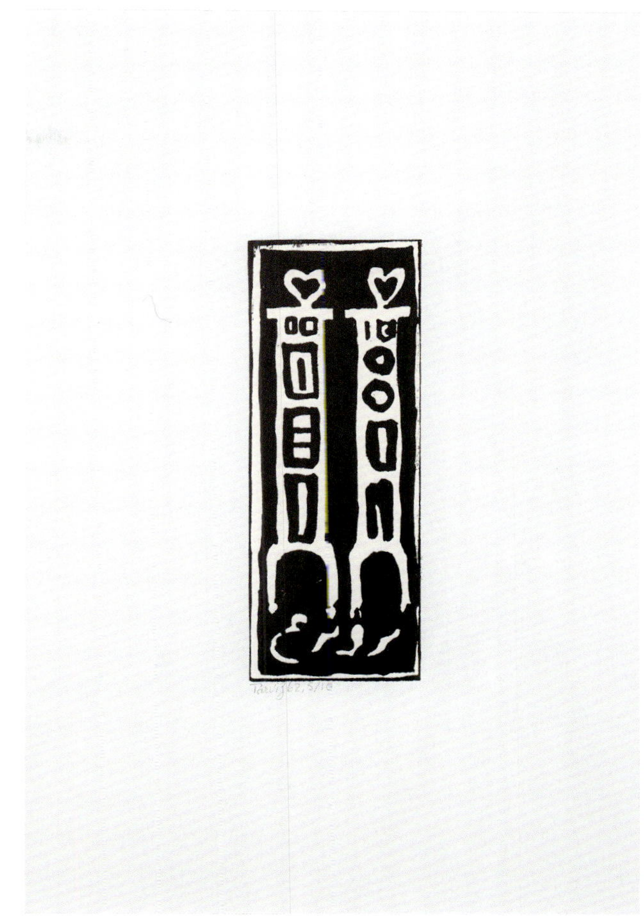

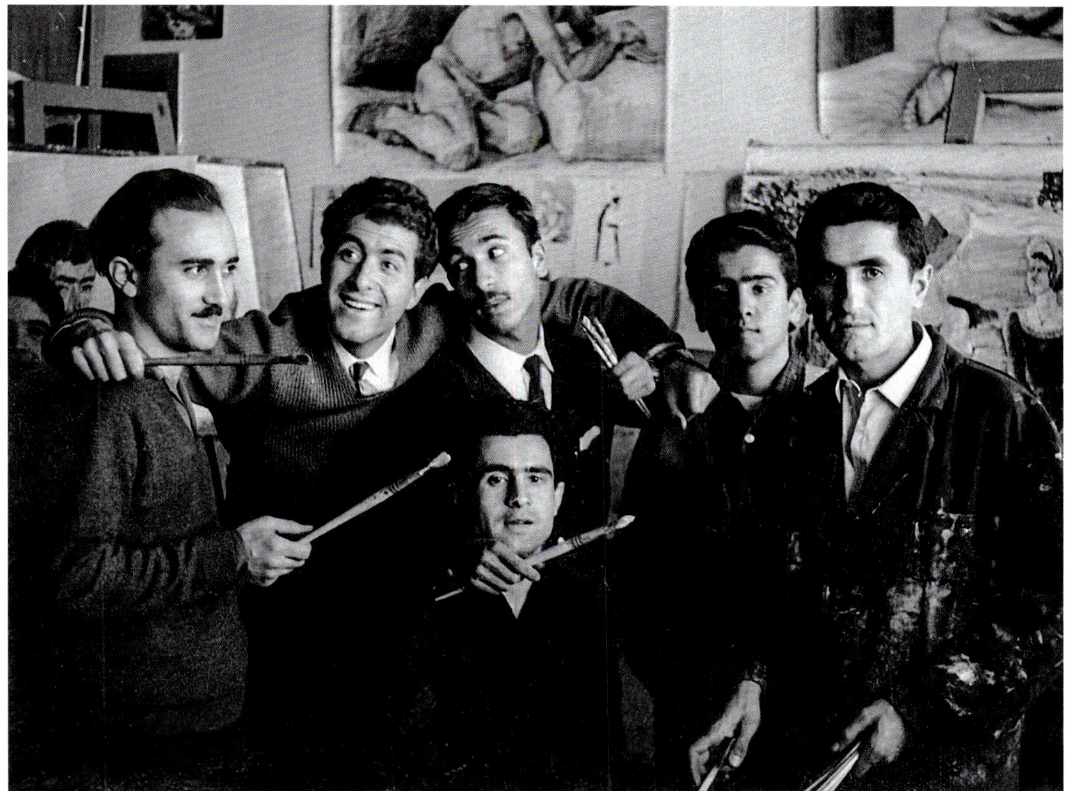

Right
Sirouss Assadollahzadeh, Ghobad Shiva, Mohammad Ebrahim Jafari, Gholam-Hossein Nami, Arapik Baghdasarian and Asghar Mohammadi, Faculty of Fine Arts, University of Tehran, 1962

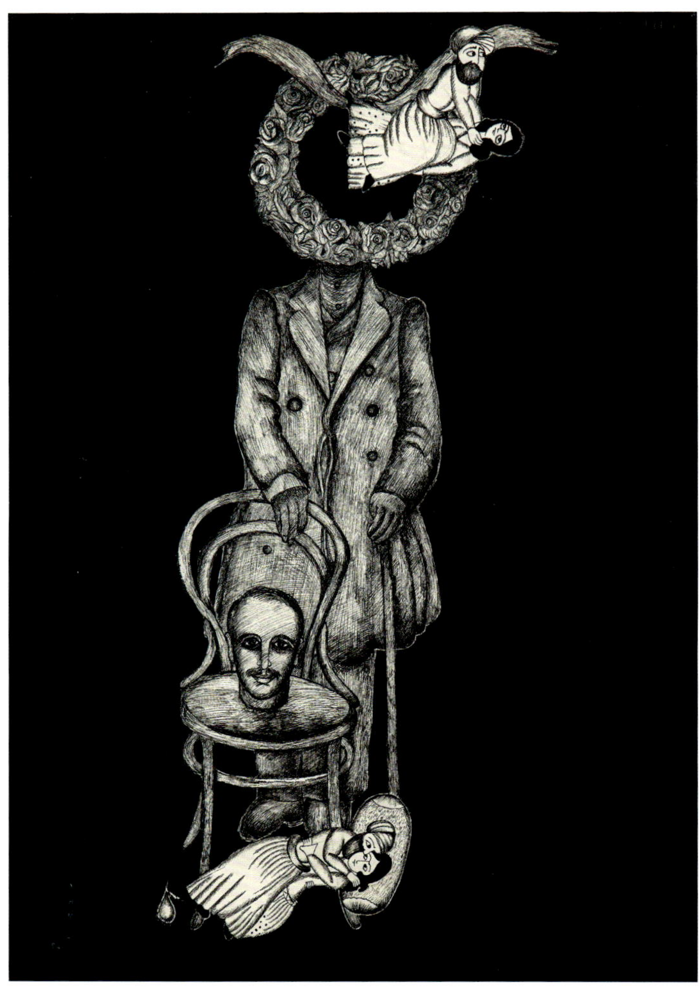

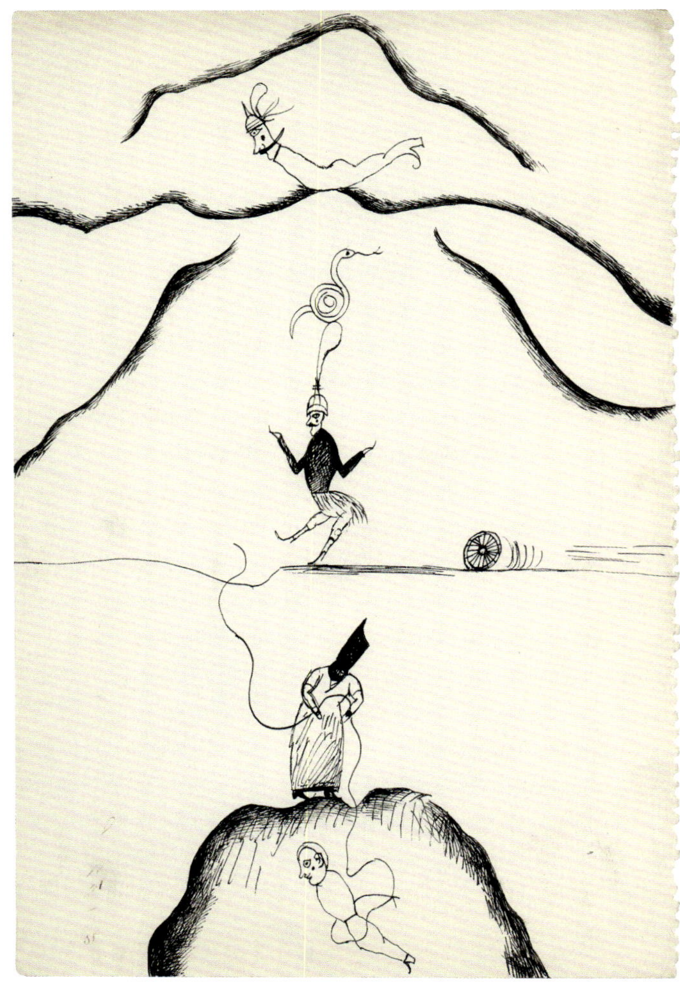

of Mohsen Foroughi's tenure as president of the school; the second, during Houshang Seyhoun's presidency, from 1962 to his resignation in 1968; and the third, coinciding with the presidency of Fazlollah Reza until the beginning of the Islamic Revolution in 1978–79. The faculty's painting workshop (which operated alongside three architecture workshops and one sculpture workshop) was run by Ali Mohammad Heydarian under Foroughi's presidency, assisted by Mahmoud Javadipour, Javad Hamidi and a French artist named Martine Amin-Ashoub. During Seyhoun's presidency, the painting workshops were divided into three groups under Hamidi, Javadipour and Behjat Sadr.

The general definition of graphic design in the 1950s and the first half of the 1960s was based on painting and illustration, to the extent that design and graphic work were known as "advertising painting." At this time, advertising agencies found their place in the business world, and institutions like Ziba Advertisement Agency, Fakopa Organization and Avazeh Advertising Organization were reputable centres for commercial advertising, while Bahrami Studio handled cultural commissions.

The launch of the Franklin Book Programs in Iran was another factor in the expansion and transformation of the country's visual culture. The Tehran branch

Left
Ardeshir Mohassess
Untitled, 1972–73
ink on paper

Right
Ardeshir Mohassess
Untitled, 1975
ink on paper

of the Franklin Publishing Institute, representing the United States' Franklin Book Programs, was established in 1953 by the writer and translator Homayoun San'atizadeh, and it began its activities in 1954. In 1957, San'atizadeh founded the Offset Printing Company to print textbooks, and later the Pars Paper Mill in 1967. The Pocket Books Publishing Organization launched in 1961 with the idea of reducing production costs and increasing print runs in pocket-book sizes. Franklin Publishing, through these initiatives, published about 1,500 original and translated books in fields such as science, technology, art and literature during its lifetime. Other activities included collaborating with the Ministry of Education to print textbooks and publish educational magazines like *Peyk*. During the history of Franklin Publishing, numerous illustrators and graphic designers worked with its Franklin Graphic Studio arm, under the direction of Hormoz Vahid. From 1965, Ali Asghar Mohajer took over the management of Franklin Publishing until its closure after the 1979 Revolution. The shares of Pocket Books Publishing were sold to Amir Kabir Publishing, and then the institution was dissolved following the Revolution. The collection of images that Iranian designers created for Franklin Publishing played a highly influential role in shaping the visual education of Iran's literate society due to their widespread distribution.

Cultural Policies and Visual Developments in Iran, 1960s–1970s
In the 1960s, culture became one of the most significant global discourses. In December 1967, the United Nations Educational, Scientific and Cultural Organization held a roundtable of experts from twenty-four countries in Monaco to address issues related to cultural policy worldwide. The preamble to the final document stated that in a civilization dominated by technology, cultural action plays an increasingly important role, complementing educational efforts and scientific endeavours. Cultural action ensures that development serves the mind.[4]

In Iran during the 1960s, the concept of culture was redefined on a broader, national scale. According to writer and translator Changiz Pahlevan, "Before the Fourth Development Plan, there was no separate chapter titled 'Culture and Art' in the first three plans. At that time, artistic activities were categorized under educational programs and collectively referred to as 'culture,' which mainly addressed educational and curriculum planning issues."[5]

Under the Third Development Plan, the first cultural reforms in Iran took place, and in 1964, the Ministry of Culture was divided into the Ministry of Culture and Arts and the Ministry of Education. With the implementation of the Fourth Development Plan in 1968, the modern and universal concept of "culture" became more widespread in society. Chapter sixteen of this plan was dedicated to culture and the arts, with a budget of 1.8 billion rials allocated. The general objectives were outlined as follows:

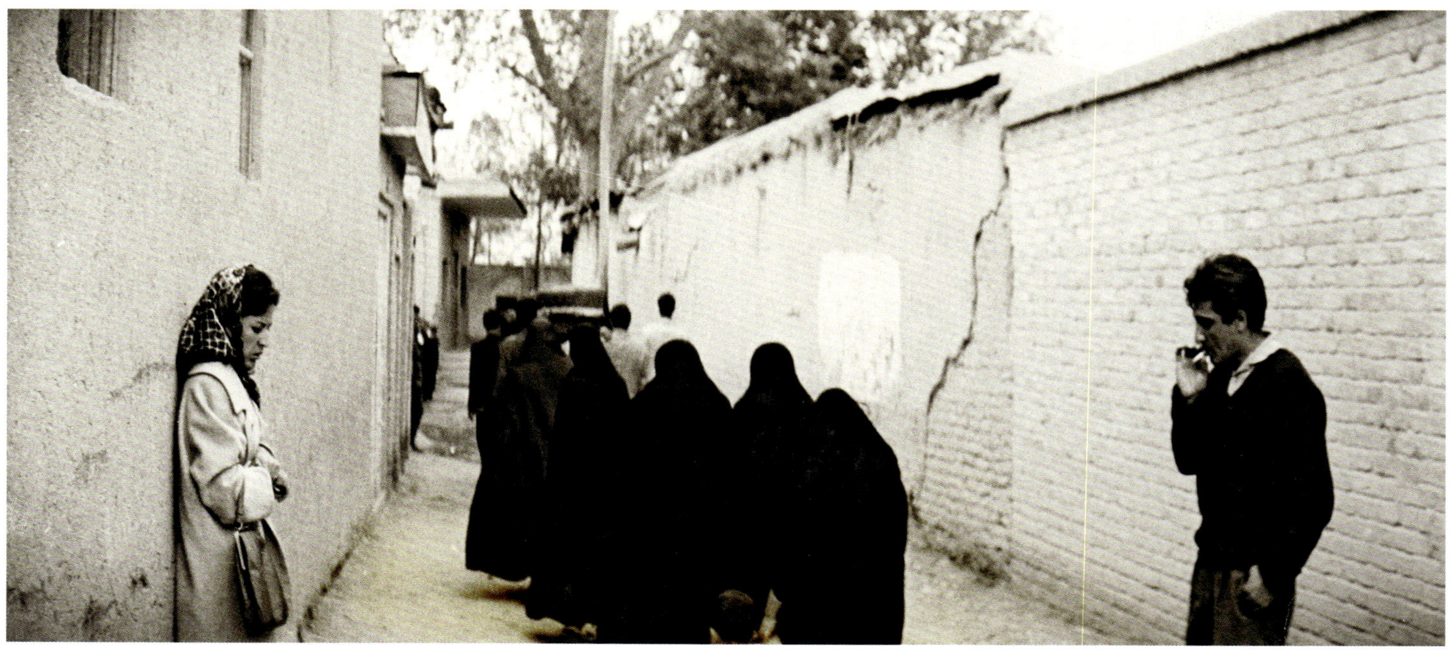

a) The advancement and promotion of the arts
b) Raising the level of public culture, especially through the effective use of audiovisual media
c) The publication and dissemination of the results of cultural and artistic research
d) Strengthening the foundations of ethnic unity and raising awareness of national culture, as well as enhancing artistic taste and understanding
e) Training artists and experts in various fields of art
f) Providing opportunities for innovation and creativity in art and literature, based on national traditions
g) Preserving national heritage, historical monuments and relics, and introducing them to the public and foreign tourists
h) Increasing the number of art students, teachers, instructors, professors and other staff in art schools and workshops from 625 to about 2,000, and increasing the number of art students from 845 to about 1,350 to meet the expected needs, with special attention to training theatre and cinema artists

Pahlevan goes on to explain: "In the Fourth Development Plan, which began in 1968, culture was considered in terms of its impact on 'strengthening the foundations of national unity.' The goal was to ensure that Iran's cultural and civilizational heritage was well recognized and efforts were made to enrich this vast national heritage."[6] In 1969, the Supreme Council of Culture and Art drafted a document titled "The Cultural Policy of the Country," consisting of seven chapters and thirty-six articles, one of which was devoted to "Culture for All."

The sociopolitical structure of Iran in the 1960s not only emphasized and supported national arts with Iranian and historical roots—showcasing them

Above
Ebrahim Golestan (director)
Brick and Mirror, 1965 (production still)

Opposite
Pasargad Advertising Company
Poster for *Night of the Hunchback*, 1965

on the global stage, such as through the Saqqakhaneh artists' works—but also needed to present Iran as a pioneering and progressive country. This dual focus emerged in the promotion of Iranian culture to the world and awareness of other global cultures, a discourse that became particularly prominent in the late 1960s and into the 1970s. The Shiraz Arts Festival[7] was perhaps the most important manifestation of Iran's redefined avant-garde status, and both focuses were reflected in the contrasting approaches of the Ministry of Culture's Theatre Department, Sangelaj Hall and the National Art Group on the one hand, and the Theatre Workshop on the other.[8]

In the early 1960s, filmmakers Ebrahim Golestan and Farrokh Ghaffari ignited a revolution in Iranian cinema by embracing modern techniques and narrative styles that redefined the moving image in Iran. Through their experimental approaches and focus on realism, they challenged traditional forms, bridging Iranian cinema and global cinematic trends. Their pioneering work laid the groundwork for a new wave of Iranian filmmakers, shaping an aesthetic that would influence generations to come.

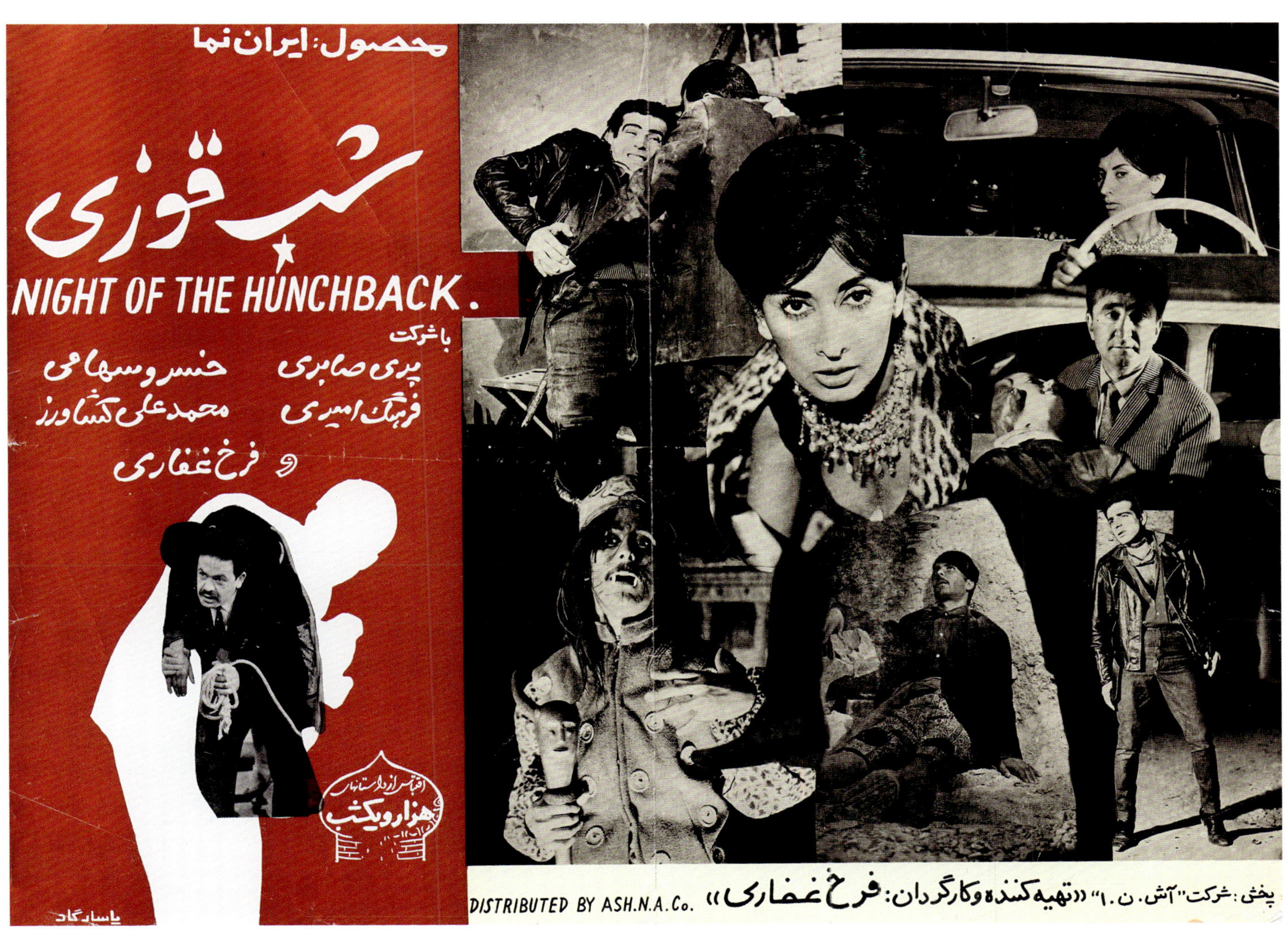

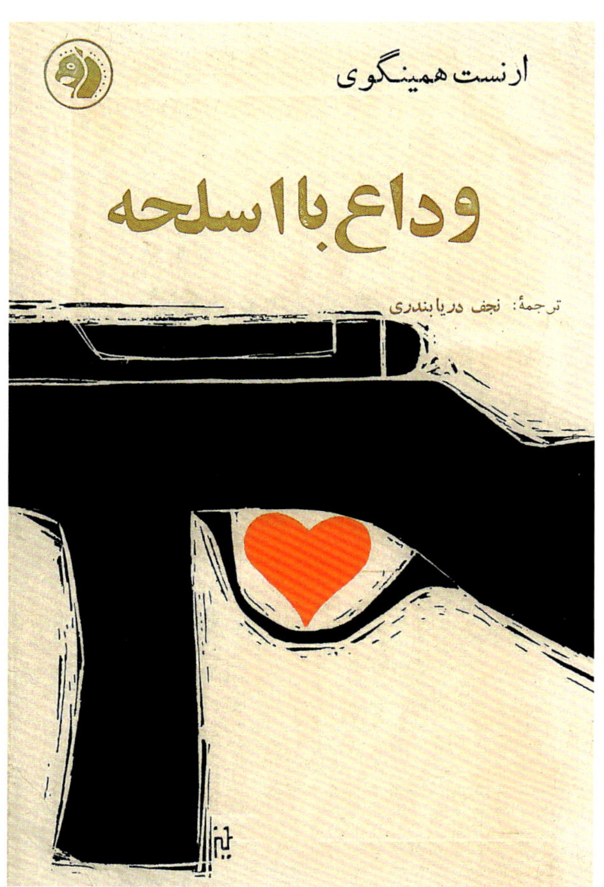
ارنست همینگوی
وداع با اسلحه
ترجمهٔ: نجف دریابندری

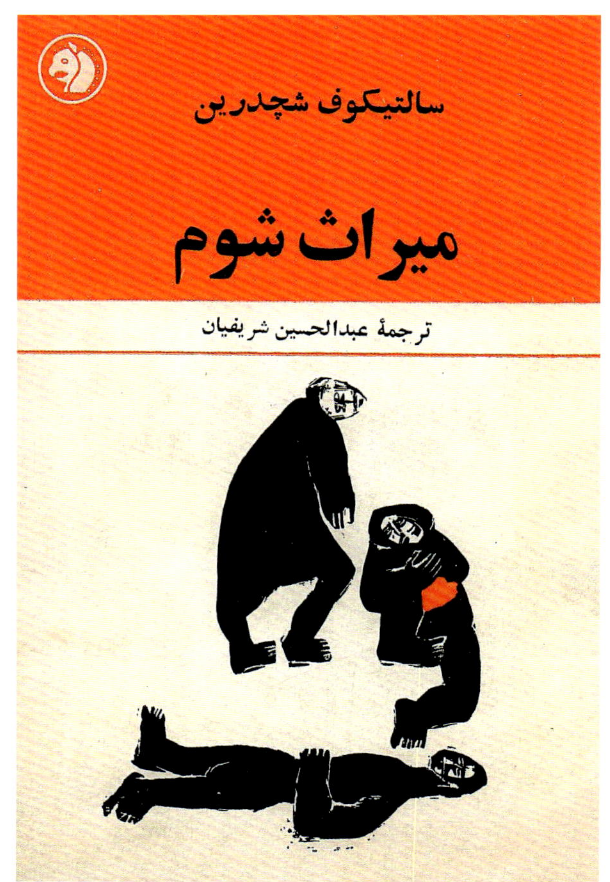
سالتیکوف شچدرین
میراث شوم
ترجمهٔ عبدالحسین شریفیان

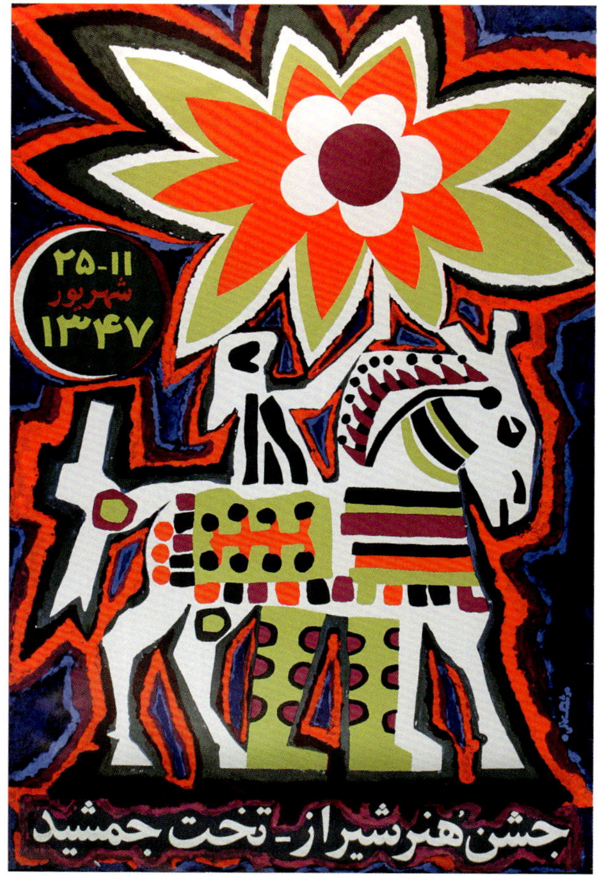
۱۱-۲۵
شهریور
۱۳۴۷
جشن هنر شیراز - تخت جمشید

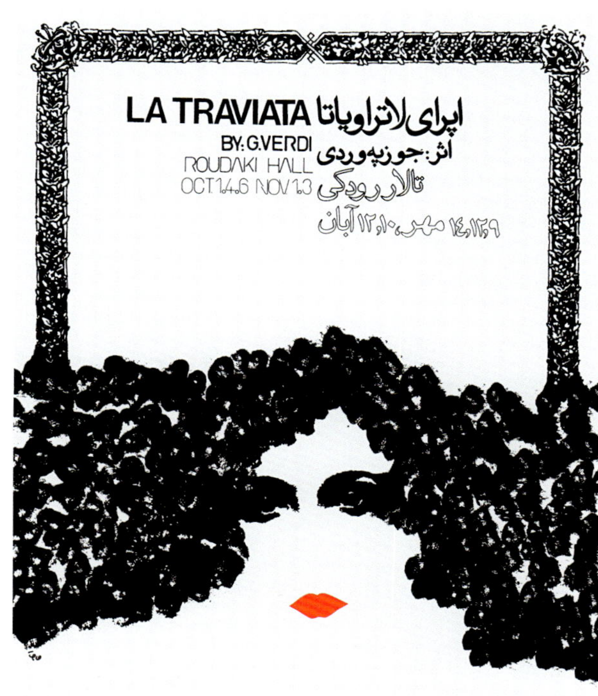
LA TRAVIATA اپرای لاتراویاتا
BY: G.VERDI
اثر: جوزپه وردی
ROUDAKI HALL
تالار رودکی
OCT 1,4,6 NOV 1,3
۱۴،۱۲،۹ مهر، ۱۲،۱۰ آبان

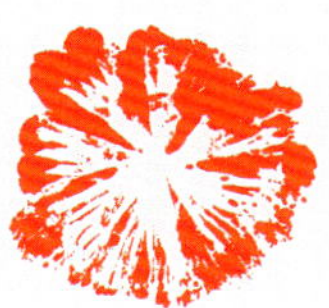

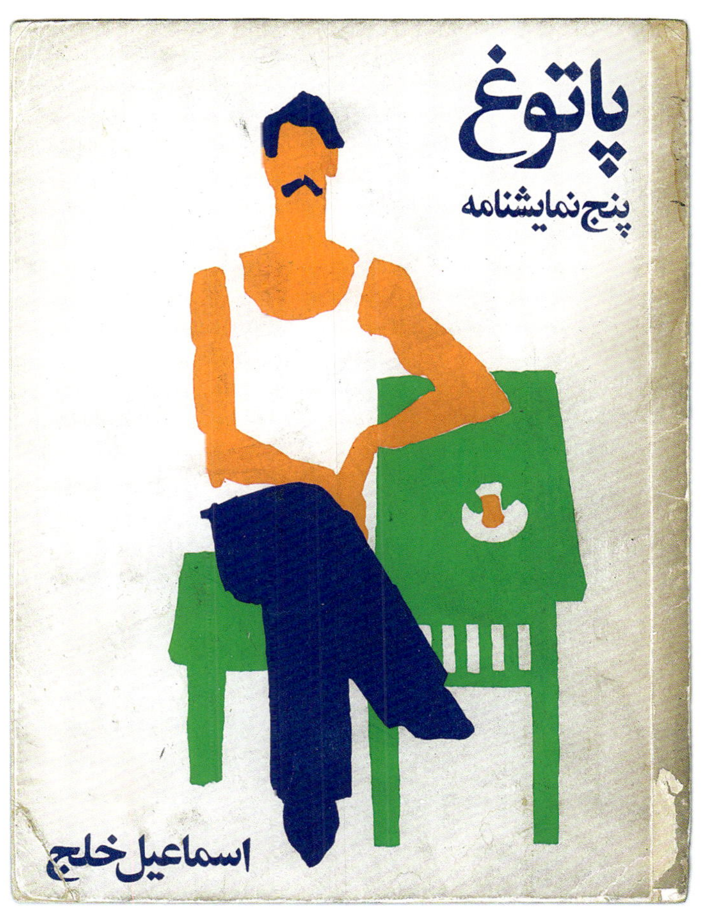

Above
Bijan Saffari
Book cover of *Patogh (The Hangout)*, 1971

Opposite, left to right, top to bottom:

Morteza Momayez
Book cover of *A Farewell to Arms*, 1965

Noureddin Zarrinkelk
Book cover of *The Golovlyov Family*, 1967

Houshang Kazemi
Poster for the 2nd Shiraz Festival of Arts, 1968

Behzad Hatam
Poster for *La Traviata*, 1975

The Shiraz Arts Festival and the Theatre Workshop were among the most influential institutions in shaping the new visual expression at the highest cultural level in Iran. Designers such as Houshang Kazemi, Ghobad Shiva and Fowzi Hassan Tehrani were involved in the Shiraz Arts Festival, while Fereydoun Ave along with Bijan Saffari, Reza Mafi and Ashurbanipal Babilla were key figures in the design of the Theatre Workshop. In reviewing the work of the Roudaki Hall,[9] this dual discourse and its visual influence were also evident: world-class performances of European operas and ballets such as *Tosca*, *Cavalleria Rusticana*, *Carmen*, *La Traviata* and *Rigoletto* alongside Iranian productions such as *Bijan and Manijeh*, Iranian folk dances, tributes to master musicians such as Ahmad Ebadi, a memorial for Abolhasan Saba and musical performances by Darvish Khan—all of which had posters and catalogues designed by Sadegh Barirani and Behzad Hatam.

From the perspective of visual culture, the selection of works exhibited in the 1976 and 1978 editions of Art Basel and ART777 Washington International Art Fair in 1977 again highlights this dual discourse in Iran's cultural diplomacy. Avant-garde figures such as Behjat Sadr, Leyly Matine-Daftary, Parvaneh Etemadi and Bahman Mohassess represented one approach, while the nationalistic side was embodied by artists like Parviz Tanavoli, Charles Hossein Zenderoudi, Massoud Arabshahi, Faramarz Pilaram, Jazeh Tabatabai and Nasser Ovissi.

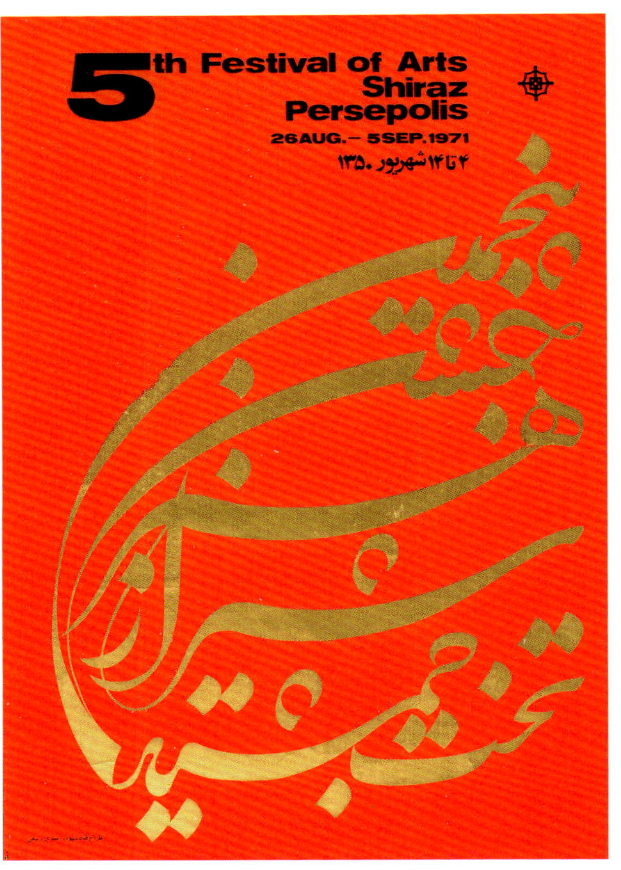

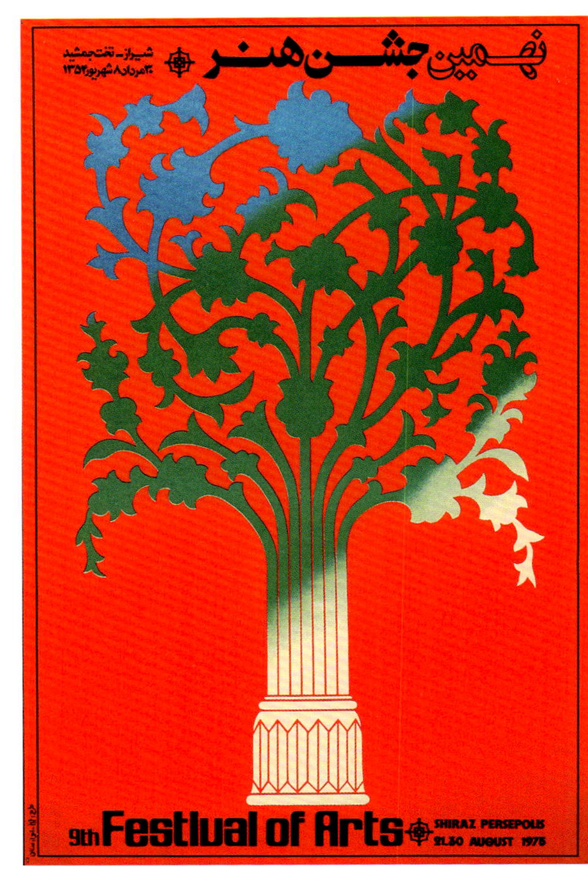

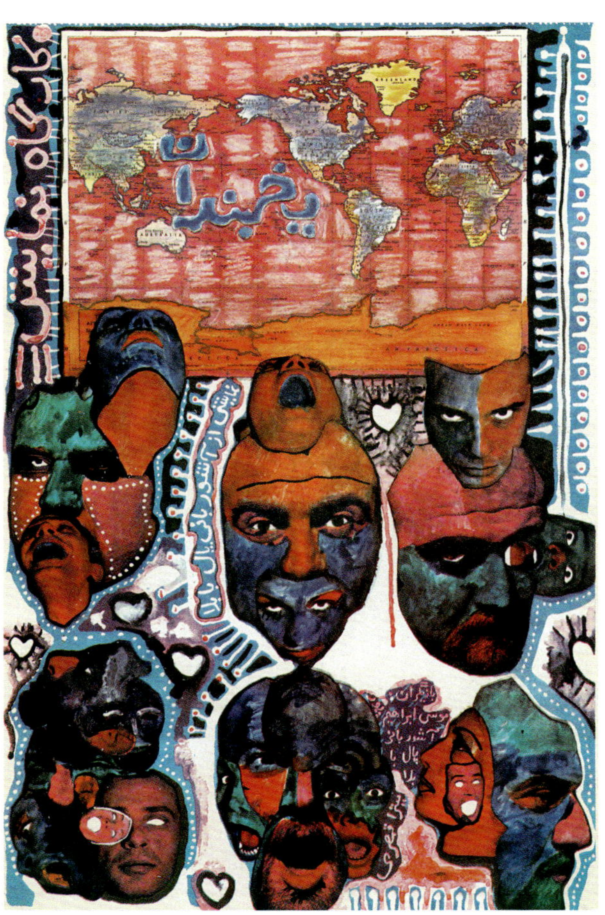

-۱۲۴۲-

شب پره۱ ، **شب پرک** - معروفست که مرغ عیسی باشد و بعربی خفاش خوانند. گویند چون او را بکشند و برزهار کودکان پیش از بلوغ بمالند منع بر آمدن موی کند و اگر او شب پره را در سوراخ موش نهند همه بگریزند .

شب بوزه۲ - با بای ابجد بر وزن هر روزه ، شب پره را گویند که مرغ عیسی باشد.

شب پوش۳ - با بای فارسی بر وزن خرگوش ، کلاه وطاقیه (۱) باشد ۴ و تخفیفه‌ای که شبها بر سر نهند - و برقع ، را هم میگویند - ولحاف را نیز گفته‌اند .

شب بوی۵ - بضم بای ابجد وسکون واو و یای حطی ، نام گلی است و بیشتر کبود رنگ میباشد وسفید والوان هم میشود وشبها بوی خوش کند وآنرا گل گاو چشم نیز گویند و بعربی عرار و عین البقر خوانند و بعضی گل خیری را شب بوی گویند .

شب پوی - بضم بای فارسی وسکون واو ویای حطی، آواز پای را گویند در نهایت آهستگی و خفت - و شبرو را شب پوی نیز گویند؛ و باین دو معنی بجای بای فارسی نون هم بنظر آمده است ظاهراً تصحیف خوانی شده باشد. الله اعلم۶ .

شب پیمای۱ - کنایه از شب بیدار - و دردمند یعنی صاحب درد وآزار - و عاشق مهجور وبیقرار باشد.

شب پیمودن - کنایه از شب بیدار بودن است بهرعنوان که باشد .

شبت۸ - بکسر اول وسکون ثانی وفوقانی، بمعنی دالان ودهلیز خرد و کوچک باشد - ورستنیی را نیز گویند که در ماست کنند و بشیرازی شود

شبی خون : نویسنده و کارگردان سیروس ابراهیم زاده کارگاه نمایش نشانی چهار راه یوسف‌آباد، اول خیابان شاه تلفن ۴۳۶۸۸ بازیگران شهره آغداشلو هوشنگ توزیع اکبر رحمتی رضا روبگری فریده سپاه منصور رضازمان محمد نوازی

۱ - از : شب + پر (پریدن) + ه (پسوند نسبت واتصاف) ، طبری shû_parprî ، مازندرانی کنونی shû_par « واژه نامه ۴۸۵» ، گیلکی shappara :
گر نه بیند بروز شب پره چشم چشمهٔ آفتاب را چه گناه ؟ « گلستان ۲۵ » .
۲ - ظ ، مصحف «شب بوزه» = شب یازه . ورك : شپوز. ۳ - رك : شپوش .
۴ - زجستی باز کرده بند کرته ز ... کج نهاده طرف شب پوش.
سنائی غزنوی. «فرهنگ نظام» .
۵ - شب بو (ه.م) = شب ابوی (ه.م.) . « شب بوی ... است زرد ، بشب بوی بهتر دهد و بتازی منثور خوانندش . فرخی (سیستانی) گوید :
خاری که بمن درخلد اندر سفرهند بچون ... شب بوی
« لغت فرس ۵۲۰» .
شب بو = Cheiri از تیرهٔ چلیپائیان است . کاسهٔ آن دارای چهار کاسبرگ مستقیم که از خارج اندکی برآمدگی دارند . جام آن چهار گلبرگ دارد بشکل چلیپا (صلیب) . پرچمهای آن شش و دو عدد کوچکتر از چهار عدد دیگر است . « گل گلاب ۲۰۷» . ۶ - صورت اخیر مصحف «شب پوی» است . ۷ - از : شب + پیمای (پیماینده) . ۸ - شود (ه.م.) = شوی (ه.م)، تهرانی shivîd شیرازی sheved « عاوی » ، مشهدی sheved ، گنابادی shevîd « گنابادی » ، بروجردی shuît « شهیدی » ، گیلکی shibit = Anethum graveolens از تیرهٔ چتریان . برگهای آن بسیار بریده و عطری ملایم دارد . « گل گلاب ۲۳۵» .

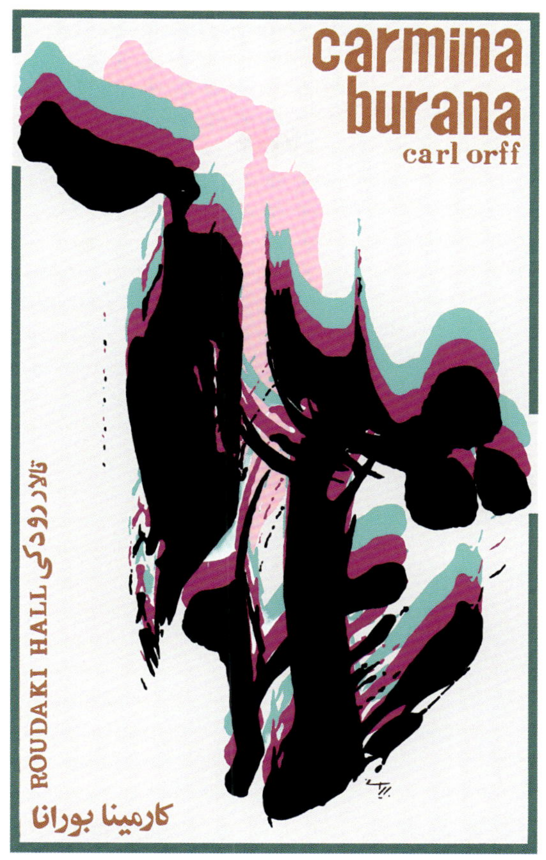

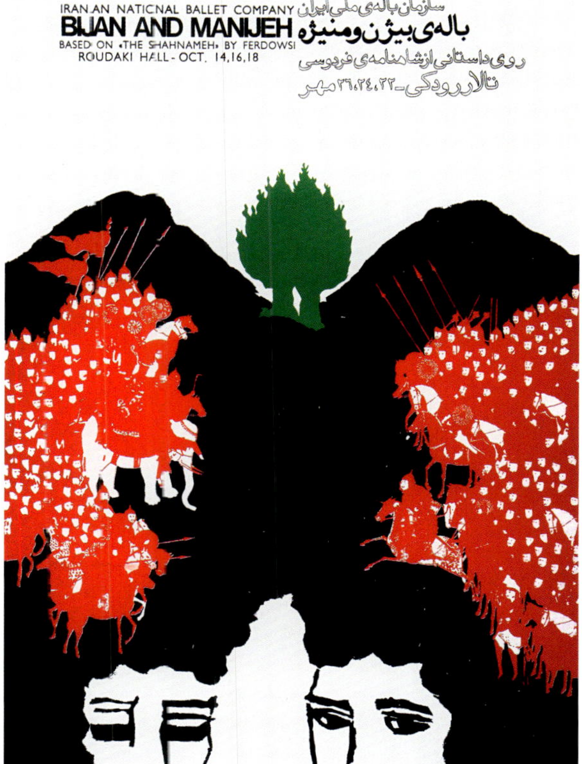

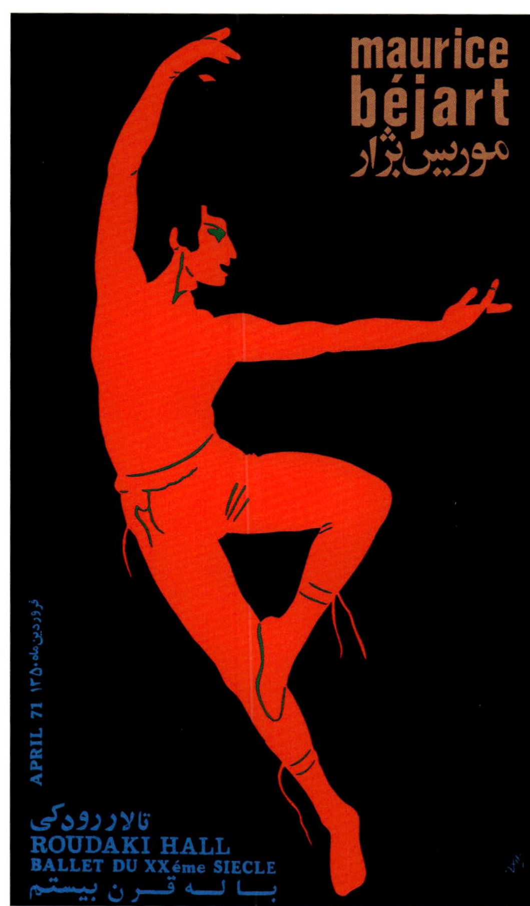

Above, left to right, top to bottom:

Sadeq Barirani
Poster for *Carmina Burana*, 1975

Behzad Hatam
Poster for *Bijan and Manijeh*, 1975

Sadegh Barirani
Poster for a Maurice Béjart performance, 1971

Opposite, left to right, top to bottom:

Ghobad Shiva
Poster for the 5th Shiraz Festival of Arts, 1971

Morteza Momayez
Poster for the 9th Shiraz Festival of Arts, 1975

Assur Banipal Babila
Poster for *The Frost*, 1977

Fereydoun Ave
Poster for *Bloody Night*, 1972

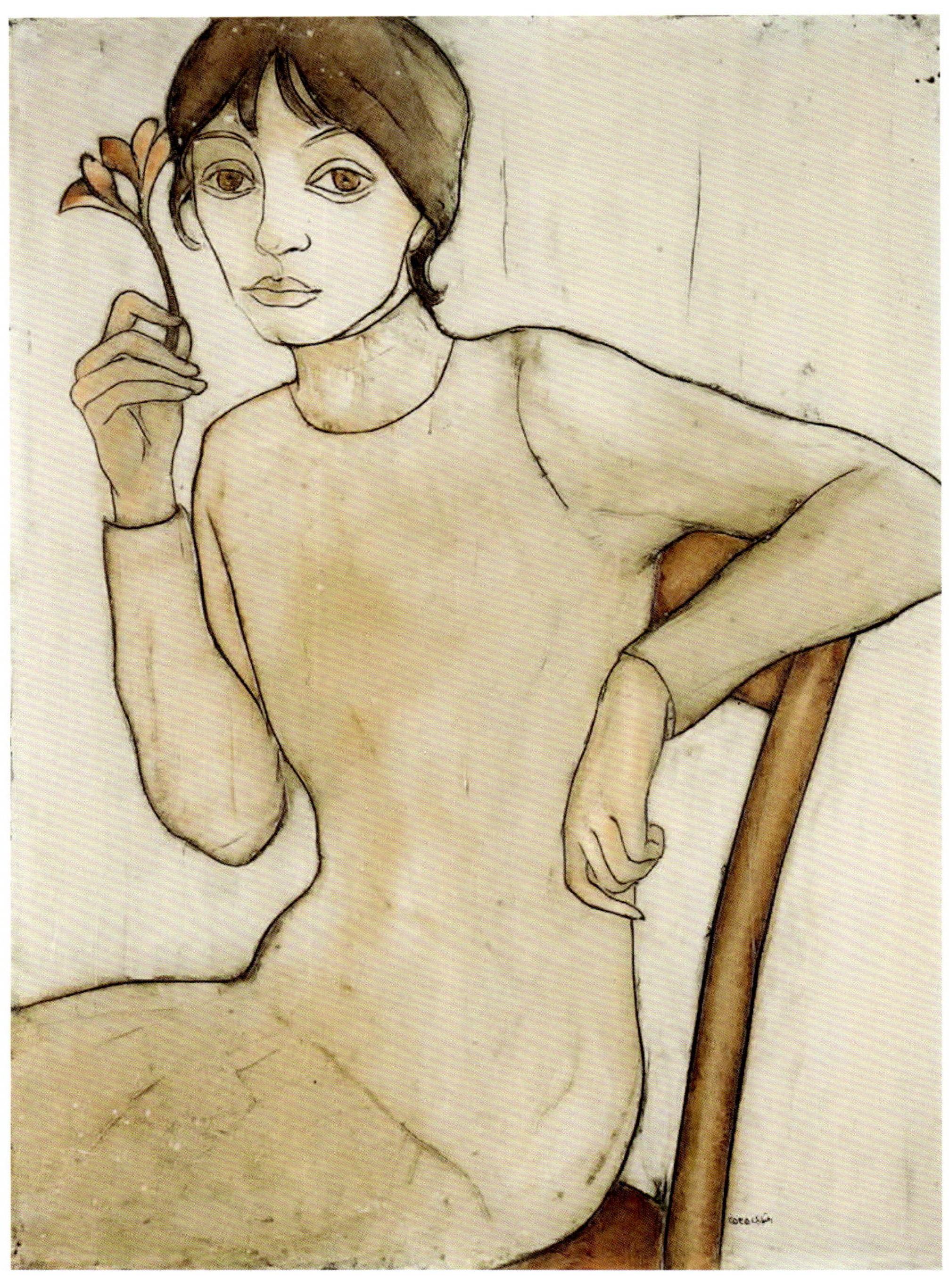

Above
Parvaneh Etemadi
Self-Portrait, 1976
oil on cement

Opposite
Leyly Matine-Daftary
Untitled, 1966
oil on canvas

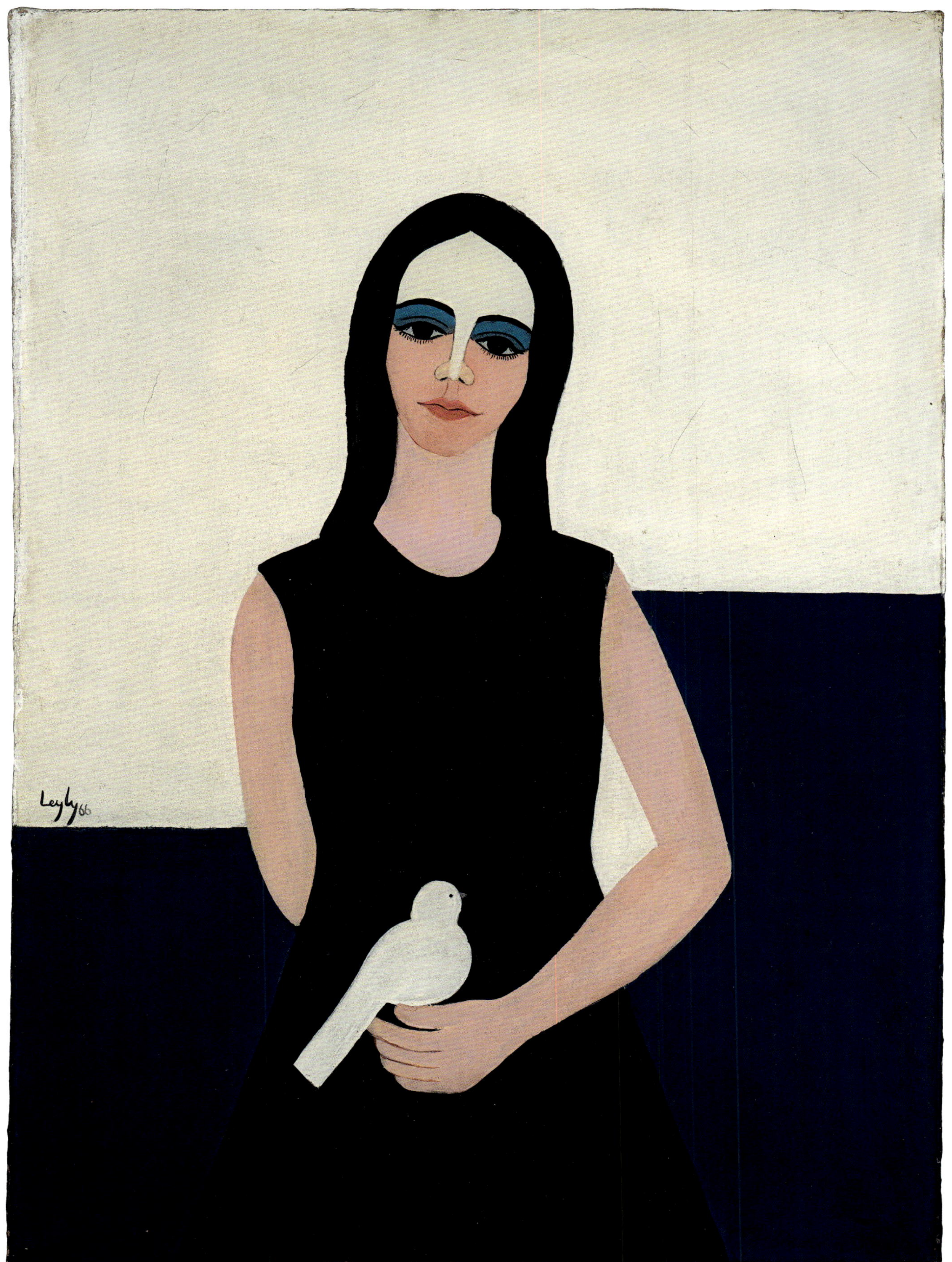
Leyly 66

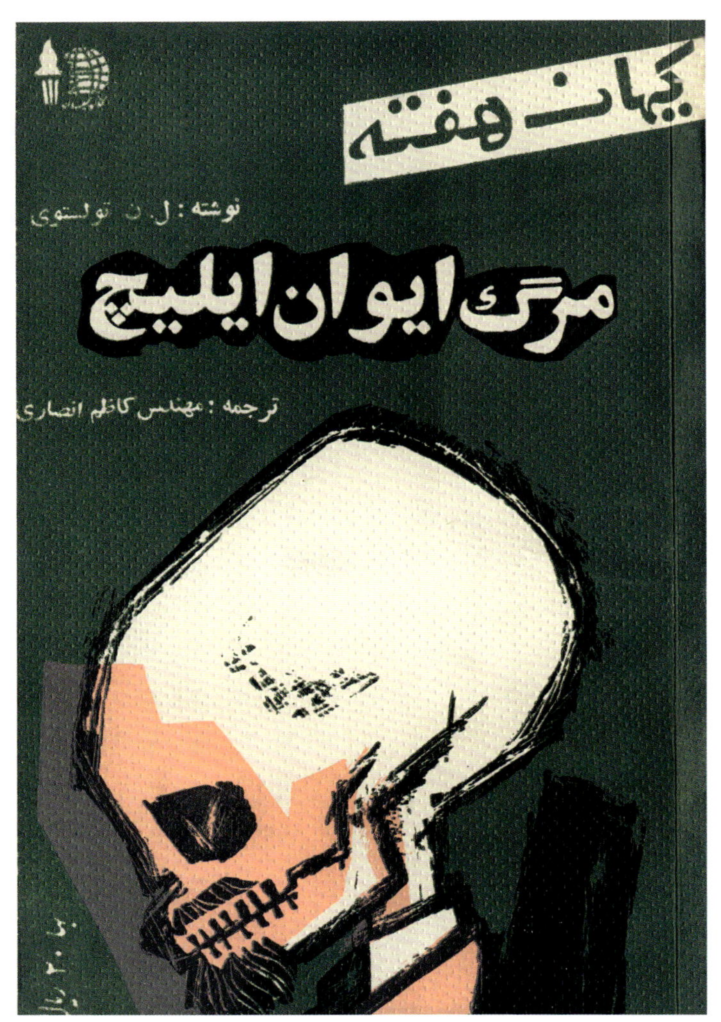

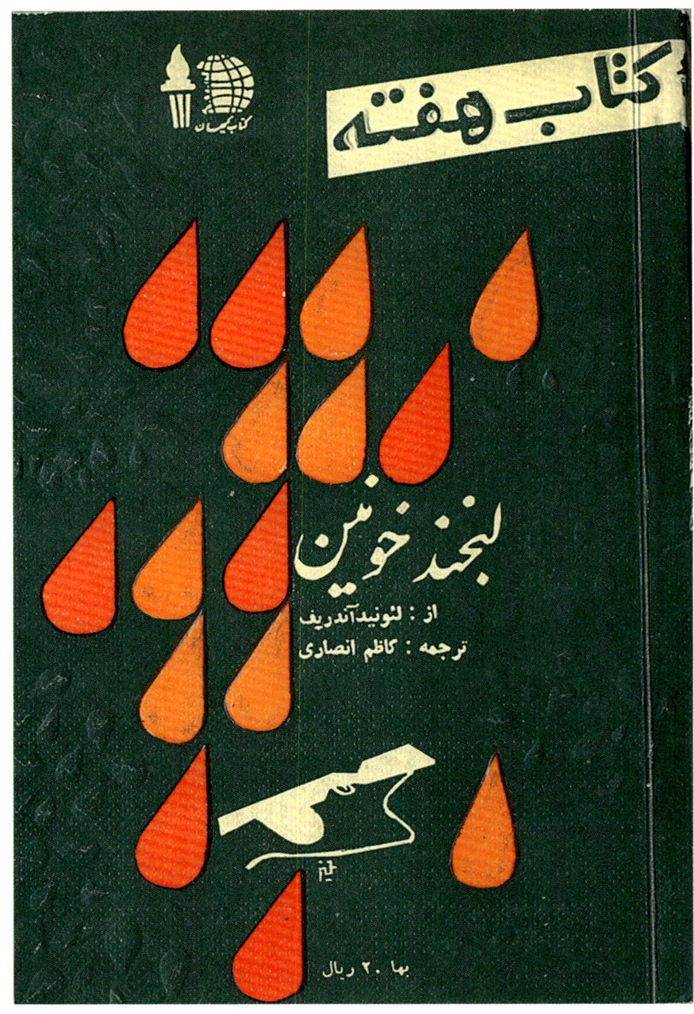

Left
Morteza Momayez
Cover of *Ketab-e Hafte*,
no. 39, 1962

Right
Morteza Momayez
Cover of *Ketab-e Hafte*,
no. 17, 1962

In graphic design, aspects of the work of Farshid Mesghali, Ghobad Shiva and Morteza Momayez demonstrated both nationalistic and global perspectives due to the fluid nature of graphic design. Momayez, in particular, played a radical role through his collaboration with the periodical *Ketab-e Hafteh*, which began in October 1961, acting as a solid bridge between intellectuals and the masses. *Ketab-e Hafteh*, which was published regularly until 1963 with 104 issues, was one of the most important platforms for expanding modern visual culture among Iran's educated population.

Another major institution that played a significant role in shaping the visual education of Iran's children and adolescents on a national scale was the Institute for the Intellectual Development of Children and Young Adults (IIDCYA). The IIDCYA was born in the winter of 1966 as a solution for shaping the free time of the younger population and providing them with educational and entertainment materials. The non-governmental organization Children's Book Council was established in December 1962 by thirty-seven experts and practitioners of children's literature. The council aimed to produce and promote children's literature, select the best books of the year and give out awards, celebrate Children's Day, hold librarian training classes and establish connections with international children's literature organizations. It also helped pass a law requiring schools to designate a room as a library. At that time, the production of books for children and teenagers was extremely limited.

From the 1960s to the mid-1970s, the social, economic and consequently cultural situation of Iranians changed significantly. The country's oil revenue increased from US$555 million in 1963 to US$958 million in 1968, then to US$1.2 billion in 1971 and eventually US$5 billion in 1974.[10] By 1976, this amount rose to US$20 billion. This revenue, through the Industrial and Mining Development Bank of Iran, was invested as loans to the private sector, as well as incorporated into the government's budget for developmental plans in the Third (1961–66), Fourth (1966–71) and Fifth (1971–76) Development Plans.

Under these plans, mass media consumption played an extraordinary role and significantly influenced urbanization and the emergence of new social classes. According to the historian Ervand Abrahamian, Iran's urban society at the time could be divided into four categories: 1) the upper class, 2) the affluent middle class, 3) the salaried middle class and 4) the working class.[11]

Between 1963 and 1977, enrollment in kindergartens increased from 13,296 to 221,896 children; in elementary schools from 241,201 to 4,078,000 students; in high schools from 369,069 to 741,000 students; in technical and teacher training schools from 14,240 to 227,497 students; and in literacy classes from 10,500 to 691,000 students. With such social and cultural expansion across different

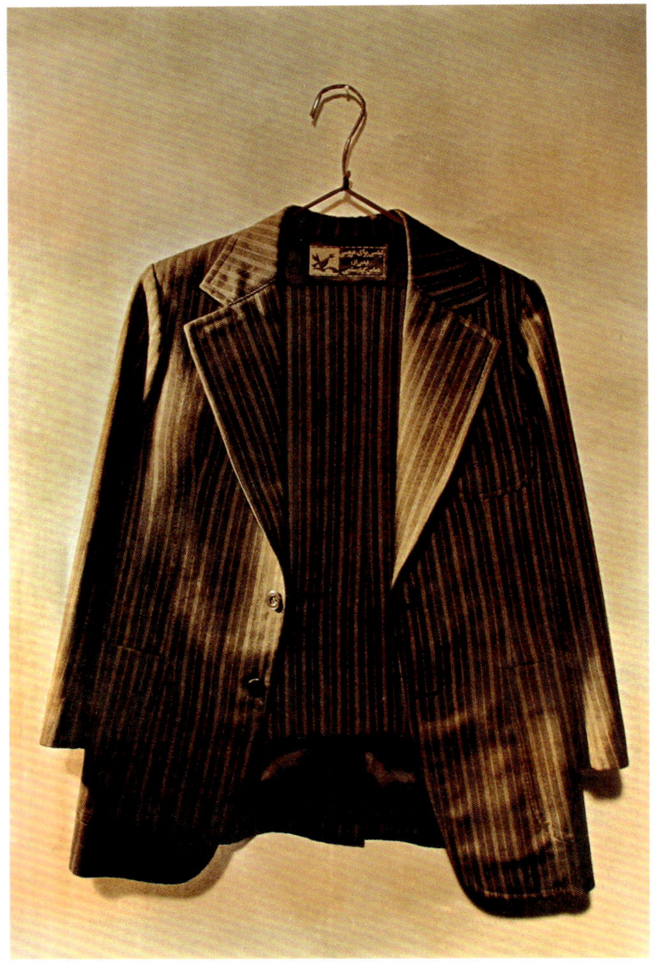

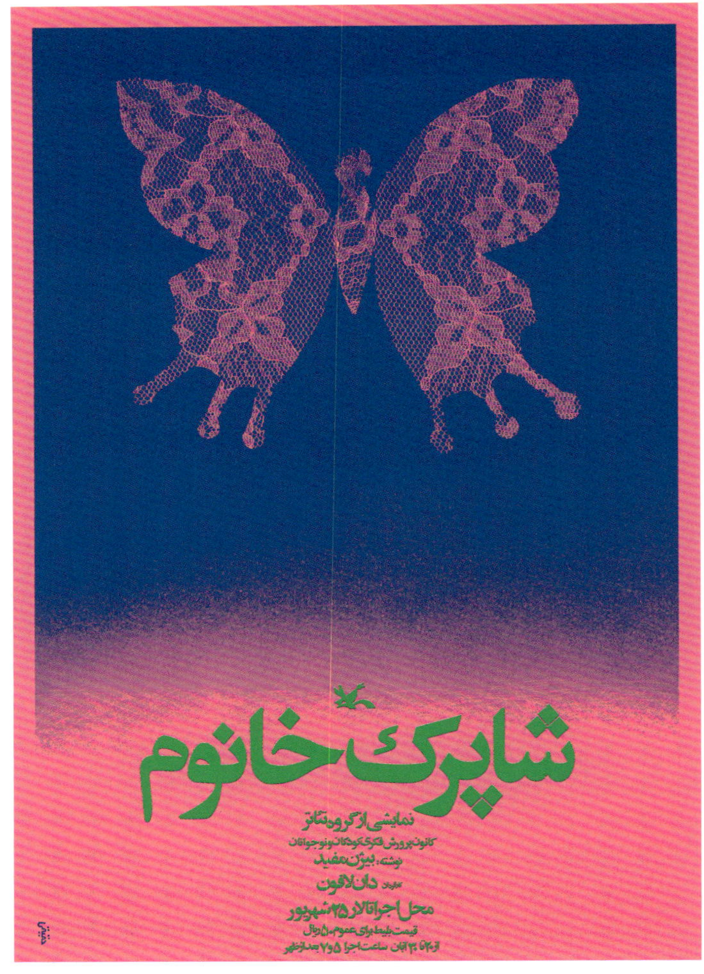

levels of society, the impact of educational and cultural needs became highly significant.[12] Educational institutions, universities, schools, vocational schools, museums, galleries, theatres, cinemas, festivals and publishing organizations were rapidly established or expanding their activities. This period prepared fertile ground for the growth of large cultural institutions such as the IIDCYA.

Lili Amir-Arjomand, after earning a Master of Library Science and Children's Literature from Rutgers University in the United States, returned to Iran. Before her move to America, she was the head of the library at the National University (now Shahid Beheshti University) in Tehran for two years. Upon her return, she became head of the central library at the National Iranian Oil Company and taught for a year in the newly established Library Science Department at the University of Tehran. Over time, Amir-Arjomand's focus shifted to publishing children's books, and thanks to her efforts, a library specifically for children was opened in Farah Park (now Laleh Park). This library became the seed for the IIDCYA. Amir-Arjomand and Homa Zahedi (the sister of Ardeshir Zahedi, Iran's ambassador to the UK and US, and wife of Dariush Homayoun, the minister of information and tourism) took over management of this new library. The library published its first book for children, *The Little Mermaid* by Hans Christian Andersen,

Left to right:

Abbas Kiarostami
Poster for *A Wedding Suit*, 1976

Ebrahim Haghighi
Poster for *Lady Butterfly*, 1973

Farshid Mesghali
Poster for Polish Animation Films, 1976

Hamid Norouzi
Poster for the 5th Tehran International Festival of Films for Children, 1970

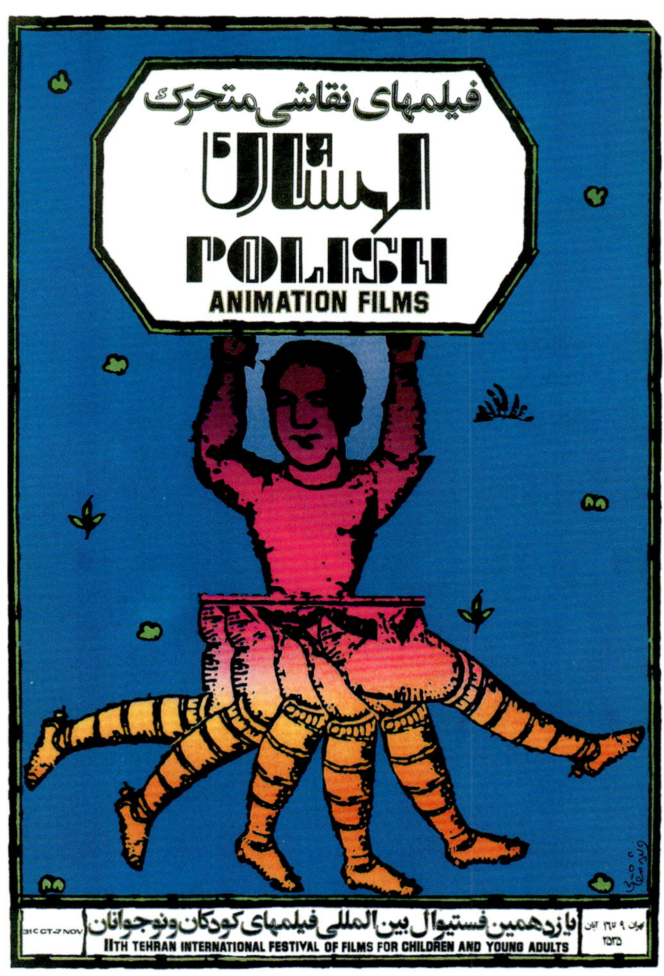

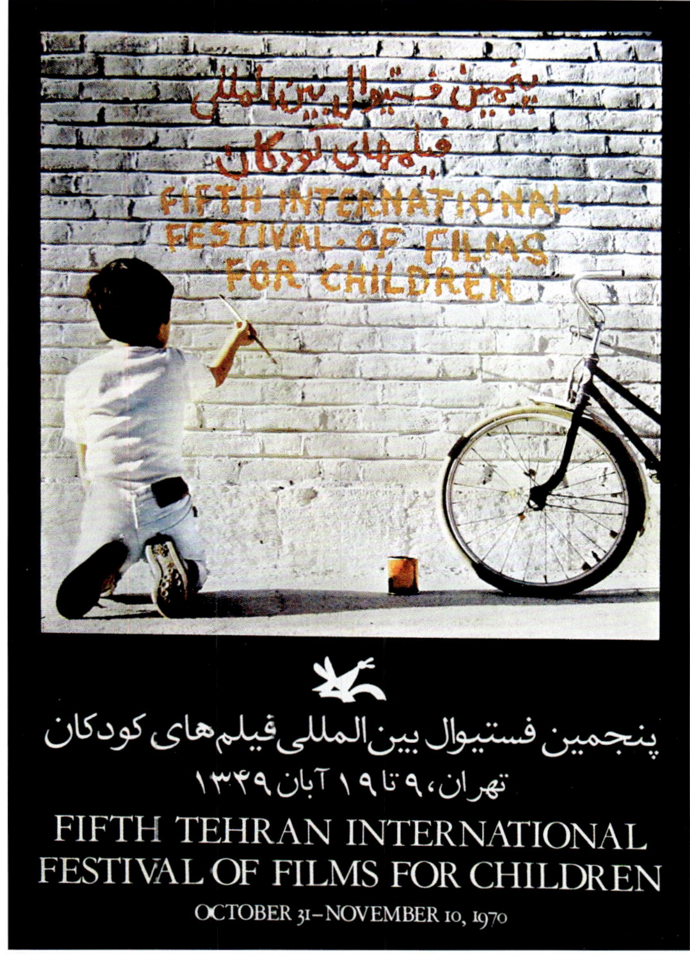

translated and illustrated by Farah Diba, in 1966. The proceeds from its sale helped launch IIDCYA's publishing arm. After the library in Farah Park, the first IIDCYA library opened in Bagh Shah, in a storage room of Shaayesteh School, in October 1966. In its first month, the library had 1,800 members, and by the end of 1968, it had 11,000 members. Amir-Arjomand's close friendship with Diba led to the formation of a board of trustees consisting of prominent figures to support the IIDCYA.

The IIDCYA's official graphic design studio began its activities in 1971 under the leadership of animator and illustrator Farshid Mesghali, with collaborators like Mohammadreza Adnani, Ebrahim Haghighi, Bahram Khaef, Mostafa Owji, Soudabeh Aghaei and Behjat Poushanchi. This studio created some of the most important visual legacies in Iranian history, from the institute's founding until 1979.

In the 1970s, important illustrated books based on ancient Iranian texts were designed and some were produced. The *Shahnameh* of Amir Kabir Publication—edited by literary scholar Mohammad Jafar Mahjoub, with calligraphy by Javad Sharifi and Seyed Mohammad Ehsaey, illuminations by Hossein Eslaamiyan and

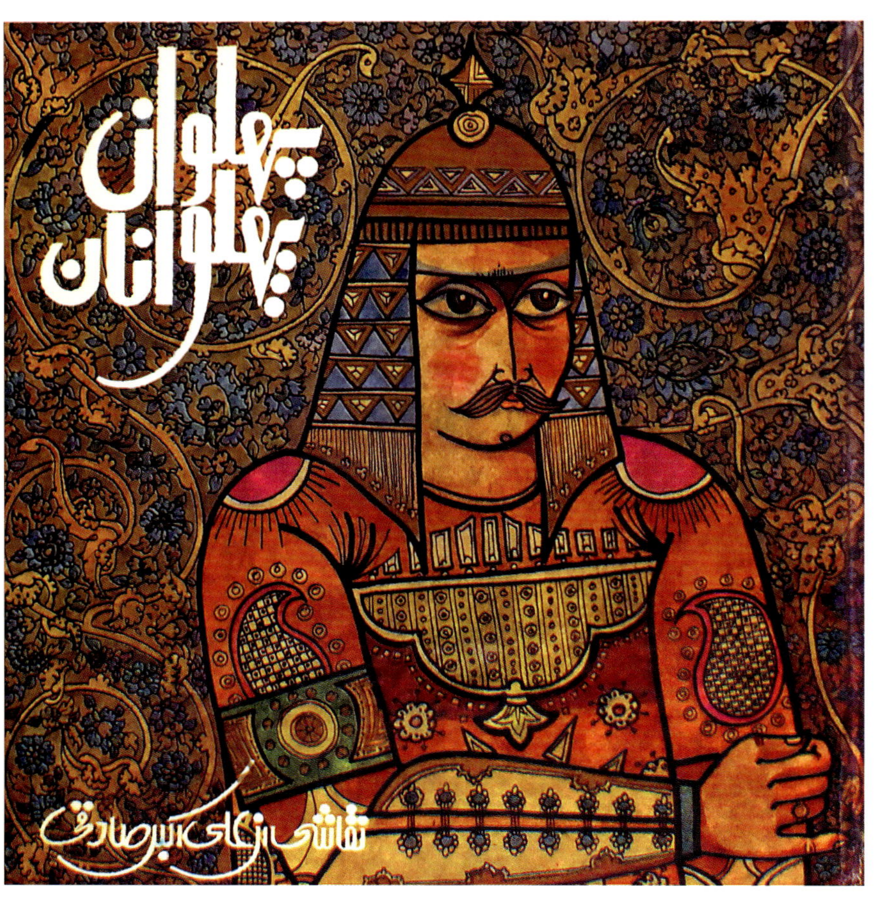

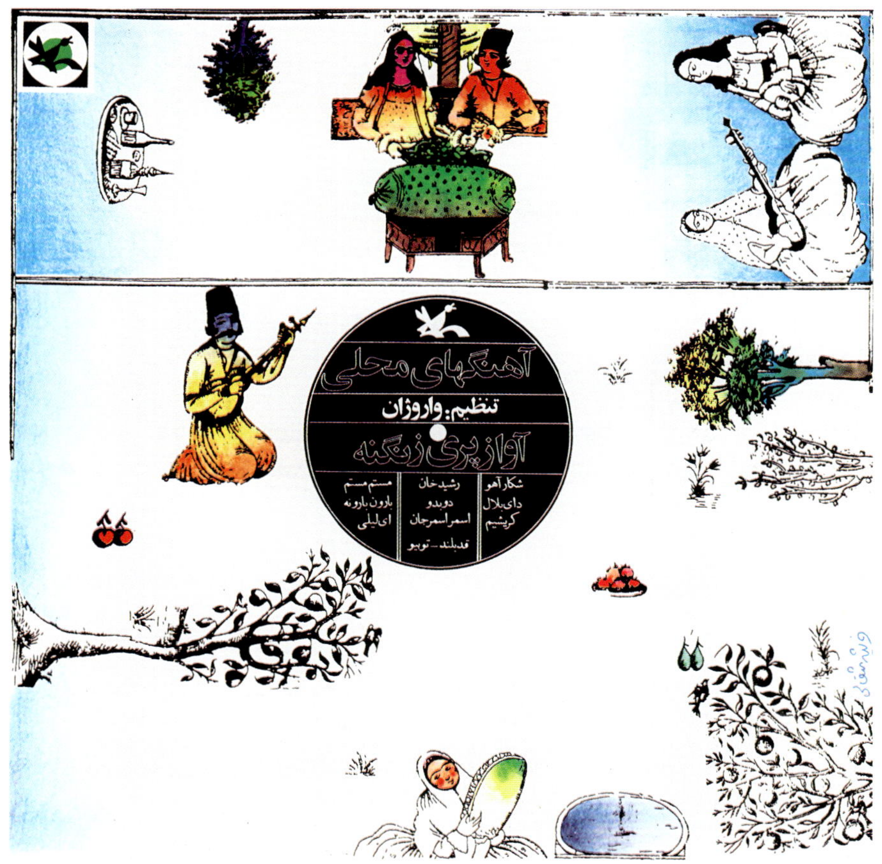

Top
Ali Akbar Sadeghi
Book cover of *Hero of the Heroes*, 1970

Bottom
Farshid Mesghali
Album cover of *Folk Songs*, 1976

Opposite
Nafiseh Riahi
Book cover of *Seven Labours of Rostam*, 1976

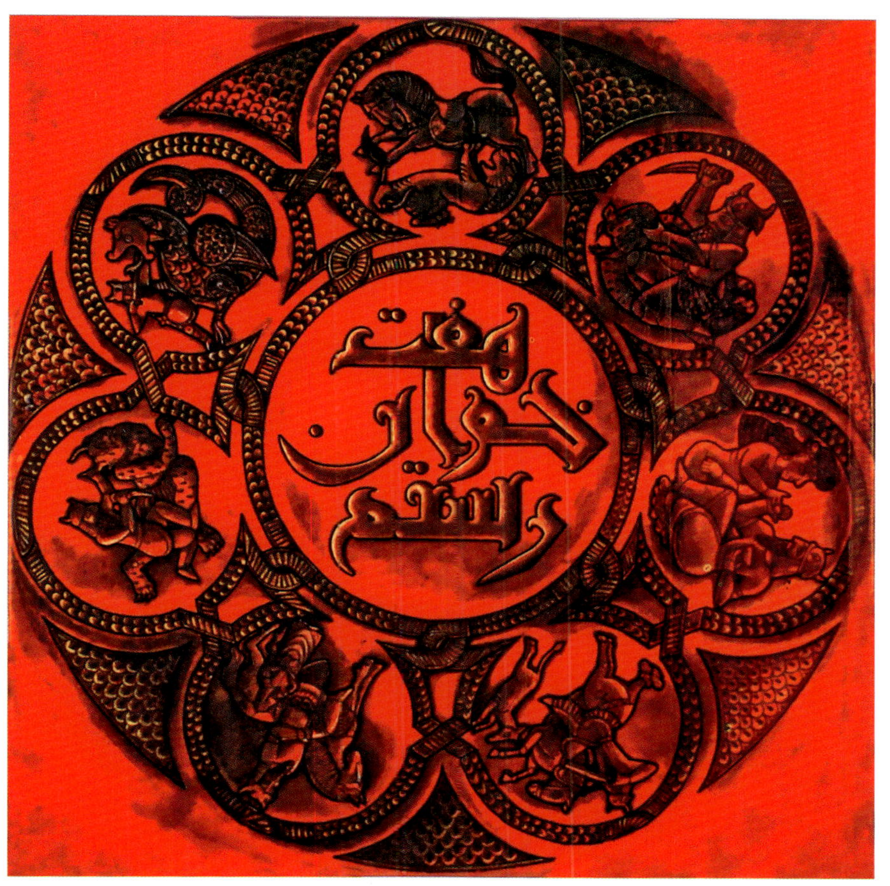

illustrations by Ali Asghar Masoumi—was printed in sixteen colours and unveiled in 1971. Madokht Keshkouli wrote *The Myth of Creation in Iran*, illustrated by Farshid Mesghali. The work of Firooz Shirvanloo and its role in shaping illustrated Iranian-universal books at Tehran's Niavaran Cultural Center can be considered the peak of this visual transformation. A new edition of the *Avesta* was illustrated with abstract paintings by Massoud Arabshahi and published by Niavaran Cultural Center in 1978. Faramarz Pilaram illustrated the *Tales of the Quran* and Nicky Nodjoumi illustrated *Arzhang Mani*, which were set to be published after the *Avesta*. However, both were left unpublished due to the events surrounding the 1979 Revolution.

Although the progress of modern visual culture did not stop with the Revolution, for nearly a decade the official visual language leaned toward a regressive, anti-design approach.

ENDNOTES

1 The School of Fine Arts in Tehran began operating in 1953 with a single mixed-gender class alongside the General Directorate of Fine Arts. The following year, the school was separated into the Boys' and Girls' Schools of Fine Arts, located in separate buildings in the Pich-e Shemiran neighbourhood, a few hundred metres apart. Both schools remain at their original locations to this day, seventy years later.

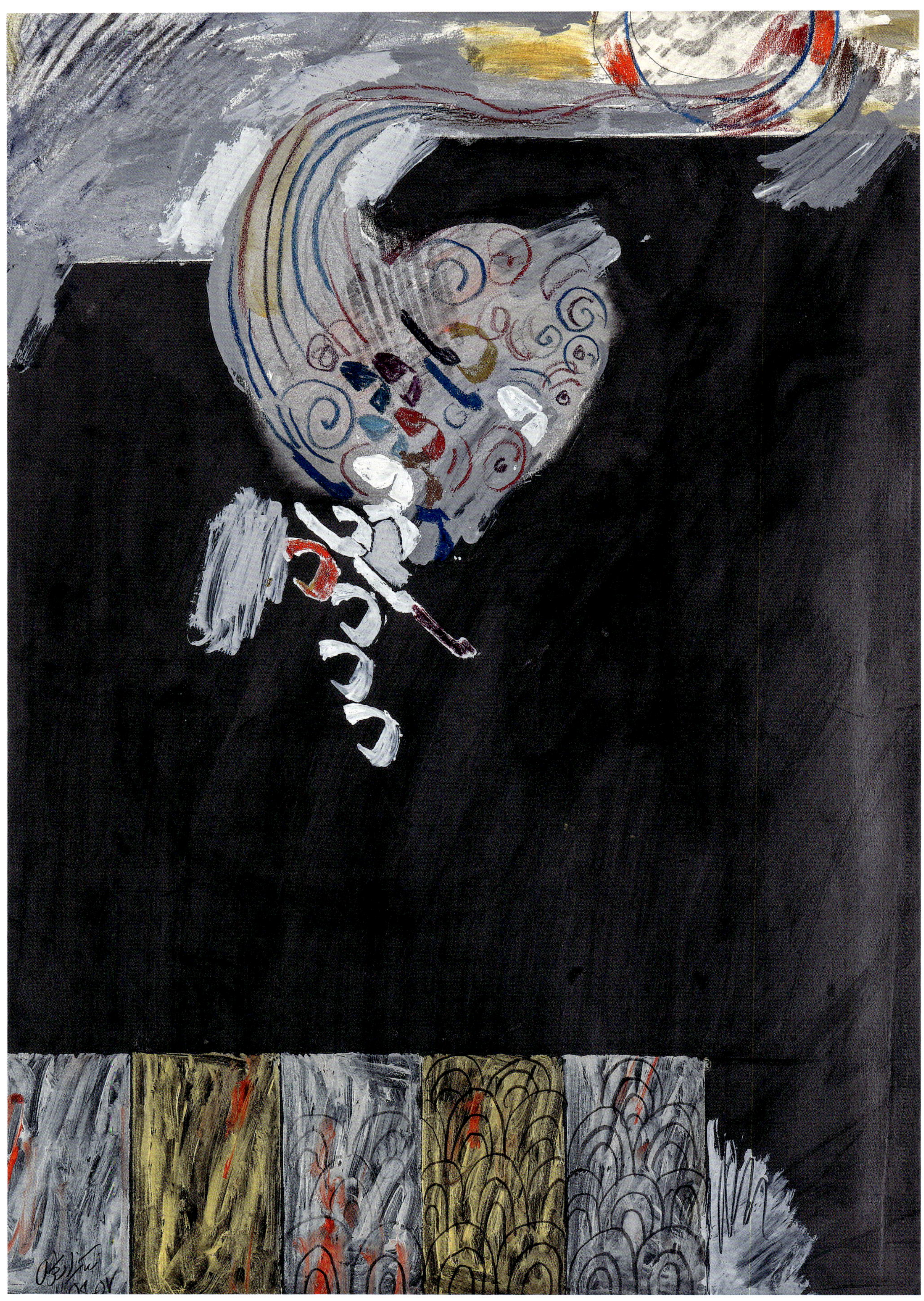

From its inception, the school had a set of administration regulations and a defined curriculum. The primary disciplines included painting, sculpture, miniature painting and decorative design (graphics), which were taught at various intervals throughout the school's history. Outstanding graduates were granted scholarships for further studies. Notable instructors over the years included Aydin Aghdashloo, Farzad Adibi, Sadegh Barirani, Mohammad Tajvidi, Mahmoud Javadipour, Ariasp Dadbeh, Shokouh Riazi, Gholam-Hossein Nami, Masoud Nejabat and Mohsen Vaziri-Moghaddam.

After the Islamic Revolution of 1979, the school continued its activities under the new name School of Visual Arts for Boys and Girls. The list of the school's graduates from inception to present day makes clear that this educational institution has played a significant role in nurturing modernist artists as well as graphic designers. Examples of such alumni include Alireza Espahbod, Mostafa Asadollahi, Farah Ossouli, Mohammad Pouladi, Parviz Tanavoli, Ghasem Hajizadeh, Hossein Khosrowjerdi, Kambiz Derambakhsh, Mehdi Rezagholi, Mehran Zamani, the brothers Koorosh Shishegaran and Behzad Shishegaran, Habibollah Sadeghi, Reza Abedini, Behzad Golpayegani, Siamak Filizadeh and Giti Navaran.

2 The Higher School of Decorative Arts was established in 1960 under the supervision of the Ministry of Culture and Arts. This institution was created to meet the educational needs of art school students and other individuals interested in higher education in the field of art, as well as to preserve and promote decorative arts. In 1974, according to a decree from the Higher Education Development Council, it was renamed the Faculty of Decorative Arts.

The Fine Arts Administration's official announcement in 1960 stated it had established the institution to "train specialists in decorative arts, whose influence on cultivating public taste cannot be neglected." Additionally, *Art and Artists News* noted: "The training of a group of decorative arts specialists will be the beginning of a transformation in Iran, with valuable outcomes gradually becoming apparent." The goal was to create a contemporary stream in the academic teaching of decorative and applied arts. The founding members, first planners and instructors included Houshang Kazemi, Bijan Saffari, Javad Hamidi, Parviz Tanavoli, Asad Behrouzan, Shokouh Riazi, Lilit Teryan, Jalal Sattari and Karim Emami.

In this faculty, after completing a general foundation year, students would choose a discipline such as sculpture, architecture, theatre and cinema stage design or "painting for book and magazine illustrations." Notable students include Charles Hossein Zenderoudi, Massoud Arabshahi, Sadegh Tabrizi, Faramarz Pilaram, Behzad Golpayegani, Abbas Mashhadizadeh, Abbas Moayeri, Mohammad Reza Aslani, Iraj Anvari, Shahrzad Esfahani, Amrollah Farhadi, Majid Akhavan and Sohrab Marzban.

3 Ebrahim Haghighi, *Face to Face* (Tehran: Khojasteh, 2011).

4 UNESCO, "Introduction," *Cultural Policy: A Preliminary Study—Round-table Meeting on Cultural Policies, Monte Carlo, Monaco, 1967* (UNESCO: 1969), 9, https://unesdoc.unesco.org/ark:/48223/pf0000001173.locale=en.

5 Changiz Pahlevan, "Cultural Programing in Iran," *Farhanh-o Zendegi*, no. 15 (1974).

6 Pahlevan, "Cultural Programing in Iran."

7 The Shiraz Arts Festival Organization was a government entity under the Office of Farah Pahlavi, which began its activities in 1967 with the first festival and held a further eleven editions, until 1977, each lasting ten days in September in the city of Shiraz. Farrokh Ghaffari headed the organization, and a large group of artistic and cultural advisors, such as Khojasteh Kia, Reza Qotbi, Fereydoun Rahnema and Bijan Saffari, collaborated with it. The festival's primary focus was music and performing arts but it also had cinema and visual arts side programs. Its approach emphasized both Western and Eastern arts, as well as the revival of traditional and folk Iranian arts.

The festival's purpose, outlined in Article 1 of its charter, was:

a) Preparing and organizing the festival programs for performing arts and music at the Shiraz Arts Festival.
b) Conducting other artistic activities to present art alongside the Shiraz Arts Festival.
c) Establishing connections and cooperation with international artistic organizations and exchanging artistic programs for the Shiraz Arts Festival.

Throughout its eleven editions, the festival collaborated with international figures such as Karlheinz Stockhausen, Iannis Xenakis, Peter Brook, Robert Wilson, Maurice Béjart and Merce Cunningham. Houshang Kazemi created the festival's logo, and designers such as Kamran Katouzian, Houshang Kazemi, Ghobad Shiva, Fereydoun Ave, Farshid Mesghali and Morteza Momayez designed the main posters for different editions of the festival. Numerous other designs were also created for side programs, book covers, brochures, invitations and festival gifts,

Nicky Nodjoumi
Arzhang, c. 1976
mixed media on paper

generally produced in collaboration with designers from the graphic design unit of National Iranian Radio and Television.

For the tenth anniversary, ten posters were commissioned from established designers and painters of the time, such as Leyly Matine-Daftary, Seyed Mohammad Ehsaey, Reza Mafi, Abolghassem Saidi and Ghasem Hajizadeh. The festival was cancelled before its twelfth edition due to the onset of protests and demonstrations in 1979.

8 The Theatre Workshop was established in 1969 after receiving an award for its performance of *The City of Tales* and *Research...* during the second edition of the Shiraz Arts Festival. Supported by National Iranian Radio and Television and the Shiraz Arts Festival Organization, it became a place for experimental and workshop theatre at the intersection of Hafez and Naderi (now Jomhouri) Streets, near Kalantari Alley. With the collaboration of advisors from Radio and Television, the workshop's charter was drafted, defining its purpose and establishing its theatre groups. The term "design," mentioned in the workshop's objectives, encompassed poster, book, brochure, costume, stage and lighting design for theatre.

During its ten years of activity, Bijan Saffari served as the head, and Abbas Nalbandian was responsible for the publishing section. The first poster printed at the Theatre Workshop was designed by Edward Arshamian for the play *The Game Without Words...* Fereydoun Ave, Arbi Avanessian, Ashurbanipal Babila and Bijan Saffari designed most of the posters for the workshop's theatre groups, while independent designers created posters for guest groups. Since the performances were repertory, the posters include no show dates or times. Venues frequented by theatre and literature enthusiasts displayed these posters as mementos, and some copies were also sold. Performance dates and times were announced via monthly program brochures, and other brochures featured the crew and photos of rehearsals and performance scenes.

Almost none of the Theatre Workshop's posters bear the designer's signature, which, according to Avanessian, was due to an emphasis on teamwork and avoiding star-making. The workshop's book designs fall into two categories: one with free designs by artists like Sohail Souzani, Ardeshir Mohassess and Hossein Valamanesh, and others following a uniform style, designed in National Iranian Radio and Television's studio under Ghobad Shiva with collaboration from Fawzi Hassantehrani. The Theatre Workshop concluded its activities after producing around seventy plays due to the 1979 Islamic Revolution.

9 The Roudaki Hall was inaugurated on October 26, 1967, with the purpose of "familiarizing the public with music and performing arts of Iran and the world, elevating the level of national culture and art, and spreading and promoting new global artistic phenomena." The building's construction took ten years, with a design by Eugene Aftandilian, an Armenian architect and professor at Tehran University.

The Roudaki Hall's programs were divided into symphony orchestra, opera, ballet, Iranian programs, recitals, chamber music and special performances. The public relations department and the monthly *Roudaki* magazine were managed by Mahmoud Khoshnam, while the publishing unit was led by Pari Safa. They were responsible for providing content and publishing magazines, books, brochures, newsletters and posters. Published books include those on composers Abolhasan Saba and Benjamin Britten.

The first phase of Roudaki Hall's activities ended with the 1979 Revolution, and since then the hall has operated under the name Vahdat Hall, continuing with various programs up to the present day.

10 Ervand Abrahamian, *Iran Between Two Revolutions*, 22nd ed., trans. Ahmad Golmohammadi and Mohammad-Ebrahim Fattahi (Tehran: Nashr-e Ney, 2014), 525.

11 Abrahamian, *Iran Between Two Revolutions*, 530.

12 Abrahamian, *Iran Between Two Revolutions*, 530.

Nicky Nodjoumi
Standing Tall, 1976
oil on canvas

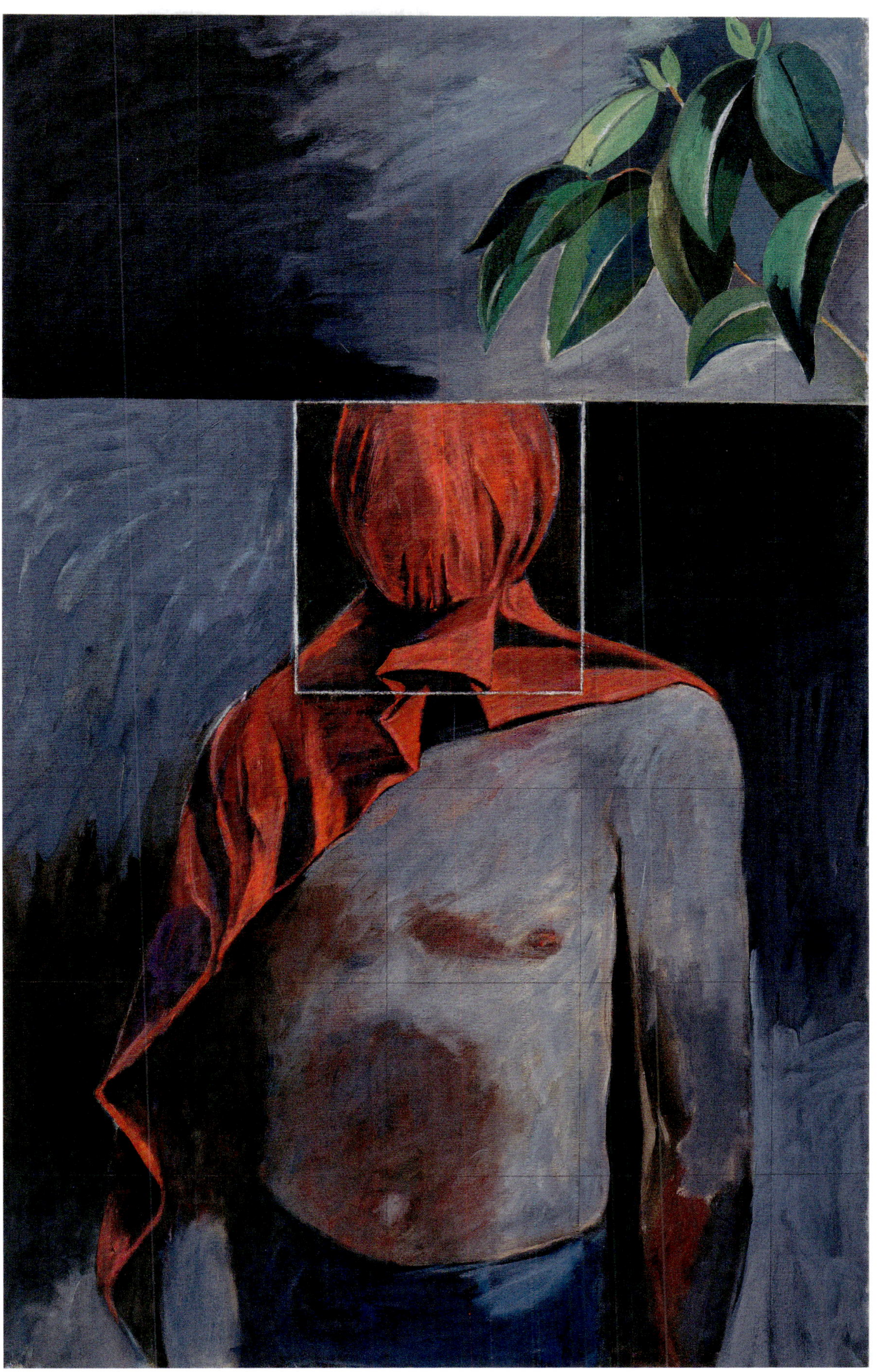

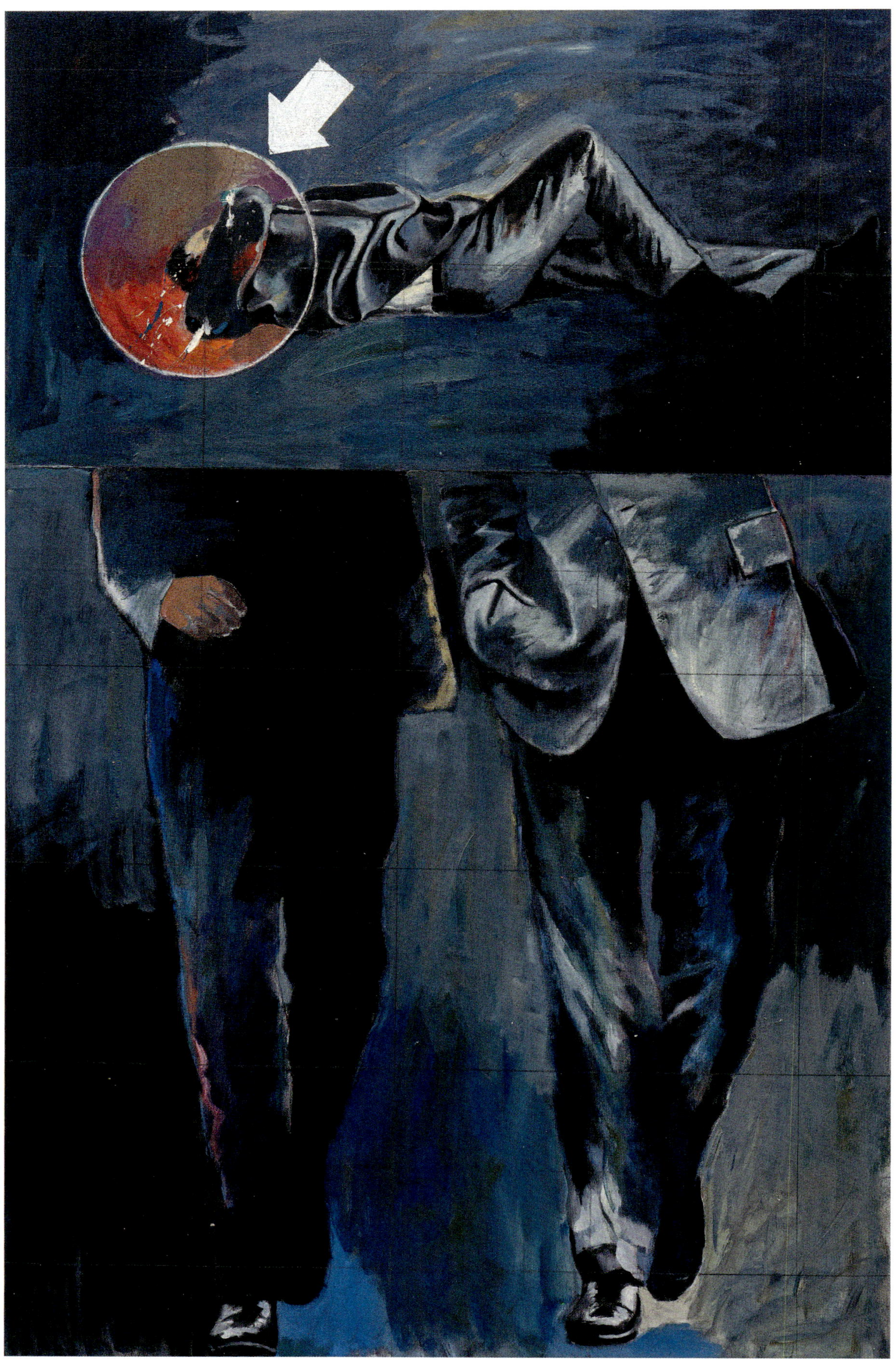

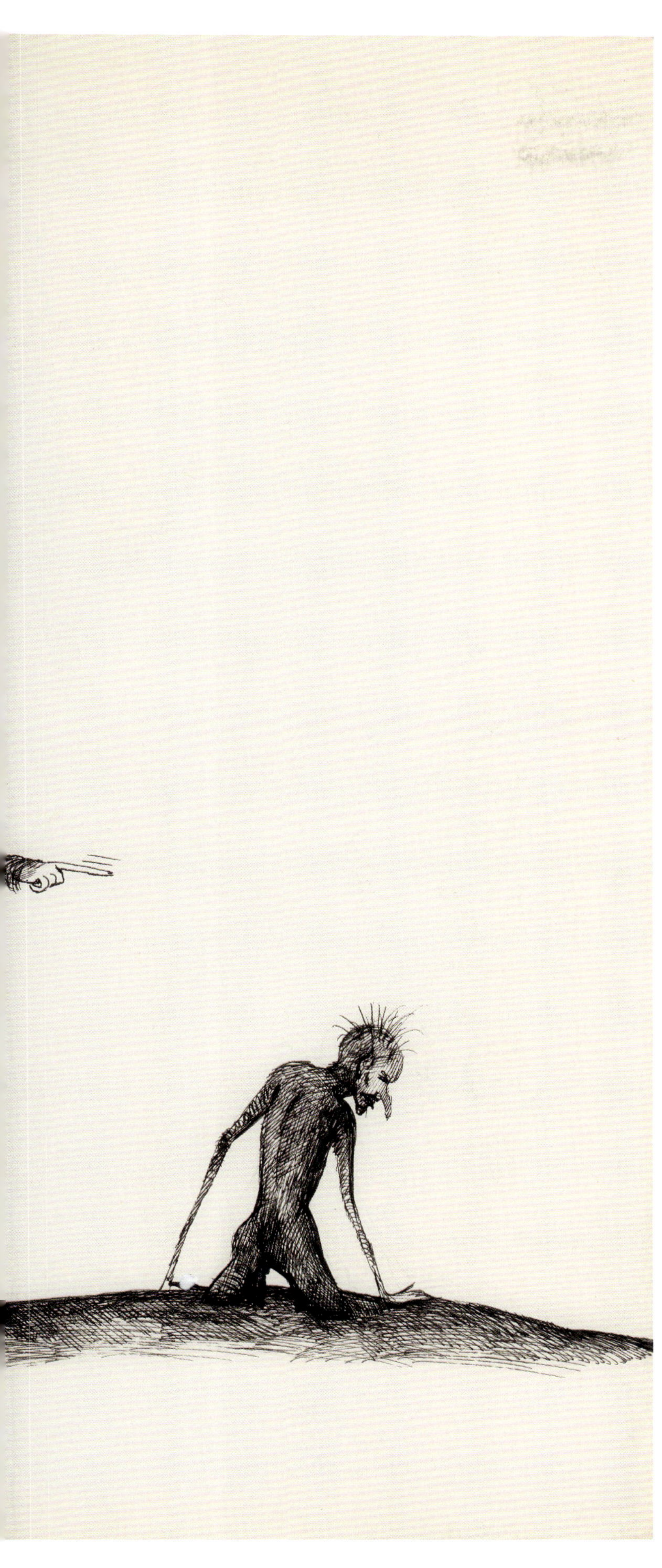

Ardeshir Mohassess
Untitled, 1978
ink and gouache on paper

Siah Armajani
Shirt #1, 1958
cloth, pencil, ink, wood

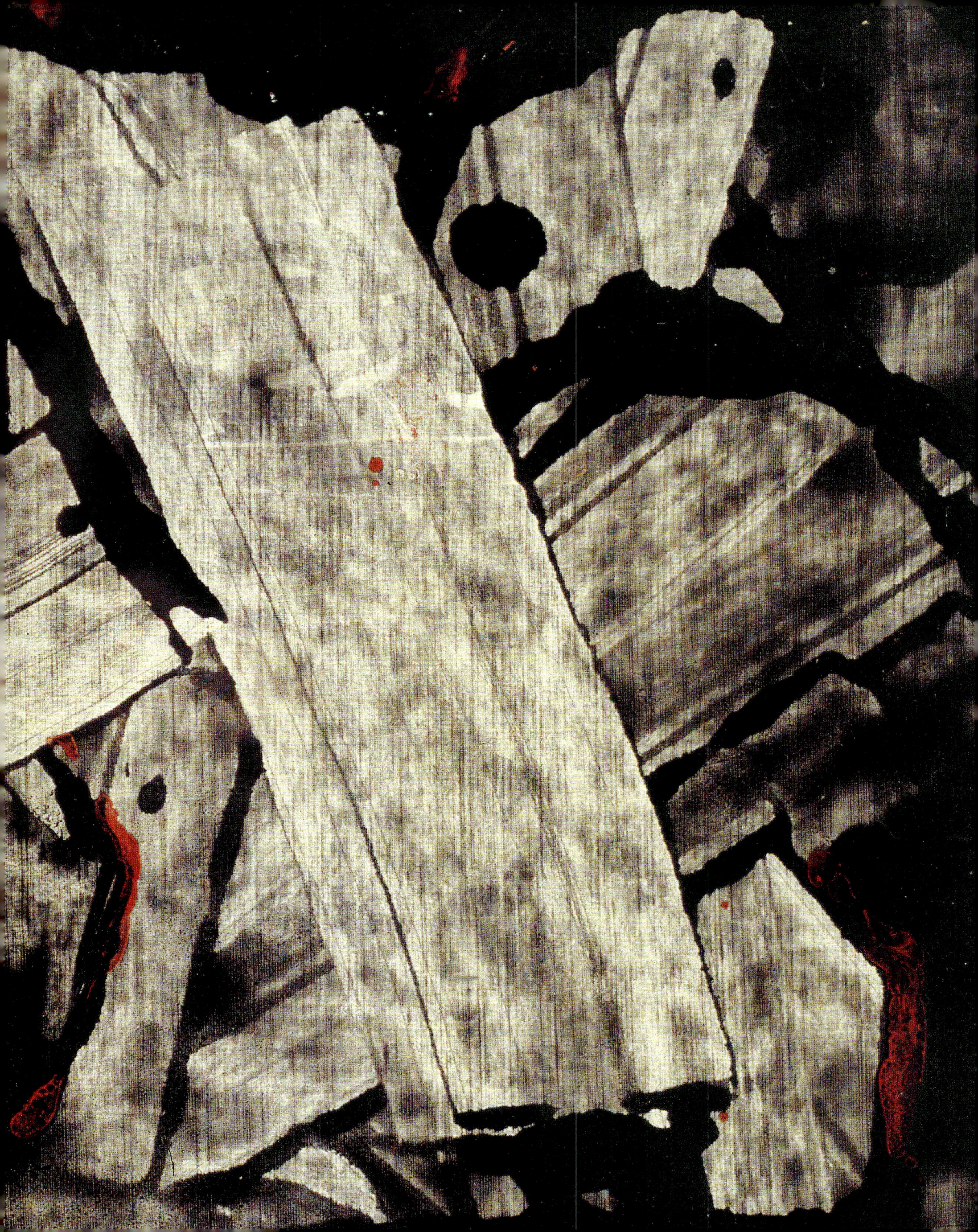

Published in conjunction with the exhibition *Modern Iran and the Avant-Gardes, 1948–78*, organized by the Vancouver Art Gallery as an initiative of the Centre for Global Asias, guest curated by Pantea Haghighi with Anna Luth, former Curatorial Assistant, and presented from December 11, 2026 to May 2, 2027.

Managing editor: Stephanie Rebick, Vancouver Art Gallery
Senior editor: Elisabeth Rochau-Shalem, Hirmer Publishers
Project management: Rainer Arnold, Hirmer Publishers
Copyediting: Jaclyn Arndt
Design: Studio Blackwell, Kelsey Blackwell with Meredith Holigroski
Digital image preparation: Ian Lefebvre and Kyla Bailey, Vancouver Art Gallery

Printed and bound by optimal media GmbH, Röbel/Müritz
Prepress: Reproline mediateam GmbH&Co. KG, Unterföhring

Printed in Germany in 2025

Cover: Massoumeh Seyhoun, *Composition #13*, 1967, enamel and lacquer on canvas, Grey Art Museum, New York University Art Collection, Gift of Abby Weed Grey, G1975.113, Courtesy Grey Art Museum, New York University

ISBN 978-1-927656-74-7 (Vancouver Art Gallery)
ISBN 978-3-7774-4476-5 (Hirmer Verlag)

Publication Support:

The Pamela and Dave Richardson Family

The Jack and Doris Shadbolt Endowment for Research and Publications

Exhibition Support:

Presented by:

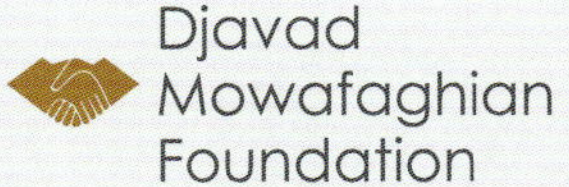

Cultural Partner:

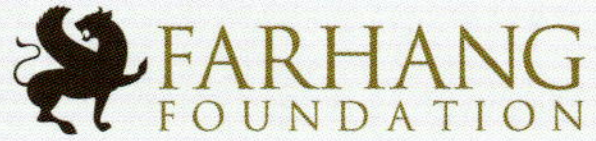

The Vancouver Art Gallery is a not-for-profit organization supported by its members, individual donors, corporate funders, foundations, the City of Vancouver, the Province of British Columbia through the British Columbia Arts Council, and the Canada Council for the Arts.

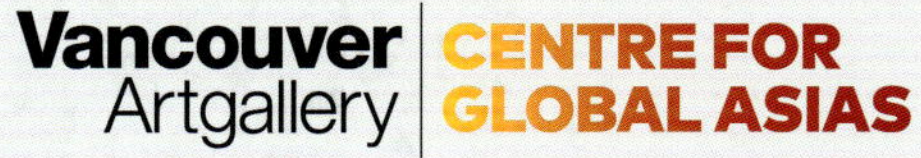

Vancouver Art Gallery
750 Hornby Street
Vancouver, BC
V6Z 2H7 Canada
www.vanartgallery.bc.ca

The Vancouver Art Gallery respectfully acknowledges its location on the traditional, ancestral and unceded territories of the xʷməθkʷəy̓əm (Musqueam), Sk̲wx̲wú7mesh (Squamish) and səlilwətaɬ (Tsleil-Waututh) peoples, and honours the Indigenous stewards of the land whose rich cultures are fundamental to artistic life in our province and the work of the Gallery.

HIRMER

Hirmer Publishers
(Hirmer Verlag GmbH)
Managing Director: Kerstin Ludolph
Bayerstraße 57–59
80335 Munich
Germany
www.hirmerpublishers.com
www.hirmerpublishers.co.uk